International Dict
Hospitality Management

International Dictionary of Hospitality Management

ABRAHAM PIZAM
JUDY HOLCOMB

EDITORS

AMSTERDAM • BOSTON • HEIDELBERG • LONDON • NEW YORK • OXFORD
PARIS • SAN DIEGO • SAN FRANCISCO • SINGAPORE • SYDNEY • TOKYO

Butterworth-Heinemann is an imprint of Elsevier

ELSEVIER

Butterworth-Heinemann is an imprint of Elsevier
Linacre House, Jordan Hill, Oxford OX2 8DP, UK
30 Corporate Drive, Suite 400, Burlington, MA 01803, USA

First edition 2008

British Library Cataloguing in Publication Data
A catalogue record for this book is available from the British Library

Library of Congress Cataloging-in-Publication Data
A catalog record for this book is available from the Library of Congress

For information on all Butterworth-Heinemann publications
visit our web site at books.elsevier.com

Typeset by Charon Tec Ltd (A Macmillan Company), Chennai, India
www.charontec.com

Printed and bound in Great Britain

08 09 10   10 9 8 7 6 5 4 3 2 1

ISBN: 978-0-7506-8385-2

Contents

Acknowledgements

This project could not have been done without the hard work and dedication of the 216 authors who wrote the original entries for the *International Encyclopedia of Hospitality Management*. Their collective work was the cornerstone for this dictionary and without their contribution this project could have never been completed. To them we extend our gratitude and appreciation.

On the publisher side, we wish to express our deepest appreciation to Ms. Sally North who guided and coached us throughout this project and had confidence in our ability to bring it to fruition.

Last, but not the least, many thanks and appreciation to our families for their patience and understanding during the many months that we worked on this project.

Abraham Pizam
Judy Holcomb
Editors

Introduction

This dictionary is a landmark book in several ways. First, it is the first ever published *extended* dictionary that is entirely devoted to the domain of hospitality management. Second, it is a comprehensive work that is comprised of entries relevant to the major sectors of the hospitality industry including lodging, foodservice, events, clubs, and timeshare. Third, its entries reflect all the main managerial disciplines prevalent in the hospitality industry namely accounting, facilities management, finance, human resources, information technology, marketing, and strategic management. Fourth, the entries reflect the global and cross-cultural nature of the hospitality industry and were written in a way that makes them relevant to most countries around the world.

The dictionary is an abridged version of the *International Encyclopedia of Hospitality Management*. As such, each of the *Encyclopedia* entries that were composed by 216 authors whose names are listed at the end of this book was revised and condensed by the current editors to an average of 150 words. The end result is a single volume that is composed of 734 entries containing over 110,000 words. Like the *Encyclopedia of Hospitality Management* this *extended* dictionary is by no means an all-encompassing reference book that covers every single aspect of hospitality management as practiced in every country around the world. It is however a serious attempt to define and shortly describe the major issues relevant to the international and multi-sectoral hospitality industry.

The easiest and most convenient method of using this dictionary is by either searching through the alphabetically arranged list of entries that appears at the beginning of the book or by searching the index that appears at the end of the volume. It is our sincere wish and hope that this dictionary like its predecessor the *Encyclopedia of Hospitality Management* will become an important and essential tool in the scientific development and professionalization of the field of hospitality management.

List of entries

À la carte
Accommodation, demand for
Accommodation, supply of
Account aging
Account allowance
Account correction
Account posting
Account settlement
Account transfer
Action learning
Activity-based pricing
Affiliate resort
Agency theory
Alarm annunciators
Alliances
Application service provider
Apprenticeship
Arbitration
Architectural plans
ARDA International Foundation
ARDA Resort Owners Coalition
Artificial intelligence
Association market
Atmospherics
Attendee
Attribution theory
Attrition clause
Auto-closing device

Automated minibar
Average check
Average daily rate
Average rate per guest
Awareness, trial, and usage

Back of the house
Back office systems
Backflow prevention
Balance sheet
Balanced scorecard
Baldrige award
Bandwidth
Banquet event order
Bargaining power
Barriers to entry
Barriers to exit
Basic elements of cost
Beliefs and attitudes
Benchmarking
Biases in consumer decision-making
Biennial timeshare
Bluetooth
Booth
Brand
Branding
Break-even analysis
Budget methods

Exchange company
Executive information systems
Executive recruiters/head hunters
Exhibit prospectus
Exhibitions
Exhibits
Expenses
Experience economy
Expert systems
Express check-out
External analysis
Extranet

Facilities engineering
Facilities management
Facilities operating and capital expenses
Fairs
Family service
Fast casual
Feasibility study
Federacion de Desarrolladores Turisticos
Festivals
File Transfer Protocol
Financial accounting
Financial leverage
Financial risk
Fire protection
Fire seal
Fire sprinklers
First-in, first-out
Fixed charges
Fixed costs
Fixed costs in foodservice operations
Fixed timeshare plan

Flexible firms
Float timeshare plan
Focus groups
Folio
Food Code (The)
Foodborne illness
Forecasting
Forecasting methods
Forecasting rooms availability
Forecasting rooms revenue
Fractional
Framing
Franchising
Free cash flow
Frequent guest programs
Front office accounting
Front office communications
Front office ledger
Front office operations
Front office organization
Front office system
Front-of-the house
Full-time equivalent
Furniture, fixtures, and equipment

Game theory
Gap model of service quality
General manager
General session
Generic strategies
Global alliance of timeshare excellence
Global distribution systems
Globalization
Glocalization

xvii

xix

xx

Aa

À la carte

The literal interpretation of *à la carte* is 'from or off the card' to order. The à la carte menu is designed to enable guests to choose the meal according to their needs and tastes. This classical format is based on the original French à la carte menu form, which in former times comprised 16 courses – with or without a choice in each course for guests to choose from. The classical French à la carte chronological course structure is as follows: appetizers; soups; farinaceous dishes; eggs; fish and shellfish; entrées (main course in the USA, appetizers or starters in the rest of the world); grills; roasts; vegetables; salads; cold buffet items; sweets; ices; savories; cheeses; and chocolates, fruits, and bonbons.

Accommodation, demand for

Development of the accommodation sector comes as a result of a healthy tourism industry attracting both domestic and international tourism that arrive at a given destination for leisure and/or business purposes. There have been fundamental changes in the demand for hospitality accommodation during the past two decades. These have been in response to general socio-economic trends, in particular:

- Increasing prosperity and/or increased leisure time in developed economies (e.g. the introduction of the 35-hour working week in France in the 1990s has impacted directly on the demand for hospitality, as customers are taking short-break holidays starting on a Thursday evening).
- Changes in the structure of family life (e.g. dual careers, smaller families holidaying together).
- Increasing urbanization.
- The transition from an industrial society to a knowledge-based society.
- Need for specialized business facilities to serve the Meetings, Incentives, Conferences and Events (MICE) markets.
- 'Mass customization' and 'personalization', in the business accommodation sector resulting in guests turning to boutique hotels in preference to the standardized product offered by hotel chains.

Accommodation, supply of

Hospitality accommodation may include hotels, motels, timeshares, guest-houses, lodging-houses, bed and breakfast, inns, pensions, and 'auberges'. Accommodation may be commercial, non-commercial, or social in character, and may include holiday camps, holiday villages, sanatoria, and villas and apartments for rent.

In recent years, several major trends have affected the supply of accommodation and therefore the structure of domestic and international hotel companies, including increasing concentration and consolidation, the increased importance given to branding, and the impact of technology. The major companies are indeed getting bigger and international companies now control an increasing proportion of the worldwide hotel supply. Owing to the effects of globalization, the industry has seen increasing competition, but with the continued dominance of major brands through companies emanating from the USA, UK, and France.

Account aging

Accounts receivable represents money owed to a hotel by its customers. To monitor how customers are paying their bills, hotels need to age the accounts and perform an aging schedule. This schedule is a table that lists the names of the customers, the unpaid account balances, and the number of days the accounts are outstanding. Unpaid account balance is the amount of funds that customers owe or have not paid to the hotel. The aim of the hotel is to keep all accounts 'young' so that they will not be aged. Generally speaking, aged accounts have a higher probability of becoming delinquent account.

Account allowance

A reduction in a hotel guest account folio for unsatisfactory service, a rebate on a discount voucher, or if a correction is to be made to a posting, which has been made the previous day (after the night audit).

Account correction

In a hotel, account corrections are normally made on the same day that a transaction has been posted (before the night audit). It corrects errors that have been made to postings (e.g. if a wrong charge was posted to a room). Depending on the error it can either increase or decrease the guest account balance.

Account posting

When guest make either payments or charges to their accounts the process is known as posting. It is the procedure used to record transactions made by the guests.

Account settlement

A term used to describe a situation that occurs when a guest account folio is brought to a zero balance (i.e. when the guest pays their account). Guests can pay their account in numerous ways namely: by cash, by credit card, by direct billing arrangement (normally arranged before the guest stay), or a combination of the above.

Account transfer

Involves transferring transactions from one hotel account to another. An example would be if one guest offers to pay for restaurant charges for another guest, the posting would have to be transferred from one account to the other account.

Action learning

The process whereby individuals learn skills through involvement in a team focusing on organization-specific problems. This is achieved through the use of questioning, analysis, and problem-solving techniques. As the individuals using this process are often working out with their normal area there is the added advantage of learning about other processes or areas of the business whilst developing interpersonal skills and, of course, improving organizational effectiveness. For example, a member of the front office team in a hotel may work in an action group with individuals from the sales and reservations teams to consider how to improve communication between the departments. The front office team member will learn about the other departments and assist in the creation of a solution for more effective communication; thus learning has taken place.

Activity-based pricing

A pricing method that combines market research data with cost accounting information to establish prices for products and services that result in designed profits. The activity-based pricing (ABP) concept emphasizes that profits can be maximized through knowing how much of a product's price is profit and through the elimination of pricing errors. For example, one method that the lodging industry uses to maximize room revenues is yield management. This technique forecasts demands for market segments that will generate the highest room rates, but it does not incorporate precise product and customer costs. ABP can improve a company's profitability by providing the marketing and accounting departments with information that allows them to cooperatively establish accurate prices.

Affiliate resort

A resort with which a timeshare exchange company has a contractual agreement to offer rooms for exchange. The basic premise underlying the exchange process is that a collection of timeshare resorts, either single site or multi-site enter into an agreement with an exchange company to offer their owners the option of exchanging their interval (commonly a week) with another member that is seeking to swap their interval. It is this agreement between the timeshare developer and the exchange company that is known as an affiliation agreement. The affiliation agreement simply means that the developer has the right, at the point of sale, to offer the exchange company's services to this new owner as an additional service. Therefore, the owner makes a voluntary decision to buy into the exchange process by paying an annual fee to this exchange company for their services.

Agency theory

A theory of corporate behavior that describes the contractual relationship between principals and agents. In the context of hospitality, the appropriate framework for understanding the contractual relationship, for instance, between a hotel operating company and a hotel owning company, is agency theory. The agent is represented by the operating company, the principal is represented by the owning company, and the two parties' relationship is mediated by a hotel management contract. Agency theory explains how to best organize these relationships in which the owning company (the principal) delegates the work to the operating company (the agent) who performs that work. More specifically, the focus of the theory is on the contract between the principal and the agent and the ways in which the contract can be made most efficient from the point of view of the principal.

Alarm annunciators

Annunciator panels or terminals are used to pinpoint the specific location of a fire. The alarm annunciator panel is located in a control center, such as the security office, engineering office, or at a main entrance to allow trained personnel to identify the exact location, or zone, of the fire. Annunciators can monitor from 8–64 points and can be mounted on racks, panels, walls, or desks. Some annunciators are flame or explosion proof and most of them come with standby power supply. The alarm annunciator at the control center is required to be audible and visible to alert employees, who might be away from their desk or concentrating on another task. Regulations in the Life Safety Code limit the size of the floor area that can be included in an alarm zone.

Alliances

An umbrella term for a wide range of cooperative arrangements that can encapsulate suppliers, buyers, and competitors. As such, it covers many collaborative organizational forms including franchising, management contracts, joint ventures, marketing, and purchasing consortia. Primarily, hospitality and tourism alliances offer organizations a basis for creating a degree of stability in their external relationships and a method to secure access to resources or competences possessed by other organizations that support the attainment of strategic objectives. Alliances may function on the basis of formal or informal agreements and can be classified into two categories: equity and non-equity alliances. Equity alliances demonstrate a mutual financial commitment and often imply a long-term commitment to the partnership. On the other hand, non-equity alliance allows for greater strategic flexibility as partners may decide to terminate an agreement and either act on their own or form an alternative alliance without the need to deal with shared equity.

Application service provider

An information technology service firm that deploys, manages, and hosts remotely a software application through centrally located servers in a rental or lease agreement. The service provision is made usually through the Internet or virtual private networks (VPN). Usually the client pays a flat fee to sign up and a monthly fee for access to the application, training, expert support, and upgrades. Other payment schemes are based on usage rates (fees per transaction, number of screen clicks, or amount of computer time). Initially hospitality and tourism firms were reluctant to adopt the application service provider (ASP) model mainly due to the perception of data control loss, current telecommunication infrastructure problems, interface challenges with legacy systems, and data transfer security. Problems are gradually being overcome and the model seems to receive greater acceptance.

Apprenticeship

Apprenticeship involves on-the-job training and work experience while in paid employment with formal off-the-job training. Traditionally, formal apprenticeships (membership in Guilds) started in Europe during the Middle Ages. These were restricted to trade occupations (i.e. tailors, blacksmiths, etc.) and were of multiple years' duration. Hospitality apprentices can learn in fields such as front office, housekeeping, food and beverage, or culinary. Apprentices enter into formalized agreements with employers known as 'training agreements'. In some countries apprentices are paid a training wage adjusted to reflect the amount of time spent learning off the job and employers have access to public training funds to assist with training apprentices.

Arbitration

6

A method of dispute settlement in which an independent third party or group (e.g. industrial or labor tribunal) considers the arguments of both sides in a dispute and then makes a decision that is legally binding on the parties. This third party or group is appointed by mutual consent or statutory provision. The difference between arbitration and other forms of dispute settlement such as mediation or conciliation (where an arbitrator attempts to find a compromise) is that decisions are legally binding. Hospitality and hotel employers generally join employer associations (such as hotel associations) that represent their interests during arbitral proceedings in industrial tribunals, though larger hotels are increasingly using their own internal human resource management (HRM) departments to conduct tribunal work.

Architectural plans

Drawings developed by architects, engineers, or consultants to provide instructions for contractors and trades personnel. They may also be used to determine the amount of construction materials needed and to evaluate the travel patterns of building inhabitants. There are several types of architectural plans:

- *Plan view*: The plan view is obtained when a building or room is cut horizontally 3′ above the finished floor.
- *Elevation*: An elevation is a vertical view of an exterior wall or an interior room.
- *Section*: A section view is generally a vertical cut through a building or piece of equipment.
- *Plot/survey*: A plot view is a horizontal view of an entire property showing the location of the building, contour lines, and landscaping.
- *Detail*: A detail view is used to show specific features of construction, such as cabinet drawers, decorative trim, or furniture design.

ARDA International Foundation

The American Resort Development Association (ARDA) was founded in 1969 to represent the interests of the resort industry in the USA. The ARDA International Foundation serves the professional and educational needs of the resort industry. The foundation provides two professional designations, the Associate Resort Professional (ARP) and the Registered Resort Professional (RRP). Other programs offered by the ARDA International Foundation are the conduct of consistent, on-going surveys, and research studies of the industry such as the Worldwide Timeshare study, and the US Economic and a Financial Performance study.

ARDA Resort Owners Coalition

One of the American Resort Development Association's (ARDA's) programs that brings together opposite sides of the timeshare industry, the developer and the consumer, to work together in achieving benefits for all parties involved. ARDA is a national US association that serves as the vacation ownership industry's sole lobbying, educational, and information source. The ARDA's Resort Owners Coalition (ARDA's ROC) is comprised of individual timeshare owners forming a united front as a legislative advocate. Since its inception in 1989, ARDA-ROC has served as a funding resource waging legislative battles across the USA. The organization is dedicated to preserving, protecting, and enhancing vacation ownership for timeshare owners.

Artificial intelligence

A branch of computer science focusing on the automation of intelligent behavior, such as reasoning, learning, and problem solving. Artificial intelligence (AI) seeks to construct intelligent machines; formalize knowledge and mechanize reasoning; make use of computational models to understand behavior of people, animals, and intelligent agents; make it possible to work with computers as easily as with friendly experts. Areas of AI are: (a) knowledge representation and articulation; (b) learning and adaptation; (c) deliberation, planning, and acting; (d) speech and language processing; (e) image understanding and synthesis; (f) manipulation and locomotion; (g) autonomous intelligent agents and robots; (h) multi-agent systems; (i) cognitive modeling; and (j) mathematical foundations. AI went through a period of success followed by failure, and is becoming a steadily growing and maturing technology now. AI has the potential of helping tourists to better plan their trips and choose the most appropriate services from huge information sources, and also support various functions within hospitality enterprises.

Association market

A body of existing or potential buyers that are associations, of specific goods or services in the hospitality industry. Associations are a subset of a type or organizations typically referred to as 'non-profits' or non-governmental organizations. More than 147,000 associations exist in the USA, including more than 127,340 local, state, and regional associations; 20,285 national associations; and 2409 international associations headquartered in the USA. Convention planning and other convention activities are the second most prevalent activity, next to education, in which 89 per cent of associations engage. With a budget of $3.6 billion per year, association-sponsored meetings and conventions account for more than 26 million overnight stays in hotels each year. Association

8

meetings and events account for a large part of the meeting industry, with associations spending more than $66.4 billion annually on conventions, expositions, and seminars.

Atmospherics

The study of the physical environment where some activity occurs. The physical environment is defined as the material surroundings of a place. For example, a physical environment may be the lobby of a hotel or the swimming pool/spa area of a property. Atmospheric studies examine the effects that the physical environment has on people's behaviors. One way of looking at the atmospheric effects of an environment is the 'Servicescapes' framework. In the service industry atmospheric researchers examine the effect of the physical environment on human response in a services delivery situation. In such situations the customer becomes part of the service-creation environment and the atmospherics becomes part of the product itself.

Attendee

A combination of delegates, exhibitors, media, speakers, and guests/companions who attend an event. It is customary to classify attendees based on their origin as follows:

- *International*: Draws a national and international event audience; 15 per cent or more of event delegates reside outside of event host country.
- *National*: Draws a national event audience; more than 40 per cent of delegates reside outside of a 400 miles (640 km) radius of event city.
- *Regional*: 60 per cent of delegates reside within a 400 miles (640 km) radius of the event city.
- *State/province*: More than 80 per cent of delegates reside in state/province event; state/provincial audiences are less inclined to use air travel and local auto-rental than regional audiences.
- *Local*: 80 per cent of delegates reside within a 50 miles (80 km) radius of the event site; local audiences typically do not require overnight accommodations.

Attribution theory

Attribution theory attempts to explain how individuals interpret causes of behavior based on their past knowledge and experiences. They can attribute behavior either to internal factors such as ability, skill, or effort, or to external factors such as rules, policies, or environment. This is known as locus of control and can influence behavior at work. For example, if a customer complains about poor service from their waiter, the restaurant manager might agree that the waiter has been slow and/or rude (internal attribution). Alternatively the manager might attribute this to the restaurant being overcrowded or short-staffed (external attribution). The attribution of these events might then influence how the restaurant manager deals with the waiter.

Attrition clause

Based on the word attrition, meaning a reduction or decrease in numbers, size, or strength, this clause is contained in most hotel contracts today. This clause specifies the fees that the organization that books an event must pay if it fails to use the sleeping room block commitment. It contains formulas that stipulate the amount of liquidated damages for which the organization will be held liable. The attrition fee is based on the difference between the total room nights booked by the organization and the total number of rooms actually used. There is often a 10 per cent attrition allowance before fees are imposed. The amount is generally multiplied by an agreed upon percentage of the room rate to calculate the fee due in terms of lost profit for the facility. Experienced meeting planners require language that stipulates that rooms resold by the hotel are not included in the penalty fee.

Auto-closing device

A device that automatically takes a fire door back to the closed position. A fire door is impaired when chocked or blocked open and is unattended. Opening a fire door and walking through it, or holding it open for materials to pass through, is not impairment as long as someone is there to close the door when done. For safety and security purposes, hotels install the auto-closing device on each fire door. When a guest walks out from the room, the auto-closing device starts its function by closing the door automatically. Furthermore, when fire breaks out in a hotel, guest floors and hallways fill with smoke. With the auto-closing device, the guestroom entrance door can prevent the spread of fire and smoke through the hallway by containing it in the compartment of origin.

Automated minibar

A refrigerator in the guest's room containing drinks and other items (snacks, sun cream disposable cameras, etc.), which the guest can purchase for a fee. Manual systems rely on the minibar being restocked daily, and the consumption noted. An automated minibar has sensors that record the removal of items. These sensors are linked to a computer, which records the removal of each item.

This produces information about consumption that is added to the guest's bill, as well as a list of items to be restocked by the hotel staff.

Automated minibars have the advantage of reducing the demand for room service. They can be locked, for instance when children are staying in the room. They ensure that items are added to the guest's bill immediately, reducing the risk of a guest checking out before the consumption is noted and charged for.

Average check

Average check is calculated by dividing total revenues by total number of customers.

$$\text{Average check} = \frac{\text{Total revenues}}{\text{Total number of checks (guests)}}$$

Average check (also referred to as 'guest check average') is one of the common tools available to the foodservice industry to measure the amount of money spent per customer. This information is extremely useful in managing a restaurant. Average check is used in foodservice operation for various purposes, including allocating labor dollars, forecasting unit sales, assessing employee productivity, measuring the effectiveness of suggestive selling, effective usage of floor space in the dining area, calculating cost percentage per meal, comparative analysis across operational units, etc. In on-site foodservice operations, average check is sometimes translated into 'average transaction'.

Average daily rate

The average (mean) selling price of all guest rooms in a hotel for a specific period of time. Average daily rate or ADR is calculated by dividing total room sales by the number of rooms sold.

$$\text{ADR} = \frac{\text{Total room sales}}{\text{Total number of rooms sold}}$$

ADR is a measure of the hotel's staff efficiency in selling available room rates. ADR is used in projecting room revenues for a hotel and is a factor in calculating gross revenue from room sales. If the supply of hotel rooms is limited considerable attention is focused on improving the ADR.

Average rate per guest

The average rate that the hotel obtains per guest. Some rooms are double rooms, some are triple and this rate indicates an average rate that each guest paid. It is calculated by dividing the total rooms' revenue by total number of guests.

Awareness, trial, and usage

A grouping of three types of questions, *awareness*, *trial*, and *usage*, which are used in marketing research to determine some of the behavioral characteristics of consumers. *Awareness* refers to the presence of the product or brand in the consumer's mind. *Trial* refers to the types of questions that ask the consumer if he or she has ever used the product or brand in the past. *Usage* of the product may refer to both the frequency of use as well as the way the product is used. Usage questions also ask how the respondent uses the product or service. Hospitality applications of usage questions may include the occasion or reason for a visit to a hotel or restaurant and the types of services that are consumed while at the hotel or restaurant.

Back of the house

An archaic term that has survived over the centuries. It was first used in the Middle Ages in England to describe the area of an inn where food was prepared, which was normally located outside and to the rear, and therefore was called the back-of-house area. Its modern interpretation is similar, as it is commonly used to describe the areas of a hotel or restaurant, which are normally off-limits to the guests (e.g. the kitchen). The modern application lies with the delineation of back-of-house employees such as cooks, laundry operators, cleaners, etc., from front-of-house employees such as front-desk clerks, concierge, or restaurant servers.

Back office systems

The IT (Information Technology) business applications that support the internal business functions of hospitality organizations. Like the customer-facing (front office) ones, these applications are instrumental in the fulfillment of the hospitality or tourism enterprise's mission – from product to service and everything in between. They are usually software packages such as Business Performance Management Tools, Enterprise Resource Planning, Supply Chain Management and Sourcing, or individual applications such as inventory management, purchasing or e-procurement, menu and recipe management (for catering operations), human resources management (e-recruitment, e-training, employee scheduling, and payroll), energy management, preventative property maintenance, and accounting. Customer-centric strategies require back office systems to have some level of integration with front office systems (mainly the property management system (PMS) in the case of hotels and the customer relationship management (CRM) system of the enterprise) in order to provide a complete outlook on customer interactions and the connected business processes.

Backflow prevention

All water distribution systems are designed to keep the water flowing from the distribution system to the customer. However, when hydraulic conditions within the system deviate from the 'normal' conditions, water flow can be reversed. When this backflow happens, contaminated water can enter the distribution system. Backflow can be prevented by the installation of a device or assembly, called a backflow prevention system which uses valves, in different configurations, to prevent, polluted or contaminated water from reversing direction and flowing backward. In the case of hotels or restaurants, the devices are used to prevent the property's water system from over pressurizing and forcing the water back into the municipality's system.

Balance sheet

A statement showing a business' financial position at the end of an accounting period. It portrays the financial position of the organization at a particular point in time. The balance sheet lists all the assets, liabilities, and owner's equity of an entity as of a specific date. It is classified into major groupings of assets and liabilities in order to facilitate analysis, for example, current assets, fixed assets, current liabilities, non-current liabilities. The balance sheet is like a snapshot of the entity. For this reason it is also called the statement of financial position. The balance sheet is useful to financial statement users because it indicates the resources the entity has and what it owes.

Balanced scorecard

A performance measurement system, devised to provide a set of measures that gives managers a fast, but comprehensive view of their business. The approach incorporates four main perspectives of which financial measures are the results of actions taken and the operational measures of customers, internal business processes, and the organization's innovation and improvement activities are the drivers of future financial performance. The balanced scorecard puts strategy and vision at the center so that the measures are designed to pull people toward the overall vision, rather than the more traditional focus on control. It is a tool for managers to ensure that all levels of the organization understand the long-term strategy and that objectives at different levels are aligned with it. It emphasizes that financial and non-financial measures must be part of the information system at all levels of the organizations.

Baldrige award

The Malcolm Baldrige National Quality Award is an internationally recognized prize given by the United States Commerce Department to businesses in manufacturing, services, small businesses, education, and healthcare for excellence in quality. The Baldrige award is highly prestigious. Applicants are subjected to rigorous review of their performance in areas such as leadership, strategic planning, customer and market focus, information and analysis, human resources management, process management, and the business' results. The only hospitality company that has won a Baldrige award to date is the Ritz-Carlton Hotel Company, which won it for the first time in 1992 and a second time in 1999. The company focused on achieving 100 per cent guest loyalty with defect-free performance, reducing employee turnover, making its strategic planning process more systematic, and developing processes and tools for quality improvement. The development of tools to measure processes and quality were developed using statistical control techniques that were previously rarely used in the services industries.

Bandwidth

A channel is a crucial component of telecommunications. It is the path through which information passes between the sending and receiving ends, and bandwidth describes the width of the channel. The amount of data that the channel can transmit at one time is directly proportional to the size of the bandwidth. Explicitly, data transmission rate is predominately determined by the transmission channel capacity, usually expressed in bits per second (bps). In other words, bandwidth represents the data rate, and the term refers to how fast data flow on a telecommunication channel. In the context of hospitality, bandwidth is considered as the communication capacity. As communication rate increases, bandwidth-intensive applications such as high-quality Internet multimedia will be benefited from rapid downloading and good quality graphical images. Hotels and guests therefore will be able to distribute and access better-quality multimedia information much faster via the Internet.

Banquet event order

The banquet event order (BEO) is sometimes referred to as simply an event order or the function sheet. It is the basis of a property's internal communication system between the various departments and the catering department. It is also the basic building block upon which the catering department's accounting and record-keeping systems are constructed. A BEO is prepared for each meal and beverage function, and copies are sent to the each department that will be directly or indirectly involved with the events. Usually all departments receive a copy of each BEO a week or more before the catered function is held. This ensures that all department heads have enough time to schedule and complete their necessary activities that support the events. A BEO should include who is responsible for what and specify the cost for every item or service and acts as the primary means of communication within the facility for the function.

Bargaining power

The relative power that either a guest or supplier has over the firm and its ability to negotiate transactions. Buyers have power if they buy in bulk and can therefore dictate terms, or if the product represents a large percentage of the buyer costs, making the buyer highly price sensitive. Suppliers have power if there are few firms supplying the product or if there is no reasonable substitute for it, or if the hotel or restaurant is of little importance to the supplier, making the supplier insensitive to the hospitality firm's needs. In periods of low occupancy hotels are often willing to lower their prices significantly in order to sell rooms to these price conscious buyers. However, as a supplier of rooms when occupancy rates are high the hotel's bargaining power is increased, allowing it to maintain a fairly firm position on room rate.

Barriers to entry

Barriers to entry block new hospitality competitors from entering the local industry. Since new hotels or restaurants bring additional capacity and the desire to gain market share, the result often reduces profitability for existing firms. This threat of entry can be reduced through seven major types of entry barriers: (1) economies of scale; (2) product differentiation; (3) capital requirements; (4) switching costs; (5) access to distribution channels; (6) competitive advantages such as proprietary products, locations, access to raw materials, etc.; and (7) government policy. If a firm operating within a local industry, high barriers are desired to block new entrants. Existing competitors can raise barriers through favorable supplier contracts, market dominance, offering unique products and/or services, or by lobby government for restrictions on building policies or licensing costs. In the hospitality industry, entry barriers are not particularly high. Opening a restaurant requires a relatively modest investment and would-be operator can usually find financing.

Barriers to exit

Exit barriers are economic, strategic, and/or emotional reasons that keep hospitality firms competing even though they might be earning low or even negative returns on investments. Such costs are viewed to outweigh poor performance. Examples of such barriers include specialized assets with high costs to transform or with limited other use (such as a hotel or aircraft), fixed costs (labor agreements), or strategic relationships that attach high importance to being in the business and would significantly impact image, marketing ability, access to capital, etc. For example, a hotel building has limited reuse other than that of a hotel. The rooms are generally too small for residential living and the building infrastructure too complex for convenient redesign. Office space or light manufacturing operations generally prefer larger, more open areas. The cost to convert such space often outweighs retaining the space as it was initially created and hospitality firms frequently find it more acceptable to continue current operations.

Basic elements of cost

Most business accounting systems classify costs in groupings of 'material', 'labor', and 'expenses' that relate to the resources consumed. Presenting cost information in the basic elements provides the basis to begin to assess business performance. For example, in a restaurant operation, basic cost elements would typically include food and beverages (material), wages, salaries and overtime (labor), cleaning supplies, energy, insurance, advertising, and depreciation (expenses). With respect to accommodation activities of a hotel we would also see other expenses such as guest supplies, laundry, travel agents' commission, etc. This type of cost classification is generally used in the routine presentation of profit and loss statements. Costs can also be classified according to their behavior (i.e. fixed and variable). Fixed costs do not change in total as a hotel's level of activity changes. Variable costs change in line with a hotel's volume of activity.

Beliefs and attitudes

A belief is a descriptive thought that a person holds about an object or phenomenon. The term 'attitude' refers to an individual's preference, inclination, views, or feelings toward some phenomenon or object. Thus, attitudes and beliefs are part of a consumer's psychological makeup. Beliefs and attitudes are important concepts in Marketing Science, since it is generally held that a person's beliefs and attitudes are related to his/her behavior. Thus, marketers are interested in people's overall beliefs and attitudes toward not only a product or service itself, but also with regard to specific brands and brand features.

Benchmarking

Originally a benchmark was a mark in a wall used as a point of reference against which other measurements could be compared. In business operations, benchmarking is the comparison and measurement of a hospitality firm's business processes against the best practices of those processes by *any* organization in *any* industry throughout the world. The objective of benchmarking is to accelerate organizational learning in order to achieve a break-through in performance. To engage in this approach to self-improvement, a firm must first identify its own value-adding activities or processes that create its value chain. Then specific areas should be pinpointed for improvement. Next, star-performing firms in any industry are examined to identify what it is they do to create their outstanding results. The focus is upon practices, processes, and operational methods for it is these aspects that enable a firm to identify how to apply their findings to their own activities. Benchmarking should be done against non-competing firms so that innovative concepts are uncovered and unworthy practices are more easily identified and avoided.

Biases in consumer decision-making

A bias is a tool that we cognitively use to ease the decision-making process. Many types of bias exist and all people have biases to varying degrees.

Bias as a result of context effects

When a decision needs to be made, the most important information in the decision may be compared against a background of other information that provides a 'frame', or context, for the decision.

Bias as a result of the simulation heuristic

Heuristics are short cuts that humans use in decision-making. It is not always possible to give a decision our full attention, so heuristic devices are used to help make decisions quickly and with a lower amount of effort.

Self-serving bias

Self-serving bias is a form of attributional bias. Attributional bias occurs when the consumers views themselves more positively than is actually the case and believes that their own contributions are more worthy than those of others.

Biennial timeshare

A biennial timeshare gives the purchaser the use of a fixed week every other year. It was developed to meet certain consumers' financial needs that normally could not afford an annual timeshare. Typically the biennial owner is classified as an 'odd' or an 'even' owner. If an owner is not going to use the week that they own, or if the owner wants to use it to exchange elsewhere, the owner can enter their week into the exchange company's reservation system.

Bluetooth

A worldwide standard in short-range radio communication technology that enables computers, mobile telephones, personal digital assistants (PDA), and other electronic devices to be connected without wires, cables, or infrared to each other or to the Internet. This technology uses radio waves at a frequency of 2.4 GHz to establish short-range networks, up to 10 m in distance, with other similar devices. Once a network has been formed the systems in the network then communicate without any interference from the user and switch frequencies automatically in order to prevent another similar device from interfering with the network. This allows multiple networks to be established simultaneously. Applications in hospitality include automated check in for guests, controlled door access with a PDA acting as a virtual key, billing of services via the guests computer or PDA, in-room wireless printing, and access to the Internet and e-mail.

Booth

One or more standard units of exhibit space assigned by management to an exhibitor under contractual agreement. In Europe, a *booth* is known as a *stand*. In the USA, a standard unit is generally known to be a 10 ft × 10 ft space (one standard booth unit, equaling 100 net square feet (approximately 3 m by 3 m). If an exhibitor purchases multiple units side by side or back to back, the combined space is also still referred to as 'a booth'. There are four basic booth types: the standard booth, which has access from one side; the perimeter booth, which is up against the wall of the facility; the peninsula booth, which is at the end of a row and has access from three sides; and the island booth, which has access from four sides.

Brand

A term, sign, symbol, or design, or a combination of them, intended to identify the products or services of one seller or group of sellers and to differentiate them from those competitors. A product or service's brand reveals its functional, pleasure, and symbolic values as a reflection of the buyer's self-image. The brand summarizes all the attributes, values, and principles infused into the product or service. Under the trademark laws, the seller is granted exclusive rights to the use of the brand name in perpetuity. In the context of the hospitality industry, a brand identifies the service provider or establishment. Hospitality brands such as Marriott, Hilton, Westin, and Ritz-Carlton identify a specific set of attributes that take the shape of a definite and unique, though intangible, service.

Branding

The process of building a positive image for a product, service, or organization that differentiates it, in the minds of current and potential customers, from other competitors. As a marketing tool branding is perhaps as old as commerce itself. Craftsmen, in an attempt to guarantee the authenticity of their handiworks, would leave a mark or '*griffe*' (translated as a claw) on the goods they produced. The primary objective for any brand is to enhance customer loyalty to the firm. This is accomplished through increasing customer frequency of use, positive brand positioning in relation to competitors, and forging a consumer's personal association with the brand. The stronger the emotional attachment, the more trustworthy a brand's promise becomes, and the greater the likelihood is that a customer will return to buy that product again. Thus, 'branding' is when the historical value of a brand, showing 'proof of ownership', becomes equally shared between the producer and the consumer.

Break-even analysis

Sometimes referred to as cost–volume–profit analysis, break-even analysis considers the interaction among fixed costs, variable costs, and revenue. When revenue is sufficient to cover both variable and fixed costs exactly, but insufficient to provide any profit (i.e. profit is zero), the operation is at the break-even point (BEP). The key assumptions are that fixed costs remain constant and that variable costs change at a constant rate with sales. Moreover, the technique requires that those costs that have fixed and variable components will be addressed accordingly. Related analyses can be performed using total revenue, number of orders, or number of covers. The BEP calculation is expressed as follows:

$$BEP = \text{Net income } \$0 = \text{Revenue} - \text{Fixed costs} - \text{Variable costs}$$

Budget methods

Budgets are a quantitative expression of a proposed plan of action. Widely used by hospitality managers for directing and controlling operations, such plans may be presented in a variety of forms. For example, 'traditional' static budgets are based on one particular planned volume of activity, such as the numbers of covers in a restaurant, which is consistent with the achievement of an organization's strategic objectives. Flexible budgets depict a range of activity levels within which management considers an organization may operate, and within which they believe cost and revenue behavior patterns will remain relatively stable. Rolling budgets are established for a full

12-month period by adding, as appropriate, a month, or quarter in the future, as the current month/ quarter ends. As a result, they encourage managers to be always looking forward and anticipating possible future developments for a full 12-month period.

Budget variances

Variance (for a period) for an organization represents the difference, on a standard cost basis, between the actual and budgeted contributions. With regards to sales, where actual contribution exceeds budgeted contribution, this is viewed as being a favorable variance – whereas if budgeted contribution is greater than actual contribution, this is termed an unfavorable or adverse variance. The analysis of budget variances enables hospitality managers to 'drill down' into the cause(s) of differences between actual and budgeted performance levels. With regard to variances in cost, typically a total variance for example food cost of sales is calculated by comparing the actual expenditure incurred with the flexed budgeted cost for the actual level of activity achieved. Where the actual cost incurred exceeds the budgeted cost, this is viewed as being an unfavorable or adverse variance – whereas if the budgeted amount is greater than the actual spend, this is termed a favorable variance.

Budgetary controls

The objectives of control are to safeguard assets, ensure accuracy and reliability of data, promote efficiency, and encourage adherence to prescribed managerial policies. Operating budgets are meaningless unless they assist in controlling the business and hence maximize profits (or minimize costs). Use of the *Uniform System of Accounts for Lodging* or similar enables departmental reports to be produced for managers for both actual and budgeted ('standard') results. These should also include both financial and non-financial ratios that will then allow common-size comparisons to be made. Variances are calculated by monetary or numerical and percentage amount and are used by managers to identify areas for concern. The process of budgetary control includes identification of variances, and determination of which are significant, then analysis of these and identification of the causes and last establishment of action to be taken.

Budgetary preparation

Budgets form a detailed operating plan that looks at all aspects of the hospitality business for the forthcoming financial year. It guides the firm toward its objectives, perhaps with the aid of a balanced-scorecard approach by making plans for the future that are then converted to financial and statistical information. The process for establishing the various aspects of the master budget requires the involvement of all managers within the organization. There are three parts to a master budget: the operating, capital expenditure, and cash budgets.

Operating budgets

Operating budgets predict the profit and loss results for the forthcoming period (usually a financial year). Once a budget has been established comparisons may be made with actual results and variances analyzed (budgetary control).

Capital Expenditure budget

A Capital Expenditure budget is prepared to acquire or upgrade physical assets such as property, industrial buildings, or equipment.

Cash budget

A cash budget is an estimation of the cash inflows and outflows of a business. Cash is not necessarily the same as profits – businesses may be operationally profitable but due to high finance charges and/or slow payment by debtors may be technically insolvent. The cash budget forms one part of the master budget, together with the operating and capital expenditure budgets and are used for monitoring cash flows, planning acquisitions and refurbishments, investing surplus cash or borrowing if required, at optimum rates. There are three approaches to budgeting: zero base, bottom up, and top down, with the bottom-up approach resulting in a greater level of commitment from managers. Zero-based budgeting is used colloquially to mean the preparation of a budget from a nil base – usually where little or no historical sales or cost information is available.

Buffet service

For buffet and smorgasbord service, the food is usually artistically arranged on a display table (possibly more than one) and guests select what they wish from a range of hot and cold foods, soups, roasts, salads, and desserts. A proper buffet service requires service staff to serve the foods, which the guest has selected, using the silver service technique. This differs from the smorgasbord service where guests are allowed to help themselves from the smorgasbord table. It is not unusual, though, for many modern foodservice operations to allow guests to help themselves from the buffet table.

Building codes

22

Building codes regulate construction methods and materials to protect the safety and welfare of the people. Three major model building codes existed in the USA prior to 1994. These were the National Building Code (NBC) developed by the Building Official and Code Administrators International (BOCA), the Southern Building Code (SBC) developed by the Southern Building Code Congress International (SBCCI), and the Uniform Building Code (UBC) published by the International Conference of Building Officials (ICBO). Codes provide minimum standards for occupancy classifications, types of construction and construction materials, interior finishes, accessibility, and fire protection systems. In 1994, the three organizations joined to form the International Code Council (ICC) to establish a uniform code. All three codes are now written in the same format so the order of topics is similar. Additionally, the intent is to phase out the three model building codes and incorporate all of the standards into one International Building Code.

Building components

Major building components include items such as:

- Foundations (located under or at ground level).
- Structural framing (usually steel but can be wood in smaller structures) or bearing walls (often poured concrete or concrete block but sometimes wood as well) providing the above ground physical support for the structure.
- Curtain walls or other types of exterior façade or fenestration (glazing) (providing a weatherproof exterior for the building).
- Roof (consisting of a roof deck and weatherproof covering).
- Interior walls (often with a steel or wood framing covered with drywall).
- Various elements of mechanical, electrical, and plumbing systems.

Some properties may also have items such as parking (either in a ground-level structure or in a parking garage) and possibly extensive grounds and landscaping. In addition, there are various elements of FF&E (furniture, fixtures and equipment) including paint, wall coverings, carpet, foodservice equipment, dining tables and chairs, and guestroom furnishings.

Burnout

A syndrome that represents a state of exhaustion caused by chronic stress, and evidences a number of physiological, behavioral, and cognitive consequences. Physical problems may include chronic low levels of energy, frequent headaches, nausea, sleeplessness, and marked changes in eating habits. Psychological symptoms may include anxiety, fear, emotional liability, and out-of-character signs of defensiveness and heightened sensitivity to any perceived criticism. Within the hospitality industry work context, burnout may frequently manifest itself in concentration problems, physical illnesses, absenteeism, and lack of interest in cooperating with others. Major sources of damaging stress leading to burnout in hospitality industry work life include role conflict and role overload or underload. Disempowerment, diminished social support, and job insecurity are also causal agents. Burnout may also be symptomatic of the hospitality employee's alienation from their work and from co-workers, and is commonly associated with uninteresting work, as well as unpredictable or unmanageable work levels and might also be engendered by dysfunctional communication processes.

Business centers

Business centers within hotels provide services to business travelers who require an office away from the office. Depending on the type of guest that a hotel targets its business center may be open 24 hours a day and it can provide equipments such as computers, facsimile machines, printers, pager systems, etc.; services such as audiovisual services, secretarial services, translation services, desktop publishing services; and facilities such as private offices, meeting rooms, lounges, and libraries. Hotel and lodging properties are rapidly moving to business centers with free usage of fax, printing, and copying equipment. A slightly higher room rate may often be justification enough to the traveler who is provided with an efficient working environment.

Business environment

The economic, political, social, cultural, and institutional conditions within which a business enterprise exists and conducts its operations. The internal business environment for the larger contemporary hospitality organizations includes inter alia production, marketing, facility management, purchasing, finance, information technology, and human resource management divisions, while as with other industries smaller firms may not be as internally differentiated. The external business environment of the firm is most often largely uncontrollable by management. Factors such as demography, economic conditions, level of competition, industry structure, social and cultural forces, political and legal forces, and technological level impact on the ability of the firm to provide its services to its intended clients and to sustain its internal business environment. Equally, external microenvironmental factors of the market, suppliers, competitors, and intermediaries all influence the behavior of the firm in the business environment.

Business-level strategy

The approach taken by an organization to compete in its chosen markets. A business-level strategy can be competitive – battling against all competitors to secure competitive advantage –and/or cooperative advantage – working with one or more players to gain advantage against other competitors. Strategies can be classified into two generic types aimed a broad segment of market. (1) *Low-cost leadership* based on efficient cost production that enables the company to charge a lower price for its product than its competitors and still make a satisfactory profit. To illustrate Accor hotels cater to large segment of the population and strive to keep costs low, while providing clean, functional, and comfortable rooms. (2) *Differentiation* refers to the ability to provide unique value to customers and create brand loyalty that lowers customer sensitivity to price. To illustrate, Marriott has been adding services available to guests once they have checked in, including in-room services and toiletries.

Business Management Institute

The comprehensive educational program of the Club Managers Association of America (CMAA). Designed as a series of courses, the Business Management Institute (BMI) offers continuing education specifically for club managers. BMI currently consists of five hierarchical courses that serve managers ranging in experience from entry-level to senior-level club professionals; additionally, eight elective programs are available. All BMI courses are intensive one-week learning experiences taught by university faculty and industry experts at seven leading universities throughout the USA. BMI today exists as an educational role model for other professional organizations. It boasts of over 5000 graduates and serves as a stepping stone for club managers who aspire to the prestigious designation of Certified Club Manager (CCM).

Business' objectives

A goal or target of a hospitality business usually considered to be obtainable.

Objectives can be considered the fundamental strategy of a business. The objectives of the business must be operational. They must be capable of being converted into specific targets and goals. They must be capable of becoming the basis, as well as the motivation, of work and achievement. In any business, there will be multiple objectives, and the role of management is to balance a variety of needs and goals to achieve the aims.

Business process reengineering

Activities that transform a set of inputs into a set of outputs. Business process reengineering (BPR) has been propelled due to recent Information Communication Technology (ICT) developments and the proliferation of the Internet. Many hotels redesign their inter- and intra-organizational processes to increase efficiency and facilitate interaction and interconnectivity. Hospitality distribution is a good example of BPR, where hotels redesign best processes to reach their customers and partners. In contrast to continuous process improvements, BPR requires process designers to start from a clean slate, disassociating themselves from current thinking and focusing on a new course of action.

Successful BPR projects require senior management commitment and support, appropriate manpower and equipment, well-defined core business processes as well as project scope and objectives, adequate funding, technological innovation and solutions taken into consideration, assumptions, and preconceptions are challenged.

Business risk

The possibility of suffering harm or loss from any means. Business risk varies across industries as well as across firms within a given industry. Demand variability or seasonality, input cost fluctuations, sales price volatility, operating leverage, and a firm's ability to keep up with competition and to adapt its sales price to absorb cost fluctuations are some factors that can influence a firm's business risk. Such factors depend partly on a firm's industry characteristics. However, a firm's management may also control these factors to some extent. For instance, the seasonality in a ski resort's demand may be industry specific. However, the management may successfully reduce such demand volatility by organizing pre-season and post-season festivals, thereby stretching the seasons. The firm-specific aspect of business risk may also be an elimination via diversification by the firm's equity holders.

Cafeteria service

In cafeteria-style service, guests select their meals from food counters, the full length of which is known as a 'race', and place these on their meal tray. These meals might be pre-bought or paid for at the end of the race at the cash desk prior to sitting down to consume the meal. Usually, cutlery, napkins, additional crockery, and beverages are collected at the end of the race before proceeding to the cash desk. Cafeteria-style service can be found in on-site foodservice, which – depending on the venue – may also serve gourmet-style food.

Call center

A centralized office of a company that answers incoming telephone calls from customers or that makes outgoing telephone calls to customers (telemarketing, sometimes referred as a Central Reservation Office (CRO). In its simplest form, it consists of a telephone and a reservation agent. Generally, call centers have the ability to place multiple reservations at the same time through central reservation systems (CRS), usually through an 800 number. Hotel companies may have call centers that serve many different properties within the corporation. Airlines and car rental companies usually have one centralized call center in each of the different countries where they operate, all interlinked through the CRS. Centralized call centers have the advantage of providing consistent service and decreasing the company's costs, such as management and training. Multi-branded companies, however, may have different call centers and, in some cases, different CRSs within their system, mostly due to mergers and acquisitions.

Capital assets pricing model

A model that describes the relationship between risk and required rate of return. The capital assets pricing model (CAPM) proposes that the required rate of return on a risky asset is composed of the risk-free rate of return plus a risk premium, which is the excess market return over the risk-free rate multiplied by the level of systematic risk of the asset. Systematic risk, often denoted as beta, is a measure of a stock's covariance with the capital market. According to the CAPM, hospitality investors expect to be compensated for bearing the systematic risk. Symbolically, the CAPM for determining the required rate of return from a particular hospitality asset, say the ith security, can be described as:

$$R_i = R_f + \beta_i (R_m - R_f)$$

where
R_i is the required return on the ith security;
R_m is the return on the market portfolio;
R_f is the risk-free rate;
β_i is the estimated beta of the ith security.

Career planning and development

The lifelong process of working out a synthesis between individual interests and the opportunities (or limitations) present in the external work related environment, so that both individual and environmental objectives are fulfilled. It is a continual process that affects both the individual and the hospitality organization. For the individual in the hospitality industry it involves career planning and career outcomes and encompasses such issues as job change, mobility, and stages of a career. Whilst for the hospitality organization it is concerned with and influences human resource planning. The demise of the traditional hospitality organizational career, with its vertical progression, has affected an individual's career development with the trend now being to develop core skills, increase marketability, and develop employability. A gradual shift has been seen from the traditional skill base (such as food and beverage) to more managerial and business skills together with the need for international experience and language skills.

Cash flow

The term often used to describe the inflow and outflow of liquid assets from operations. A cash flow statement is one of the top three financial statements used in hospitality operations, along with income statements and balance statements. Neither the profit and loss statement nor the balance sheet shows the amount of funds available to meet current financial obligations, which is the purpose of a cash flow statement. For that reason, most financial institutions insist on healthy cash flow statements as an indication of their ability to meet current obligations. According to generally accepted accounting principles, cash flow statements can be prepared by the *direct method* or the *indirect method*. The direct method takes into consideration only the cash receipts and payments from operations. The indirect method considers all receipts and payments irrespective of the source.

Cash flow statement

An overview of the cash inflows and outflows of an organization. While the profit and loss statement can provide one perspective on the organization's profit performance, it fails to provide an indication

28

of the organization's cash flows. This is because the profit and loss statement is prepared on the basis of accrual accounting and not cash flow accounting. The statement of cash flows can thus be seen to provide useful supplementary information to that provided in the profit and loss statement. In the statement of cash flows example presented below, cash flow from operations represents the normal trading operations' cash receipts minus the cash payments associated with normal trading activities. The remainder of the terms used in the sample statement below is relatively self-explanatory.

Table 1   Cash flow statement for the ABC Hotel for the year ending December 31, 200X.

	$	$
Net cash flow from operations		210,000
Cash flow from investments and for servicing finance		
Interest on loan capital	(5,000)	
Drawings	(125,000)	
		(130,000)
		80,000
Investing activities		
Fixed assets purchased	(54,000)	
Proceeds from fixed assets sales	22,000	
		(32,000)
		48,000
Sources of finance		
Capital introduced	18,000	
Loan raised	4000	
		22,000
Net cash flow for the year		70,000

Casinos

A public room, hotel or building for gambling and other entertainment. Casino hotels have been one of the most rapidly growing and expanding sectors of the lodging industry over the past 15 years. Casino hotels vary in size from limited service-like 150/200 room hotels in small markets such as remote Native American reservations (Eagle Pass, Texas, some areas of North and South Dakota) or smaller riverboat jurisdictions in Iowa and Louisiana to large opulent hotels worthy of five star or diamond ratings as are found in Las Vegas and Connecticut. Four of the seven largest hotels (rooms wise) in the world are casino/hotels. These large casino/hotels can be found amongst the commercial casino brand names such as MGM Grand, Venetian, Caesars, and Native American casinos such as Foxwood's and Mohegan Sun, both of which are in Connecticut.

Centralization

An organization structure where elements of a system are united and consolidated under a single center. This type of organization can be applied to computer systems, networks, employees, accounting operations, and business facilities, as well. Centralization arose in the 1980s, when computers became able to establish better control in organization departments. The advantages of centralization are: increased organization of a system, cost reduction due to standardization of equipment and procedures, and increased efficiency. The downside is inflexibility and slow implementation of structural changes. Hotel reservation systems are sometimes made for smaller individual hotels, while for hotel chains they have centralized reservation facilities. When several reservation systems should be integrated, their infrastructure could be organized according to the decentralization principles.

Centralized guestroom HVAC

Centralized guestroom HVAC (heat, ventilation, and air conditioning) systems utilize fan coil units installed either vertically (usually adjacent to a window) or horizontally (usually immediately over the entry area within the room). The fan coil units consist of a copper pipe with fins to enhance heat transfer and a drip pan and drain to collect condensate that may occur during cooling operation. There is also a fan to circulate air through the unit and out into the room and a filter to remove airborne dust. The fan coil units are connected to pipes which deliver chilled or hot water to the rooms. Rooms with two pipe fan coil units can only deliver heat (if the pipes are connected to the boiler) or cold (if the pipes are connected to the chiller) with the connection decision made based on the climate season (chiller connection in common cooling seasons and boiler in common heating seasons).

Chain restaurants

Chain (also called *multi-unit*) restaurant companies dominate the modern retail landscape, but for all intents and purposes the chain restaurant segment is a post-World War II phenomenon. There were multi-unit operators prior to 1950, but they were few and far between. Since 1954, chains have been slowly growing to the point of now representing more than one out of every two dollars in US foodservice sales.

Probably the greatest contribution to the ideas we now accept as defining the chain restaurant came from industry pioneer Howard Johnson. He began quite modestly, selling ice cream to beach goers at a traffic circle on US Highway 1 in Quincy, Massachusetts in the early 1920s. Howard Johnson was completely focused on operational excellence, and it is generally accepted that he was the first to describe each of the units in his system as being like a 'link in a *chain of restaurants*'.

Change management

Change management is usually seen as the planned organizational response to two objectives: response to external and internal environmental factors and improvements on performance. External factors include political, economic, social, and technological events or circumstances which influence the environment in which an organization functions. Within the hospitality and tourism sector these include the impact of regional conflicts, regional or global recession, demographic changes, property prices, increased leisure spend, increasing globalization, the emergence of markets, and new business centers in newly industrialized countries and the increasing use of the Internet by both businesses and individuals. Internal factors can be such things as a change in ownership as a result of mergers and acquisitions, procedural or policy changes to reinforce brand differentiation or customer focus, restructuring to achieve greater job flexibility, expansion or downsizing. The key to change management is not only to be able to respond to these drivers of change but also to anticipate them.

Characteristics of service

The following are 15 characteristics that are unique to the production and delivery of services by hospitality firms where success is achieved through differentiation from their competition:

1. Service is an experience for the customer.
2. Service is a performance by an employee or product.
3. When service is delivered, the guest and service provider are both part of the transaction.
4. Service quality is difficult to control and evaluate.
5. The customer and the organization often measure quality of service differently.
6. When service is delivered, there can be no recall of the guest's experience.
7. Estimating the cost of service delivery is difficult.

8. Excess production of service cannot be placed in inventory.
9. Service delivery and demand can be individually customized.
10. Successful service delivery can be achieved with different viewpoints.
11. The delivery of service is viewed as a series of tasks.
12. Service is a strategy.
13. Service is often provided as a value added to a physical product.
14. Service has an aspect of time.
15. When purchasing services there is limited or no ownership.

Checkout

The process by which a guest settles his account and leaves the hotel. This is the last stage of the guest cycle and is one of the last contacts that a guest has with the hotel. The main objective here is to settle the guest account, to update room status information and to create a guest history record. Due to changes in technology there are other check out options available, namely express checkout and self-checkout. *Express checkout* is the process by which the guest authorizes the hotel to charge his/her credit card without stopping by the front desk to physically checkout. *Self-checkout* involves the (credit card) guest actually checking themselves out of the system through terminals located in the lobby area or via in-room systems which may be connected to the front office computer.

City ledger

In hotels, a set of accounts for groups, non-guests, and unsettled guest accounts. In accounting terms, the city ledger is part of the accounts receivable balance on the balance sheet. When the guest or group checks out, the balance is transferred to the back of the house accounting systems for the accounting department to begin the collection process.

Cleaning schedule

Scheduling is the housekeeping departments' most important management function. Without a clear and well thought out schedule every day may present one crisis after another. Since the housekeeping department is responsible for cleaning so many different areas of the hotel, scheduling the work of the department must be done with a systematic, step-by-step approach. Scheduling includes:

- Creating inventory lists of all items within each area that will need housekeeping's attention.
- Determining the frequency or number of times the items on the inventory lists are to be cleaned.

- Creating performance standards which clearly state not only what must be done but detail how the job must be done.
- Identifying productivity standards that describe the acceptable quantity of work to be done by the departments employees.
- Providing appropriate equipment and supply inventory levels to insure that the employees have the necessary equipment and supplies to get their jobs done.

Clicks and mortar

The term *clicks and mortar* (alternatively known as *bricks and clicks*, *surf and turf*, *cyber-enhanced retailing*, and *hybrid e-commerce*) refers to supplementing physical outlets of traditional *bricks-and-mortar* businesses with e-commerce capabilities on the Web. Potential sources of synergy between physical and virtual channels include common infrastructure, common operations, common marketing and sales, common buyers, and other complementary assets (e.g. existing supplier and distributor relationships, experience in the market, and a customer base). This enables the business to take better advantage of an innovation like e-commerce. In the hospitality industry, the role of trust in consumer purchasing is paramount and the use of the Web to capitalize on strongly branded products, for example international chain hotel brands, in responding to the needs of carefully researched markets cannot be underestimated.

Club board of directors

The governing function of private equity clubs is assigned to a board of directors otherwise known as board of governors. A club's board is comprised of directors and club officers (i.e. president, vice-president, treasurer, and secretary). These positions are typically elected on a rotating two-year basis so that there is never a complete replacement of the entire board in any given year. Members of the board are elected either by (a) an election by the club's membership or (b) an election held by the present board officers. In an effort to preserve the consistent provision of club services the board of directors sets forth club bylaws concerning club operation, fiduciary responsibilities of the club as reflected in financial statements, operational and reserve budgets, membership nomination, committee of standing committees, and in some settings the hiring of key management personnel such as the recreational professionals (i.e. tennis, aquatic, golf, clubhouse manager, and general manager).

Club corporation

A renowned developer of private clubs and golf courses throughout the world. Founded in 1957, Dallas-based ClubCorp has approximately $1.6 billion in assets. Internationally, ClubCorp owns or operates nearly 200 golf courses, country clubs, private business and sports clubs, and resorts. Among the company's nationally recognized golf properties are Pinehurst in the Village of Pinehurst, North Carolina (the world's largest golf resort, site of the 1999 and 2005 US Opens); Firestone Country Club in Akron, Ohio (site of the 2003 World Golf Championships – NEC Invitational); Indian Wells Country Club in Indian Wells, California (site of the Bob Hope Chrysler Classic); the Homestead in Hot Springs, Virginia (America's first resort founded in 1766); and Mission Hills Country Club in Rancho Mirage, California (home of the Kraft Nabisco Championship). The company's 19,000 employees serve the nearly 210,000 member households and 200,000 guests who visit ClubCorp properties each year.

Club entertainment

A critical part of club member satisfaction is directly related to the process of entertaining club members. This is important to note because well-designed entertainment entices the members to utilize the club while enhancing the perception that the club is an exciting place to be. Designing club entertainment is not a haphazard process, instead the design and deployment of an entertainment program requires a thorough assessment of club members' needs, wants, and expectations. This is a challenging and rewarding process because entertainment can range from children's programs, graduation parties, honeymoon celebrations, weddings, holiday parties, to debutante celebrations each of which requires unique planning, physical arrangements, ambiance, and personnel requirements. Entertainment can be of two varieties. First is the special event type of entertainment that is a one-time event or second, the cyclic event that is largely conducted using internal staff, club members, or management. All planned entertainment must be approved by the appropriate club committee and overseen by management.

Club fitness programs

The primary objectives of a private club's physical fitness program are the improvement of the general health and well-being for those individuals that choose to engage in a structured physical fitness program. The secondary benefits of a member fitness program encompasses enhanced social interaction with other club members, a means of allowing members to entertain clients while promoting the club, and a means of interacting with family members in a private setting. Common fitness programs include general physical conditioning (including weight training), aquatics, and tennis. The oversight of a club's fitness program varies with the type of fitness services and how responsibilities are assigned to each of the fitness areas. The physical fitness area of a club encompasses a fitness area, exercise area, sports area, and spa areas.

34

Club management

A profession that involves managing all of the different areas and departments in a club. A club manager generally supervises the following departments and/or staff: accountant/comptroller, upscale dining, casual dining, banquets, lounge/bar, maintenance, locker rooms, kitchen, membership, aquatics, and tennis. If the manager is a general manager than the golf program/golf professional and golf course maintenance/golf course superintendent also report to the general manager. The manager implements the policies set by the board and oversees the operation of the club. Club managers need skills in multiple areas such as guest service skills, good supervisory skills, financial skills, personnel and legal skills, and knowledge in food and beverage. Manager of golf or athletic clubs should have some knowledge of the sports and activities they will be overseeing. It should be enough knowledge so that they can interact with the professionals working in those departments.

Club manager certification programs

In an effort to keep private club management current with trends and issues in the private club industry, the Club Managers Association of American (CMAA) offers professional development courses that lead to educational and professional designations. This type of program is important to note because a private club manager's success within a club setting requires a willingness and commitment to professional development. The professional development programs offered through CMAA are multi-level courses that are designed for entry level to senior management. These certification programs are university-based courses that are structured as one-week courses as composed of five unique levels of Business Management Institute (BMI) I–V. The titles of the five levels are: BMI I – *The Basic Club Management School*; BMI II – *The Leadership Edge*; BMI III – *The Chief Operating Officer Concept*; BMI IV – *Managerial Excellence: Tactics for Today*; and BMI V – *Strategies for Tomorrow, Realities for Today*.

Club Managers Association of America

A professional, non-profit membership organization whose mission is to 'advance the profession of club management by fulfilling the educational and related needs of its members'. The Club Managers Association of America (CMAA) is an association with a membership of over 6000 dues-paying club professionals who belong to more than 50 regional chapters throughout the USA and around the world. CMAA serves to unify an otherwise fragmented industry, and it has played a pivotal role in evolving the job of a club manager into a highly respected profession. The objectives of the association are to promote and advance friendly relations between and among persons connected with the management of clubs and other associations of similar character; to encourage the education and advancement of its members; to assist club officers and members, through their managers; and to secure the utmost in efficient and successful operations.

Club membership categories

The following category definitions apply to an equity club type of operation only. While not all equity clubs will offer these classifications, these membership categories are readily accepted within the private equity club sector:

- *Absentee* membership, for members who are out of the country for an extended period of time.
- *Associate* membership, also known as a non-resident membership, applies to out-of-state members that desire to use the club on a seasonal (e.g. infrequent) basis.
- *Clergy* membership is offered to local clergy.
- *Founder* membership applies to an individual or individuals that provided the funds that established the club.
- *Golf* membership for individuals that want nothing more than to use the golf course facilities of the club.
- *Honorary* memberships are offered to individuals that are respected leaders in the community.
- *Junior* membership applies to individuals that are under a specified aged as noted in the club's bylaws. This classification only applies to the children of club members.
- *Regular* membership within an equity club means that members pay an initiation fee to join a club of preference with either none or at least a partial part of the initiation fee being refunded upon the member's separation from the club.
- *Reciprocity* membership is an agreement between clubs that are commonly geographically remote.
- *Senior* membership is available to individuals that have been members for a specified number of years and have reached a certain age.
- *Social* membership classification appeals to those individuals that seek out social functions within the club while not desiring to use recreational services (i.e. golf course, tennis, racquet, and etcetera).
- *Surviving spouse* classification is a special membership where the surviving spouse of a member assumes the membership classification of the deceased member.
- *Temporary* membership category in cases where visiting dignitaries are in the area.

Club membership nomination

In general the initial step in gaining club membership is to submit a formal application to the club. Before an application will be considered the prospective member must be sponsored by a club member. The role of this member sponsor is critical to the receipt and acceptance of this inquiry given the selective nature of the application process. The sponsoring member ensures that all the necessary information is contained in the application and then forward the application to club management or to the membership committee. In many clubs the prospective member's application is sent out for scrutiny to the club membership. This is important to note because the club's members can accept or reject the applicant based on personal reasons, stature in the community, fit with values of the club, or some other pertinent reason. In all cases, the general consensus of the membership is strongly considered before the membership committee levies their vote for approval or rejection.

Club membership process

Access to a private club is restricted to members, their immediate families, and guests of the members. To join a club a candidate for membership must be sponsored by a current member. In addition, the applicant has to provide letters of recommendations from other members that are in good standing. The application is then carried forward to management or the membership committee for consideration. As such, the member that forward the nomination must be a strong advocate for the applicant. The candidate or nominee for membership is then evaluated by the membership committee to ensure that the candidate is a good 'fit' for the club and the applicant meets the criteria for club membership. In some private clubs the candidate may have to meet and interview with the board members.

Club officers

The governing body of a private equity club is comprised of a group of club officers that preside over the club's operation. This policy-making function is clearly delineated within the club's charter as recorded with the state in question. The president performs the function of directing the club officers within their policy-making capacity for the club. The vice-president serves in an advisory function to the president and replaces the president when he or she cannot attend a board meeting. The secretary sets the meeting agendas, records all meeting minutes, and distributes meeting reports to the board members. The treasurer files reports of the club's financial status as disseminated from the finance/budget committee. The sergeant in arms is given the role of ensuring that the board of directors follows proper rules of conduct which is formally Roberts Rules of Order.

Club professionals

The skills required to run a private club correspond directly to the complexity of services offered through the club's departments. Given that the clubhouse is the social hub for the club, the most influential person in satisfying members' culinary tastes is the executive chief. Another person that is critical to the delivery of quality service within the clubhouse is the assistant general manager, also known as the clubhouse manager. The duties of an aquatics director entail management of daily aquatic center operations, maintenance of aquatic facilities, and supervision of aquatics staff. The primary golf professional at a private club is called the golf director or golf pro. The grounds superintendent of a private club plays a critical role in the maintenance of the grounds and in staffing grounds personnel. The tennis professional at a private club handles the daily management of tennis facilities which includes hiring, training, and performance appraisal of tennis staff. The last but not least to be mentioned is the club's general manager. The general manager, or chief executive officer, of a private equity club plays a pivotal role in communicating operational concerns with the club's board of directors.

Club reciprocity

When private clubs enter into a reciprocity agreement the respective members have the right to use the facilities and services of a reciprocal club while traveling in that area whether locally, nationally, or internationally. When planning to exercise their reciprocal usage rights the member must notify management of the receiving club of the time and duration of their travel plans. Another example of a reciprocal agreement is when a private club is undergoing a major renovation that requires the club to close down of an extended period. In this instance a reciprocal use agreement is sought so that club members do not experience a discontinuation of services while the renovation process is taking place. However, the entire club does not have to be under renovation for this type of agreement to be put into effect. A reciprocity agreement can also be exercised when club services are only partially under renovation.

Club types

The following are brief definitions that delineate the different club types:

- *City club*: A club that typically offers its members food and beverage service and is usually located in a downtown or urban location.

- *Country club*: A club that typically offers its members and families a variety of activities and services. And is usually located in the country or suburbs because of the large amount of land needed for the golf course.
- *Yacht club*: A club that is typically on a body of water with members who have an interest in boating (sailboats or powerboats).
- *Golf club*: A club that is similar to a country club but usually only has golf as its sole recreational activity.
- *Health club*: A club that offers it members access to personal use of fitness equipment and physical conditioning programs.
- *City-athletic club*: A city club (business food and beverage) that usually has sports facilities.
- *Member-owned club*: A club that is usually owned by its members which means that the members have invested in the club.
- *Corporate club*: A club owned by a company, partnership, or individual.
- *Developer club*: A club started by a real estate developer. The club is usually sold or given to the members (becoming a member-owned club at that time) after the developer sells and develops the majority of the real estate lots in the development.
- *Military club*: A club that is usually open to a specific branch of the military for its officers and enlisted personnel (e.g. Army Navy Club, etc.).
- *University club*: A club that is usually open to faculty, staff, alumni, and students of a specific university. Some clubs that have the name the University Club in a city are not directly affiliated with a specific school.
- *Equity club*: A club where the members or shareholders receive a portion or all of the up-front fees paid when a member resigns or leaves the club.
- *Non-equity club*: A club that does not have any liability to resigning members for repayment of up-front joining fees.
- *Semi-private club*: A mixed-use club that caters to both the general public and private members.

Clubhouse

Part of the club's physical structure that offers a centralized place whereby club members can meet and socialize. Depending on the type of club, the clubhouse can be rather austere in ambiance and furnishing up to the most lavishly adorned facilities with granite, marble, antique displays, libraries, smoking rooms, card rooms, formal dining, informal or casual dining facilities, bar and cocktail lounge, piano bar, small to large meeting rooms, aerobic rooms, fitness areas, and a spa. This is not an exhaustive list because the range and quality of the club's facilities is a direct reflection of the club members' desires. Due to the influence of socializing within a private club, the food and beverage function plays a critical role to the clubhouse experience. The clubhouse also plays a critical role in the establishment of loyalty via member satisfaction and in promoting the club to non-members.

Coaching

A directive process by a manager to train and orient an employee to the realities of the workplace and to help the employee remove barriers to optimum work performance. Coaching can be a cost effective alternative to formal training in the development of services/experiences staff in hospitality organizations. Coaching focuses more on the personal development needs of employees enabling them to perform at a higher level in the organization while consulting focuses on helping employees achieve a particular desired organizational result. Given the unique nature of services, coaching can be very effective in developing empowered employees. Coaching is particularly important in organizational change and when particular competencies are desired or needed in an organization. It can also be an effective way of socializing employees.

Co-branding

Co-branding occurs when brands from different organizations (or distinctly different businesses within the same organization) combine to create an offering in which each plays a driver role. One of the co-brands can be a component or an ingredient brand (McDonald's New Premium Salads with Newman's Dressings) or an endorser (Fairmont Hotels offer the Porsche Experience). The design and implementation of co-branding efforts is complex and the returns in terms of finances and brand building cannot be pre-determined. Forces affecting one brand can result in a blurring of the other brand. The key to successful co-branding is to find a partner brand that will enhance the offering by complementary associations. It is important to consider the individual brand associations, ways to leverage them, benefits for each brand, and how the alliance will fit into their existing business models. Achieving effective, complementary associations can enhance and strengthen the overall position of both brands.

Cognitive dissonance

In the field of marketing, cognitive dissonance refers to doubts that may occur shortly after the purchase of a product or service when the buyer questions whether or not he or she made the right decision in purchasing the product. The consumer typically ponders the question of – Did I make a good decision? Did I buy the right product or service? (or) Did I get a good value? During the post-purchase evaluation stage of the consumer decision process, a buyer may experience cognitive dissonance. Hospitality and tourism companies generally minimize these questions with several strategies. Cognitive dissonance may be reduced through effective communication with the consumer and following-up with the consumer after the purchase. Hospitality providers may also reduce consumer uncertainty by quickly responding to and rectifying any problems identified by the consumer as a result of a purchase as well as offering satisfaction or money-back guarantees or service warranties.

Collective bargaining

The process of bipartite negotiations between parties (hospitality managers and employees) who bargain directly with one another, usually unaided by either a mediator or industrial tribunal. In some countries collective bargaining can occur with direct legislative support and intervention where industrial legislation provides procedures for bargaining such recognizing the role of bargaining agents (trade unions), allowing either party to take industrial action during a 'protected' bargaining period (protected from common law damages under tort) and an obligation by the parties to bargain in 'good' faith by attending meetings, providing information, and negotiating the agenda in good faith.

Combined heat and power cogeneration

The simultaneous production of heat (hot water or steam) and power (electricity). There are two primary types of combined heat and power cogeneration (CHP) units. In one type, water is heated in a boiler and the resultant steam is used to turn the blades of a turbine. The turbine is connected to a generator that produces electricity and the heat generated can be recovered for use at the property. A second type of CHP unit uses an engine or turbine driving a generator with heat captured from the engine. The engine captured heat from both types of CHP may be used for water heating, space heating, or to power an absorption chiller. Some of these cogeneration devices are sized to provide electricity and domestic hot water for hotels, motels, and even restaurants.

Comfort zones and human comfort

Comfort zones delineate specific combinations of temperature and relative humidity (RH) ranges where statistical tests have shown 80 per cent of the tested population to be comfortable. These zones are different for winter and summer conditions. Higher RH necessitates cooler dry bulb temperatures to be in the comfort zone. It is more energy efficient for a facility to have a lower temperature with a more humid environment during the winter, and a dryer but higher dry bulb temperature during the summer. The temperature and humidity ranges defined as the comfort zone are rather wide. The winter comfort zone is between 68°F (20°C) with 90 per cent RH and 76°F (24.4°C) with 25 per cent RH. The summer conditions are between 74°F (23.3°C) with 90 per cent RH and 81°F (27.2°C) with 25 per cent RH. Additional factors influencing comfort include room air movement, activity level in the room, clothing worn by room occupants and the temperature of the room surfaces.

Commercial home

The provision of commercial hospitality within a home setting. The traditional private home setting is highly significant as a temporal and cultural construct suggesting a relationship between the host and the home setting. The home and its artifacts act as a reflection of the householder's personality. The type of home setting can be classified as of three types: traditional, virtual reality, and 'backdrop'. Traditional is where the private home setting is strongest, for example host families, bed and breakfasts, self-catering properties, small family-run hotels, or religious retreats. Virtual reality is where the home setting as a construct is reproduced artificially, for example timeshare accommodation, town house, or country house hotels. Backdrop homes refer to the use of the home setting and its associations for commercial purposes, for example a house used as a visitor attraction, or a house used as a film set.

Commitment

The extent to which an employee identifies with an organization and is committed to its goals and objectives. Higher levels of employee commitment have been linked to higher levels of productivity and service quality, a vital factor in a service industry like hospitality. The use of power has also been linked with commitment, with positive management styles being associated with commitment, whereas more coercive styles are associated with compliance rather than commitment. The challenge for hospitality managers is building a culture of commitment within an industry traditionally perceived as a poor employer, with long hours and poor rewards. Levels of organizational commitment amongst employees may vary according to sector and nationality. For example, levels of commitment may be higher for employees of international, luxury hotel chains, whereas, smaller, local hotels might struggle to keep employees who feel that they have little to offer them in terms of career development.

Common-size financial statements

In order to undertake meaningful comparisons of financial results between businesses of different sizes or scale of operations, it is important the comparisons are assessed on a like-for-like basis, that is on a level playing field. In terms of implementation, the issue of operating efficiency can be addressed by the presentation of profit and loss statements in what is termed 'common-size' format. Total revenue is taken to represent 100 per cent and the various individual expense items are expressed in 'relative' terms as percentages of the total revenue. With regard to hotels, however, the nature of the business offers another approach to the presentation of common-size profit and loss statements, based on the 'per available room' (PAR) concept. The PAR concept neutralizes the influence of capacity (size) and allows a hotel's financial results to be compared (benchmarked) against (say) other mid-market hotels (with differing numbers of rooms) PAR results in the same company.

Communication

The exchange of information and understanding. Effective communication is vital for organizational success and is positively correlated with employee job satisfaction and performance. Communication is particularly important for service encounters, as without effective communication, service quality will suffer. However, there is always a balancing act between enough communication with a customer to ensure friendliness and warmth, but not so much that staff appear impolite and disrespectful. Within the global hospitality industry, there are several factors that complicate the communication process; hospitality managers might work for foreign-owned companies, deal with non-native guests or customers, manage a multi-cultural and multi-lingual workforce and collaborate with other managers around the world. They, therefore, have to be able to deal with a multiplicity of communication behaviors in many different contexts, languages, or cultures.

Comparative statement analysis

An effective technique for the comparison of financial results with either past or budgeted results, or industry norms. For example, the comparison of actual results with budgeted results is carried out as follows:

$$\text{Actual result} - \text{Budgeted result} = \text{Absolute variance}$$

If a hotel achieves actual room sales revenue for a month of $68,600 against a budget of $70,000 the comparison will show an 'absolute' (numerical) variance of −$1400

($68,600–$70,000). In order to improve the understanding of the absolute variance resulting from the revenue shortfall, it is necessary to determine the 'relative' (percentage) variance by:

$(-\$1400/\$70,000) \times 100 = -2\%$ and presented as follows:

	Actual	Budget	Absolute variance	Relative variance
Room sales revenue	$68,600	$70,000	−$1400	−2%

The room revenue variance of −$1400 represents a 2 percent shortfall against budget, thus providing additional insight into the relative comparison by relating the absolute variance as a proportion of the budgeted rooms revenue.

Compensation

In the USA compensation is defined as all salary, wages, and other money payable to an employee or member of an organization for duties performed for an employer but not including reimbursement for other expenses such as travel or moving or. In other English speaking countries such as Australia, Canada, and UK, compensation refers to payments or reparations made to employees for lost wages due to personal loss or injury on the job. In the USA, the equivalent term for this type of compensation is called 'worker's compensation'. Monetary compensation for workplace injury or illness or psychological injuries has been an accepted form of dealing with workplace injury, however, today there is greater emphasizes on prevention and rehabilitation strategies to help individuals return to work. Compensation is paid irrespective of whether the employee was negligent or not (with some exceptions including intoxication and self-inflicted injuries). The notion of injury is broadly defined and can extend to items of personal property, which may have been damaged as a result of a personal injury. In many countries, there are mandatory workers' compensation schemes and employers who fail to comply risk heavy non-compliance penalties. Emphasis is on the implementation of risk assessment strategies in order to control workplace hazards and risks. In the hospitality industry, areas of work that are generally considered high risk include rooms (back and stretch injuries), kitchens (slips, sprains, and heat), and cleaning (chemicals and repetitive train).

Competencies

The collective learning in the hospitality firm, especially how to coordinate diverse production skills and integrate multiple streams of technology throughout the hotel or restaurant. In addition, it is

44

about the organization of work and the delivery of value, communication, involvement, and a deep commitment to working across organizational boundaries. Most often, core competencies are process or skills rather than physical assets or technologies. They are the central skill sets used by the firm to produce its products. For numerous organizations in the service industry core competencies include functional aspect of service (how) rather than technical (what). Competencies are built over time through the complex integration of organizational activities and are difficult to imitate.

Competency profiling

A method used to identify specified skills, knowledge, attitudes, and behavior necessary to fulfilling a task, activity, or career. Competencies can be graded or profiled according to the level of novice, apprentice, competent, or expert.

- *Novice*: A basic level of understanding but employee has not performed the task before.
- *Apprentice*: Employee has performed task with help or has understanding and limited practical experience.
- *Competent*: Employee has depth of understanding and consistently performs task to required standard.
- *Expert*: Consistently performs task to the required standard and looks at ways of improving ways to working, has in-depth understanding and could train others.

Competition-based pricing

A strategy of pricing based on what the competitors' charge. Also called price matching. The strategy is highly prevalent in the travel and tourism industry. Very often hotels, restaurants, and airlines follow the pricing strategy of the competition with the fear that they will price themselves out of the market. It is also based on the belief of those who used this strategy that somehow the competition knows something that they do not know. In this scenario, market leaders often set the price level and others follow the lead.

Competitive advantage

The set of factors or capabilities that allow a hospitality firm to consistently outperform its rivals. Not all hospitality firms have a competitive advantage. Businesses may enjoy a sustained competitive advantage if their capabilities are valuable and rare, lack substitutes and are difficult to imitate. Usually, the advantage is a process or skill but occasionally it can be an asset. For example, Hyatt has created a competitive advantage through the use of innovative architectural design of their hotel buildings. In contrast, location might become a competitive advantage. The Plaza Hotel in New York City is the only hotel that can occupy that prestigious corner lot on 5th Avenue across from Central Park. A competitive advantage may be created through an accumulation process that includes time, an interconnectedness of capabilities, steady investment, building upon past successes, and shrouding the advantage from the view of competitors.

Competitive position

A firm's competitive position can be looked on as how successfully a company competes in the marketplace relative to its competitors. Thus, the competitive position concept is concerned with how strongly the firm holds its present position and if it is positioned to maintain or improve this position in the future. The resource-based view asserts that a strong competitive position is created by firms committing tangible and intangible resources, which become a bundle of unique products and capabilities. A defensible competitive position can be formed when this process creates value to the customer and cannot be easily imitated by competitors.

Managers make resource allocation decisions to implement competitive methods addressing 'what' portfolio of products and services will be offered, 'how' these will be offered and implemented to maximize value to the customer, and 'how' this portfolio can be consistently delivered to maintain a strong competitive position relative to industry or segment competitors.

Competitive strategy

A comprehensive master plan of 'what' an organization intends to accomplish and 'how' it plans to implement and achieve its mission, goals, and objectives. The formulation of what an organization intends to achieve is referred to as strategic ends. Types of strategic ends include mission statements, business purpose, key strategic goals, market share objectives, financial target objectives, and key result areas. The formulation of how an organization intends to achieve its mission, goals, and objectives is referred to as strategic means. Strategic means can be described as strategies, policies, alternatives, programs, and action plans. Strategic ends and means make up the overriding competitive strategy for a firm. When properly formulated, the competitive strategy maximizes the competitive advantage for the firm and minimizes any competitive disadvantage.

Computer

An electronic machine, which comprises hardware and software as the major components. Hardware refers to the collection of chips and other electronic devices of a computer system, which are the identifiable and movable elements. In order to drive the operations of hardware components, a set of computer programs known as software is needed to control the electronic devices. A typical computer processing cycle consists of four stages: input, process, output, and storage. An input device gets computer accessible data, and transfers the data to a processing unit. The electronic circuit of the processing unit then transforms input data to information. After that, an output device produces the user-required information in a human comprehensible form. Lastly, an internal or external storage device can store data and information.

Computer reservation system

Computer reservation systems (CRS) are primarily used for inventory management by airlines, hotels, and other tourism and hospitality enterprises. Enhanced and sophisticated CRS configurations and functionality offer companies an integrated solution for several processes including managing sales, bookings, customer relationship management and service, other marketing practices, yield management, payments, and accounting even at a one-to-one customer basis. Integrated CRS aim to organize companies internally by enabling organizational reengineering/restructuring changes that in turn streamline processes and foster functional efficiency and effectiveness. Moreover, the term central reservation system refers to the CRS developed by hotel chains for centralizing the reservation process of all their affiliated properties and enabling multi-chain management. The major benefits of such systems are operational efficiencies and staff reductions. Through terminals and systems interconnections, enhanced CRS configurations can allow direct access to stock and price inventories to intermediaries and/or final customers for checking availability, making bookings, and payments.

Computerized maintenance management system

A software application designed to provide logical, easy to use tools to manage all maintenance functions of the engineering department. A computerized maintenance management system (CMMS) supports and enhances the responsiveness and effectiveness of the engineering department. Typically, these systems provide a variety of modules including diagnostic and equipment history data, staff scheduling and productivity reports, scheduled and preventive maintenance tracking, work order backlog control, inventory tracking, purchase order generation, supplier information, communication within the department and with departments outside of the engineering department, and information regarding adherence to standards and regulatory compliance. Typically, a service request is entered into the CMMS after it is received by e-mail or phone. The service request generates a work order number, which is then assigned to a maintenance engineer who then responds to the request. A request by e-mail generates a return e-mail with a brief description of the request and the work order number.

Concept mapping

A technique that provides a more complete understanding of relationships among ideas, concepts, and even business operations. The traditional approach to concept mapping involves linking related ideas unidirectionally and expanding the number of ideas while brainstorming or investigating complex clusters of interrelated ideas. Concept mapping is also instrumental in analyzing units on the basis of dimensional attributes.

It is this latter application that offers utility to hospitality operators. For example, suppose a restaurant operator is considering entering a new market, he/she may want to know what type of restaurants are currently operating in that market, separating each on the basis of cuisine style and average entrée price while also considering the size of each restaurant in the analysis. As shown in Figure 1, such a map readily identifies gaps in the market. Here the size of each unit is depicted by the diameter of the associated data point and the color equates to the type of cuisine.

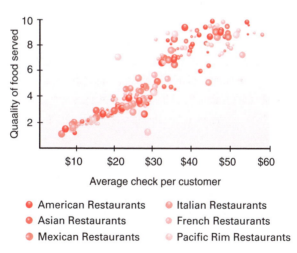

Figure 1   Quality of food served versus average check.

Concierge

A hotel functionary that assists the guest with most problems concerning accommodations, handles their mail, and facilitates special requests with the front desk agent and other hotel personnel. Typically, the concierge reports to the front office manager. The concierge assistant, bell captain, and doorman report directly to the concierge. The concierge establishes policies and procedures and writes job descriptions, training manuals, and procedures for all areas of guest services, including bell service, doorman service, guest paging, baggage and package handling, guest tour and travel services, and special guest requirements. Additional responsibilities include assisting guests with the many unscheduled guest service needs (theater tickets, car rentals, sight-seeing tours, travel information, etc.); coordinating with the assistant manager, the senior assistant front office manager, and other departments; supervising and coordinating the parking of guest cars, and the coordinating with the laundry manager to ensure quality laundry and valet service.

Concurrent sessions

Concurrent sessions in meetings and conferences are two or more plenary or breakout sessions which run concurrently, or at the same time as others with the understanding that participants will select or be assigned to those sessions. Concurrent sessions are much the same as breakout sessions. Concurrent sessions typically differ in complexity, themes, subject matter, and/or target audience, but also typically, run on an identical time schedule to assure that break times and transitions to other sessions are not disrupted. While concurrent sessions are different in context, they are designed to bring people together with a common interest or need and provide educational enhancement for participants. Concurrent sessions are typically in a conference-style format and typically serve groups of 150 or more and last between 1 and 1.5 hours. Group discussions may also be incorporated into the session. By utilizing concurrent sessions, meeting planners can provided options for attendees and are better able to meet event objectives.

Condominium

A condominium describes the absolute ownership of an apartment in a multi-unit building based on a legal description of the air space the unit actually occupies. Common areas such as the land, the physical structure, the lobby, and any amenities are owned jointly by all condominium unit owners. Common charges and fees for operational and managerial expenses are allocated among the owners of the condominiums based on the square foot percentage of each owner's unit.

Condominium hotel

Buildings whose suites are individually owned but are collectively marketed and operated as a hotel. Typically, condominium hotels offer housekeeping, front office and security services, and full or limited food and beverage facilities. In some condominium hotels the units are rented for a minimum stay of one week. Typically, investors in condo hotel suites are motivated by tax write-off opportunities, personal free use of their unit during a limited period of time each year and the potential profit share derived from the yearly rental of their unit to tourists.

Conference

A meeting characterized by its participatory nature, designed for the discussion of subjects related to a specific topic or area that may include fact-finding, problem-solving, and consultation. It is an event used by any organization to meet and exchange views, convey a message, open a debate, or give publicity to some area of opinion on a specific issue. No tradition, continuity or specific period is required to convene a conference. Although not generally limited in time, conferences are usually of short duration with specific objectives. Conferences are generally on a smaller scale than congresses and/or conventions and do not have exhibits. Conferences may be held in a variety of venues, including conference centers, conference hotels, convention centers, universities, and resorts. A conference may be organized by an association, a corporation, a for-profit company, a not-for-profit organization, or any other entity that wants to produce it.

Conference Center

A facility dedicated as an adult learning environment and designed for the comfort of the meeting participant. In order to conform to the 'universal criteria' of best practices as established by the International Association of Conference Center (IACC) it should provide ergonomic furniture, state of the art audio-visual and computer equipment, leisure time activities and offer unique and plentiful food and beverage choices. Most conference centers are also residential and provide guest rooms although this is not a requirement of the IACC. In addition to companies like Marriott and Hilton, conference centers may be owned and operated by corporations for in-house staff training and education, managed by a university, or privately owned. Often times the fees for a conference center are based on a CMP or Complete Meeting Package. This is usually a per person/per day fee, covering the cost of the sleeping room, food and beverage, meeting space rental, and audio-visual equipment.

Conference plan

A roadmap for the overall programming of different sessions held during a conference. The plan takes into account the broad goals and specific objectives of the conference organizer or producer. It helps in the development of individual session content and plays an important role in the overall success of the individual sessions. Sessions for meetings, conferences, and training events are all different in context and purpose, but the development for each is much the same. One key element in the plan is to require the session content developer to submit an outline which includes measurable objectives for the session. This outline will assist the planner on keeping the development of instructional material on track for the session.

Configurations

In the field of organizational behavior, the notion that organizational effectiveness is not attributable to a single factor, but the intercorrelation between a number of factors. Performance is thus seen as dependent upon the development of a compatible mix of organizational characteristics – a configuration – for example, a particular blend of structure, culture, and management style. The researchers most closely associated with configurations are D. Miller, and P. H. Friesen, who focused upon developing archetypes of strategy formation. They argued that change in organizations is not an incremental process, but a quantum one whereby many elements are changed concurrently – a strategic revolution.

This 'quantum theory of change' is a sharp contrast to the idea of the learning organization and its view that change is a continuous process involving small incremental adjustments.

Confirmed reservation

An oral or written confirmation by a hospitality supplier such as a hotel, that it has received and will honor a reservation. Confirmations can be given over the telephone but this is not as good a method as putting the response in writing. The letter of confirmation has certain advantages, that is it allows the hotel to inform the guest of the details of the request and includes information such as the rate(s) quoted, gives information on cancellation procedures, suitable methods of payment, and any special requests made. A confirmed reservation will only be held until the cancellation hour deadline after which the reservation will be released for sale to the next interested customer.

Conflict (work related)

A generic term that usually refers to various forms of inevitable organizational conflict. The Marxist approach presupposes that conflict is inherent in the employment relationship because both employers and employees are trying to maximize a return for their efforts. Neither party can be fully compensated for this. There are a number of ways of classifying, vertical conflict is that which occurs between managers and workers and concerns power differentials. Horizontal conflict occurs between people at approximately the same organizational level. Other ways of describing conflict include overt and covert. The former is often collectively based and organized and usually refers to strikes, go slows, picketing, stop work meetings, etc. Covert conflict is individually based and unorganized and usually refers to absenteeism, sick leave, absence without leave, sabotage, poor productivity and work attitude, etc.

Congress center

Referred to as convention centers in North America, congress centers in Europe are facilities that are designed to accommodate multiple groups of varying sizes and primarily host congresses and meetings. They consist of one or more fixed-seat theatres, a ballroom, and a large number of smaller meeting rooms for breakout sessions. Congress centers typically have catering facilities and are non-residential in nature (i.e. they do not provide sleeping rooms). Until recently the majority of congress centers in Europe did not have dedicated exhibition space, with exhibitions traditionally being held in separate trade-fair buildings. However, as associations in Europe have begun to realize the revenue potential of exhibitions concurrently run with congresses, existing congress centers are adding exhibit halls and new centers include them in their initial design, either as part of the center or being linked via a bridge or walkway.

Consortium

A group of companies that form a partnership to establish a certain task. For instance, in the late 1990s, organizations formed procurement consortia to achieve buying power within their respective industry, reduce procurement costs, and streamline their supply chains. The underlying assumption was that if multiple organizations bought products as one entity, a better price could be achieved because of the increased volume. Procurement consortia are also known as online exchanges. These consortia frequently act as independent organizations collectively owned by the interested parties. For example, in 2001, Marriott International and Hyatt Hotels formed a buying consortium named Avendra. Consortia are not limited to purchasing. In fact, many large players formed consortia for research and development and information systems years prior to forming consortia for procurement. Procurement consortia came to light in the late 1990s because of the technological advances in software and the Internet.

Constructive dismissal

In Australia and a few other countries of British heritage, the term refers to the abrupt termination of an employee's common law contract of employment that initially appears as if the employee resigned, but in reality, under certain circumstances, may be regarded as a dismissal by the employer. Circumstances amounting to constructive dismissal at common law include attempts by the employer to change worker's duties or location and a reduction of wages and other benefits without appropriate consultation. This is known as a 'fundamental unilateral variation to employees' terms and conditions. Other situations may include false accusations of theft and 'forced resignation' where the employer threatens to dismiss the worker if they fail to accept a particular ultimatum. However, there is no clear picture of what actually constitutes a forced resignation.

Consumer buying process

To arrive at a decision as to which product/service should they purchase, consumers go through a process called *Consumer Buying Decision Process*. This decision process is a useful tool that hospitality and tourism companies use in order to more accurately understand and predict the buying behavior of their customers. To understand consumer buyer behavior is to understand how the customer interacts with the marketing mix inputs, that is, the four Ps of price, place, promotion, and product. The consumer buying process is a five-stage purchase decision process that includes (1) need/want recognition, (2) information search, (3) an evaluation of alternatives, (4) purchase, and (5) post-purchase evaluation. The consumer buying decision process is important because if marketers can identify consumers' buyer behavior, they will be in a better position to target products and services to meet their needs and preferences.

Consumer rights in timeshare purchasing

The laws of some jurisdictions require that all or a portion of the funds or other property received by a developer of a timeshare plan from a purchaser of a timeshare interest in the timeshare plan must be deposited in an escrow account with an independent escrow agent prior to completion of the purchase transaction. The purchaser is entitled to the return of the funds or other property if the developer defaults under the purchase contract, including the developer's inability to deliver the accommodations and facilities of the timeshare plan as promised. Some jurisdictions permit developers to access purchaser funds or property prior to meeting the conditions for releasing the funds or property by providing an alternative assurance covering the purchaser funds or property.

Contextual effects in consumer behavior

Contextual refers to the environment surrounding a situation and effects refer to the response of the consumer to that surrounding environment. Ultimately, marketers are interested in the impact material surrounding an advertisement, product, or service will have on the consumers' interpretation. For example, in a case involving an advertisement for the Four Seasons hotels, the company might consider the *Architectural Digest* magazine because of its reputation for luxury and wealth. The type of magazine impacts the readers' perception of the Four Seasons advertisement and even articles and other advertisements within the magazine will have an effect on the readers' perception of the this advertisement. Other examples are television or radio advertisements that are aired during specific shows or programs to minimize or maximize the contextual effects.

Contingency theory (in organizations)

A theory which claims that there is no best way to organize a firm or corporation. An organizational style or form that is effective in some situations may be ineffective in others. In other words, the optimal organizational form or style of a hospitality firm depends upon various internal and external situational factors. Situational factors – referred to as 'contingency factors' – include environmental, technology, size, strategy, and others. Overall, structural contingency theory can be considered to be a functionalist theory in that organizational structure is seen as producing (causing) certain outcomes such as effectiveness, innovation, and so on. Organizations are thus seen as being required to adopt the structural form that fits with the contingency factors if they are to be effective. The term contingency theory can also be applied to leadership and decision-making styles in that there is no best way to lead a group of people or to make an effective decision.

Continuous improvement

A set of processes aimed at getting work done with minimum errors (i.e. zero defects). The concept of continuous improvement gained prominence with the onset of the total quality management (TQM) movement with the term used in relation to processes that involve everyone in an organization working in an integrated effort toward improving performance at every level. For example, in a hotel continuous improvement would involve every department from housekeeping to the front office, guest services to food and beverage operations as well as support areas. According to management guru Peter Drucker, continuous improvement ultimately transforms an organization by leading to product and service innovation. Continuous improvement eventually leads to fundamental change.

Contract of employment

A legal term describing the (common law) of contract in which the employment relationship between an employer and an employee is determined and the conditions set out. A contract of employment has expressed terms in relation to the rights of each party that specifies and defines the nature of the employment relationship such as hours of work, duty, pay, holidays, etc. A contract also has implied terms written into them (through the application of common law) such as the employer duty indemnify the employee, to pay wages for work performed and to provide a safe workplace. Employees have a duty to obey lawful instructions, to look after the property of the employer, and a duty of fidelity. In many industrial jurisdictions, the (common law) contract of employment has to be applied in the context of other statutory mechanisms such as industrial awards, industrial determinations, and employment statute that may also set out mandatory employment conditions.

Contribution margin

In conceptual terms, contribution margin is the amount contributed by a product to meet an organizational objective after paying for raw materials. It can be calculated by deducting the cost of all variable expenses from the revenues generated by a product. Products with higher levels of contribution margins are given greater importance in planning decisions. Contribution margin is calculated not only at the individual product level but also at aggregate levels. For example, one could calculate contribution margin for a meal period such as breakfast. Such information can be used in identifying 'profit leaders' or 'loss leaders' to make appropriate corrective actions. In foodservice operations contribution margin is used extensively in making menu engineering decisions such as selecting a food item for a menu, setting price levels for food items, selectively promoting menu items to improve overall profitability, etc. Contribution is also used in determining such particulars as management compensation or managerial bonus calculations.

Controllable and non-controllable costs

Controllable costs are costs that can be driven by a unit and non-controllable costs are costs that are not under the control of a unit. Most costs in a hospitality organization are controllable by someone. However, the term 'controllable' refers to a responsibility centre and not to the organization as a whole. Cost are controllable for a responsibility centre when are under the influence of the manager of the centre. A cost is controllable if the amount of cost incurred is significantly influenced by the action of the manager of the responsibility centre. However, sometimes costs are controllable by more than one manager. For example, for a Rooms Division manager, the only controllable costs are those related to the efficiency of the personnel in the services provided within his or her area of competence. In other words, controllable costs are those directly affected by the management of the organizational unit.

Controllable costs in foodservice

As defined in the previous entry, controllable costs are those expenses that fall *directly* under the control of unit management. Controllable costs are among the most commonly watched numbers in the foodservice industry. Common examples of items with controllable costs include food, beverages, labor, paper, linens, glassware, cleaning supplies, and services. Unit management often has direct control over the rate of usage of these products and services. Two of the most prominent controllable costs are food and beverage cost and labor costs. Since these two costs contribute nearly 70 per cent of the controllable costs in a typical restaurant, they are often referred to as prime costs. Most foodservice organizations make controllable costs a primary consideration in calculating compensation. The lower the percentage of controllable costs, the greater the possibility of achieving higher net profits.

Convention

An event where the primary activity of attendees is to attend educational sessions, participate in meetings/discussions, socialize, or attend other organized events. Some conventions may also have a secondary exhibit component. Normally organized by an association, the convention is usually an annual or biannual event for members. The convention program would likely include several different kinds of sessions: general sessions, keynote addresses, and breakout sessions. There would also be meetings of the association leadership, such as board meetings and committee meetings. Very often, special events, such as awards ceremonies, are also included in convention programming. Attendees pay a registration fee that covers general sessions and other scheduled events, including some meals. Conventions may be held in a variety of venues, depending upon the size of the audience. Sometimes they are held in convention centers, sometimes in convention hotels or in conference centers.

Convention and visitors bureau

A membership organization representing a city or urban area in the solicitation of business and tourism travelers is known as a convention and visitors bureau (CVB). These organizations promote the image of its community and market the destination to tourists and to groups hosting meetings, conventions, and trade shows. They provide information about hotels, special event venues and other host facilities, conduct sales tours (also known as familiarization or FAM trips), and promote local service providers and vendors to the planner. CVBs assist groups with preparations, may lend support throughout the meeting, and aid in the marketing of the event to the attendees. In addition, a bureau provides valuable research data to local governments regarding tourism and convention attendance, spending, and revenue generated. For the tourist, a CVB encourages visitors to its historic areas, cultural events, and recreational attractions. Most CVBs are 'not-for-profit' membership organizations.

Convention catering

Receptions, banquets, breakfasts, luncheons, refreshment breaks, and hospitality suites are an important part of any meeting. They serve as a focus for social interaction to meet new associates, renew old acquaintances, exchange ideas, and develop positive attitudes for the overall meeting experience. Costs of food and beverage functions can have a major impact on a meeting budget. In planning foods and beverages for meetings, it is necessary to have a basic understanding of different foods because attendees have become much more health conscious in recent years. Food and beverage affect the brain's ability to produce substances that stimulate, energize, or calm. Alcoholic beverages produce a delayed sluggishness. The food selections provided to attendees will have as much effect on their mental awareness, retention, and sharpness as the methods of presentation used.

Convention center

A facility that consists of exhibition halls and meeting rooms, and is used to host conventions, tradeshows, consumer events, and other large meetings and assemblies. In many countries, the primary purpose of convention centers is to generate economic activity. Convention centers are built in various shapes and sizes, and sometimes encompass several city blocks. Exhibition space usually contains moveable walls that can create exhibit halls of varying sizes, each having loading dock access. Meeting space typically consists of multiple breakout rooms that total 20–40 per cent of the exhibition space. Other common architectural elements include registration areas, pre-function spaces, and food courts. In Europe and some other parts of the world, convention centers are called congress centers and they are usually used to host meetings without exhibitions. Congress centers often contain one or more fixed-seat theaters, since they host more diplomatic and plenary sessions than their North American counterparts.

Convention Industry Council

An international organization composed of 31 associations that represent more than 98,000 individuals and 15,000 firms and properties involved in the meetings, convention, and exhibitions industry. The Convention Industry Council (CIC) was formed in 1949 to provide a forum for member organizations seeking to enhance the industry. It facilitates the exchange of information and develops programs to promote professionalism within the industry and educates the public on its profound economic impact. CIC is a forum for leadership to productively and cohesively move the industry in an ever-changing economic and political environment. By serving as the 'United Nations' of the meeting, convention, and exhibition industry, CIC enables its delegates to review the state of the industry and its role in today's economy.

Convention service manager

1. The facility manager who is responsible for planning and servicing meetings and conventions held at a hotel, conference center, convention center, or other meeting property. This person is the liaison between the meeting planner and all of the departments at the facility, and is responsible for meeting room setup, including tables, chairs, décor, audio-visual equipment, etc. The convention service manager is the primary contact with ultimate responsibility for the success of an event. Once the sales department confirms the event has been booked, a convention service manager is assigned to handle all group needs from initial planning to the post-meeting report.
2. A person that works for a convention and visitors bureau (CVB), and services meetings and conventions, which book their hotel(s) through the CVB. The convention service manager at a CVB assists the meeting planners in selecting hotel(s) once they have selected the destination.

Cook–chill

In a cook–chill production system, food products are prepared in bulk in a central location, packaged while hot, and quickly chilled to an internal temperature of 32–37°F (0–3°C) using specialized cooling equipment such as blast chillers and tumble chillers. Once chilled, food can be held under refrigeration for up to 30 days or more, depending on the product. This process allows a foodservice operation to use fewer skilled personnel to produce a wide range of food products that can be taken from inventory as required and, if necessary, distributed to other locations. Large facilities such as hospitals, correctional facilities, and centralized kitchens for school systems often use cook–chill production, although the practice is also being applied in smaller venues such as hotels and restaurants with great success.

Cook–freeze

The process of preparing, packaging, and freezing a food product for later distribution and reheating. In cook–freeze production, food products are cooked in bulk and packaged while hot into either single portions or bulk packs. The packaged food is then blast frozen to a final temperature of 0°F (-18°C) within 80 minutes and held at that temperature for up to two months. Products may be held even longer at -22°F (-30°C). It is common to use, at the point of service, a convection or microwave oven to bring the product to a safe internal temperature of 176°F (80°C) within 30 minutes, after which the dish can be plated and served. Typically undertaken in a central production facility, cook–freeze allows skilled personnel to prepare a wide range of products in quantity, hold them in inventory, and then ship them while still frozen to another location for reheating ('rethermalization') by less skilled staff just prior to service.

Corporate event

In the past, corporate events were mainly used as a medium for imparting internal corporate communication such a company's future plans, prospects, policies, and procedures. Today, corporate events have become dynamic sales, marketing, and public relations tools used by businesses of all sizes. Corporate events are being used as means to solicit new business, create a corporate or brand image, retain and build loyalty with existing suppliers and customers in addition to being used to elicit peak performance from employees and produce camaraderie and teamwork among co-workers. Companies today are actively pursuing, identifying, and analyzing new business and marketing opportunities that can be achieved through the application of corporate events and the scope of corporate events is widening. Traditional corporate events include board meetings, business meetings, client appreciation events, conferences, conventions, corporate shows, employee appreciation events, and tradeshows. Expanded corporate events include custom training seminars involving emotional and physical challenges, executive retreats, gala fundraising events, incentive travel and premium programs, naming rights, product launches, product placement, special events, and teleconferencing.

Corporate-level strategy

As they grow, organizations often pursue businesses outside their core business areas through, intrapreneurship (the application of entrepreneurial skills and approaches within or by a corporation), mergers, and acquisitions or joint ventures. Corporate growth strategy typically evolves from concentration to some form of vertical integration or diversification. Vertical integration, which expands an organization's involvement in multiple stages of the industry supply chain, can be accomplished through either backward integration (e.g. a restaurant that acquires a bakery supplier) or forward integration (e.g. a hotel chain that becomes a travel distribution service provider). Diversification refers to growth through entry into different industries. Diversification that stems from common markets, functions served, technologies or services to achieve synergy, is referred to as related diversification. Examples of related diversification include hotel companies that branch out into a variety of related businesses, including real estate. Unrelated diversification is not based on commonality among the corporation's activity.

Corporate meeting

An officially sanctioned and required meeting for employees of a specific corporation. Corporate meetings are often held off site of the corporate location and require employees to travel to the meeting. Expenses associated with the meeting, such as transportation, meals, and hotel accommodations are paid for by the corporation. Corporate meetings differ from association meetings in that attendance is required for corporate meetings and not required for association meetings. There are a variety of corporate meetings which include but are not limited to: incentive events, training seminars, sales meetings, and board of director meetings. An incentive event is a corporate sponsored meeting to reward performance of employees. Training seminars are structured learning sessions for employee while sales meeting focus on motivating staff and introducing new products. Board of director meetings focus on the leadership of the organization by setting long-term goals and objectives.

Cost–benefit analysis

A managerial tool used to assess the potential benefit of current or future investments. The primary objective of conducting cost–benefit analysis is to understand the return, realized or potential, of current investments. In financial terms, cost–benefit is also called 'ROI' (return on investment). ROI can be used to compare the performance of various projects within a company or across the industry. When ROIs are compared across the industry, a hospitality organization may gain competitive advantage by adjusting its cost–benefit numbers. Growth plans done without proper cost–benefit analysis may lead to disastrous consequences. In the early 1980s, for example, a restaurant company had expanded from a single-unit operation to an over 500 unit operation in less than six years. Such an uncontrolled growth phenomenon resulted in business failure and the eventual bankruptcy of the company.

Cost-informed pricing methods

60

A set of pricing methods including *cost plus, full cost, direct cost plus*, and *gross margin*. In *cost-plus pricing* businesses set prices on the basis of the cost of a product or service plus a margin for profit. The cost is typically a standard, or fully allocated, cost concept based on some assumed level of output. The margin for profit is usually a percentage mark-up that can be expressed as follows:

$$\text{Mark-up} = \frac{\text{Price} - \text{Cost}}{\text{Cost}}$$

where the numerator is called the profit margin. Solving the mark-on equation for price provides the expression that determines price in a cost-plus pricing system:

$$\text{Price} = \text{Cost} (1 + \text{Mark-up})$$

Full cost or average cost pricing is a term used to describe a number of pricing procedures which allocate all costs to individual products or services and, hence, are decisive for the final prices.

Direct cost-plus pricing implies establishing selling prices at a certain percentage above the direct, or traceable, costs of the product or service. This percentage mark-up is designed to cover an allowance for indirect costs (i.e. the overheads associated with operations) and to provide for net profit.

Gross margin pricing can be used when the material cost is the only direct cost that can be identified (when labor and expense costs can only be identified as indirect costs, that is overhead or burden). The pricing procedure involves the calculation of direct materials per product plus a mark-up percentage to cover overhead expense and net profit. When the range of products or services is heterogeneous, such as in a restaurant, it is quite often very complex and uneconomical to estimate the direct labor and expense costs per type of product on an item-by-item base.

Cost of goods sold

In the foodservice industry, cost of goods sold (COGS) is typically considered to be the sum of food and beverage expenses. It is the cost of items used to generate all food and beverage revenues over a specified time period. To determine the COGS for a given establishment, inventory at the beginning and end of a particular time period must be calculated. An establishment must also keep track of all food and beverage purchases during that time period. COGS calculations are done separately for food and beverage categories, and sometimes COGS are calculated for subcategories within these areas (e.g. wine, spirits, bottled beer, draft beer, meat, produce, dairy, fish, frozen products, etc.). The general calculation for COGS is:

$$COGS = Beginning\ inventory + Purchases - Ending\ inventory$$

Cost of sales

Cost of stock items sold during the accounting period. In a hotel, the items comprising the cost of sales would include food stocks purchased and consumed in the production of food sold through the restaurant and also the cost of beverage stock sold in the bar. Where there is a shop in the hotel complex, cost of sales would also include the cost of all merchandise sold in the shop. However, food provided to staff as part of their remuneration is a labor cost, that is part of wages and salaries and, as such, is not available for consumption by customers. Therefore, in order to obtain a more accurate indication of the true cost of food consumed by customers, the cost value of staff meals should be deducted from cost of sales and added to labor cost.

The following example shows how the cost of sales can be calculated in a restaurant:

Cost of opening stock balance	$12,000
Total purchases of stock	$180,000
	$192,000
Less: returns to suppliers	$3000
Net stock available for sale	$189,000
Less: closing balance of stock	$14,000
	$175,000
Less: staff meals	$5000
Net cost of sales	$170,000

Cost strategy

A cost strategy is when a firm intends to become the low-cost producer in its industry or competitive group. The cost strategy creates a competitive advantage when industry rivals and new entrants cannot duplicate established cost advantages. Michael E. Porter (a Harvard Business School academic who focuses on management and economics) describes two types of cost strategies: cost leadership and cost focus. The strategic basis following cost leadership requires a broad scope and that a firm becomes the cost leader rather than one of many in an industry. Cost leadership can be derived through the pursuit of economies of scale, the use of technology, access

62

to particular suppliers and distribution channels, or other factors. A cost focus strategy refers to a narrow target market or scope. This narrow focus can refer to either a particular segment within an industry or a regional focus. Firms such as McDonald's, Motel 6, and Southwest Airlines are examples of well-known hospitality/tourism organizations that have achieved significant success following a low-cost strategy.

Cost–volume–profit analysis

An analytical tool that describes the relationships between costs, revenues, profit (income), and volume. It is based on the definition of Profit = Total revenue – Total cost. Since total revenue as well as total cost depends on volume, the definition of profit can be expressed as:

$$\text{Profit} = p \times Q - v \times Q - F$$

where

p is price per unit;

Q is volume;

v is variable cost per unit;

F is fixed cost.

The simple form of cost–volume–profit (CVP) model assumes linearity, that is that price per unit, fixed cost, and variable cost per unit do not vary with volume. The model also assumes that it is possible to categorize total cost into the two categories fixed cost and variable cost, which often is difficult to apply to a practical situation. Other assumptions are that productivity and the methods of production and service remain unchanged.

Credit card guarantee

An assurance to the guest that the hotel will hold a hotel room reservation. From the hotel point of view, credit card guarantee reservations are a system that guarantees the hotel payment for no-show reservations. All guaranteed reservations are assured a room and the charge for the room is credit card guaranteed by which the payment for the room is guaranteed should the guest not check in. Credit card guaranteed reservations are the most common form of guaranteed reservation, especially for city center hotels. Unless a credit card guaranteed reservation is cancelled by the guest before a stated cancellation hour, the hotel will charge the guest's credit card for the amount of the room's rate, or a stated no-show charge.

Critical incidents technique

A set of procedures for systematically identifying behaviors that contribute to success or failure of individuals or organizations in specific situations. Organizations normally encourage customers to provide feedback concerning their service encounters. Some of the popular methods for customer feedback are: toll free numbers, comment cards, and surveys. In addition, employees are encouraged to report any service failures and detail their responses. Finally, a third party could be contracted to observe a firm's operations and comment on critical incidents. One popular approach used by hotels and restaurants is to hire a firm that conducts a 'mystery shopping' program. Trained professionals will stay at hotels or dine at restaurants and evaluate the experience (see also Service failures).

Critical success factors

The limited number of areas in which 'things must go right' in order to ensure that predetermined 'goals' are achieved. The critical success factor (CSF) approach has been in existence for some considerable time, mainly in the information systems field, and in later years, its application was extended to the generic management field. Thus, CSFs represent priority areas for on-going information provision and form the basis for a company's management decision-making. The approach is based on a framework of 'goals-CSFs-measures' called 'CSF analysis'. For example, in a hotel business, if the goal is to improve room revenue, then the key (CSFs) elements to be managed are essentially the number of rooms sold and the room rate charged, thus involving the measurement of room occupancy, average room rate, and RevPAR to monitor the results.

Cross-selling

Sales activities that identify, suggest, and sell related items such as accessories or services to a prospective or existing customer. Cross-selling techniques exist in almost every field. There are many different types of cross-selling, for example, if a customer is buying a meal in a restaurant, the waiter might recommend a bottle of wine to go with the meal. Other examples in the field of hospitality and tourism are attractions that recommend or sell hotels; hotels that provide packaged weekends that include meals and tickets to shows, etc. Cross-selling not only introduces customers to other products which can have an impact on company's '*share of customer*', but it also helps the company to attract new customers. The foundation of cross-selling is based on the already established relationship between the company and its customers.

Customer centricity

64

The capacity of an organization to focus on providing customers opportunities to be involved in every aspect of the business. It is achieved through effectively responding to the ever-changing needs of the customer. Customer centric organizations are committed to the conviction that the customer is at the center of all that they do. They involve the customer in their organization with a great amount of communication and trust. They respect customers as part of company culture; thoroughly train and motivate employees; and empower customer-facing employees to fix problems when something goes wrong. Organizations that are truly customer centric do not hold the more limited view of serving the customer, but rather view the customer as a partner in their organization.

Customer complaint behavior

Most marketers wonder why some dissatisfied customers are reluctant to complain and whether complaint behavior is due to some clearly defined factors such as cultural traits.

The causes of customer complaint behavior are numerous and profiling the complainants is a difficult task. Also, the silent majority who is reluctant to show dissatisfaction explicitly may exit or engage in negative word-of-mouth behavior. Studies show that about two-thirds of the customers do not report their dissatisfaction. If a customer does not complain, it remains a concern to the management as the firm loses the opportunity to remedy any problems and improve the product and enhance quality through customer feedback. It also damages the firm's reputation because of negative word of mouth. Therefore, it becomes important for hospitality firms to provide an environment where customers can express their feelings and be able to complain. This means the first step of a complaint resolution process is to create an atmosphere that encourages dissatisfied customers to seek redress, both implicitly and explicitly.

Customer expectations

The concept of customer expectations is intertwined with that of service quality. The role of customer expectations in service quality was first conceptualized by Parasuraman, Berry, and Zeithaml in their widely quoted gaps model and a measurement instrument called SERVQUAL. Applications of the concept of customer expectations in hospitality and tourism disciplines are dominated by the essence of the original SERVQUAL model. They focus on the comparison between *desired service* and *perceived service*. Representative of such applications are the two measurement scales of LODGSERV developed by Knutson, Stevens, Wullaert, Patton, and Yokoyama; and DINESERV by Knutson, Stevens, and Patton. The LODGSERV and DINESERV provide a score that indicates the desired or ideal level of performance by hotels and restaurants with regard to each of the service items, as well as an index that indicates the desired or ideal level of performance with regard to each of the five dimensions.

Customer lifetime value

A key component of relationship marketing (see Relationship marketing) is keeping loyal customers. The costs associated with taking care of loyal customers decline over time, while sales from loyal customers' increase. Customer lifetime value, a common way to quantify this customer loyalty, highlights the importance of keeping good customers (see 80–20 Customer pyramid). Some researchers such as Shoemaker and Lewis provide a detailed explanation of calculating customer lifetime value. In essence, they estimate how much a customer will spend with a company over their lifetime minus the costs of supporting the customer and providing the products and services. Important parts of this calculation are the probability that the customer will stay with the company and how much the customer will spend.

Customer loyalty

A loyal customer is one who values the relationship with the company enough to make the company a preferred supplier. Loyal customers do not switch for small variations in price or service, they provide honest and constructive feedback, they consolidate the bulk of their category purchasers with the company, they never abuse company personnel, and they provide enthusiastic referrals. A loyal customer can also be defined as one who feels so strongly that a given firm can best meet his or her relevant needs that the competition is virtually excluded from the consideration set and the customer buys almost exclusively from this firm. The customer focuses on this brand, offers and messages, to the exclusion of others. The price of the product or service is not a dominant consideration in the purchase decision, but only one component in the larger value proposition.

Customer relationship management/marketing

A management philosophy or a strategy that calls for the reconfiguration of a firm's activities around the customer. It is a company-wide business strategy designed to reduce costs and increase profitability by encouraging customer loyalty. Customer relationship management (CRM) requires cross-functional integration of operations, marketing, and technology. CRM extends the concept of selling from a discrete act performed by a salesperson to a continual process involving every person in the company. CRM differs from traditional marketing initiatives in that, while the latter take a predominately short term, transactional approach, CRM focuses on maximizing revenue from each customer over the lifetime of the relationship by getting to know each customer intimately. CRM is also, by definition, a cross-functional philosophy that calls for substantial business integration. In a hospitality context, then, the operator – usually chains – no longer merely markets to customers, but rather fosters a relationship with them through programs that span marketing, operations, information systems, accounting, and other organizational functions.

Customer satisfaction

The ability of an organization to fulfill the needs of its customers. In other words it is a measure of the degree to which a product or service meets the customer's expectations. Customer satisfaction may be measured directly by surveys and expressed as a percentage of customers satisfied or by the number of complaints, etc. If the customer's expectations of product quality, service quality, and price are exceeded, a firm will achieve high levels of customer satisfaction and will create 'customer delight'. If the customer's expectations are not met, customer dissatisfaction will result. Customers' satisfaction can be examined by considering the foodservice 'Big Three': *food, service*, and *décor*. *Food* is a tangible element and customers evaluate food on the basis of flavor, texture, aroma, presentation/appearance, portion size, temperature, and overall perceived quality. While none of these elements is likely to lead to satisfaction or dissatisfaction by itself, customers process their perceptions of these elements relative to their expectations. *Service* is much less tangible than food quality. Effective service delivery involves a combination of reliable communication, timing, accessibility, and conviviality. The last of the 'Big Three' factors that influence customer satisfaction is the *décor* or the environment in which the service experience takes place. Issues such as lighting, color schemes, table layout and spacing, hard and soft finishes, noise level, music/entertainment, and other ambient factors set the stage for the effective delivery of service elements. Finally, customer satisfaction is ultimately a result of interaction between service providers and customers.

Cycle menus

Cycle menus (rotating menus/cyclical menus) are generally used for on-site foodservice and volume catering, such as in hospitals, industrial operations, shipping, and large venue catering. The recipes are usually standardized for a set use, quality and quantity of ingredients, method of preparation and cooking, and method of service. Cycle menus are designed for specific periods.

The average cycle with most institutional operations is 28 days, after which the whole cycle or sequence of menus is repeated. Some operations run their cycles for five- or seven-day periods before they are repeated. Again, the menu format, menu quality, menu price, and cycle period are developed for the specific needs of the operation. Since cycle menus are repeated, the menu structure and the choice of dishes must be carefully selected. Repetition should be avoided as much as possible. Careful attention to nutrition and season of the year should be observed.

Daily operations report

This report contains a summary of a hotel's financial activities during a 24-hour period. The daily operations report provides a means of reconciling cash, bank accounts, revenue, and accounts receivable. The report also serves as a posting reference for various accounting journals and provides important data that must be input to link front and back office computer functions. Also included in the daily operations report are room statistics and occupancy ratios and comments and observations from the accounting staff. The hotel's night auditor prepares the daily operations report, from which the general manager and different department heads can review: (a) revenues, (b) receivables, (c) operating statistics, (d) front office cash receipts and disbursements, (e) departmental reports on revenue and expenditures and, (f) a credit report, which lists guest accounts remaining unpaid three days after billing, and any unusually large guest charges or balances.

Data envelopment analysis

A benchmarking technique based on linear programming that explicitly considers multiple outputs and inputs, producing a measure of performance. Data envelopment analysis (DEA) is a non-parametric (mathematical programming) approach that optimizes on the basis of each individual observation, calculating a piecewise frontier occupied by the most efficient units. Moreover, DEA integrates the variables simultaneously – including discretionary input variables that are under management's control and non-discretionary variables that are uncontrollable. Through an iterative calculation process, DEA produces a single relative-to-best productivity index that relates all units under comparison. Applied to a restaurant chain, for example DEA allows for the assessment of contingent productivity, which takes into account the differing environmental or situational factors of each restaurant under comparison. Thus, operators can use the best-performing units as the bases for evaluation.

Data mining

A process that employs a combination of machine learning, statistical analysis, modeling techniques, and information technology to discover hidden facts, previously unknown patterns of behavior, and trends. Companies can use this knowledge to make business decisions in their marketing, sales, customer service, production, credit, and finance activities more quickly, more accurately, and with higher confidence. As a marketing tool, data mining is often used to study customers and their purchasing behavior in order to look for patterns that describe the behaviors and permit businesses to perform market segmentation in new ways. Through intelligent segmentation and response analysis data mining has helped companies to retain customers and to become more relevant, by designing products and services that meet the needs of customer 'segments' and to communicate with them more effectively. Moreover, data mining assists the improvement of customer relationships through profiling, profitability, value, and loyalty analysis.

Data warehouse

A copy of the data contained in a company's operational databases, transformed and reorganized specifically for query and analysis purposes. This, in turn, enables data mining: the analysis of data for relationships which have not previously been discovered – often using advanced artificial intelligence tools. An example is the Australian Tourism Data Warehouse: a system for storing tourism product information, in a standardized and integrated system, in a single repository, for access by interested parties worldwide. Subscribers then have the ability to: access a wide range of product and destination information from a single source in a common format; analyze that data using data mining tools; publish data through individual websites without external links and publish in a variety of languages. Data warehousing and data mining are critical for the implementation of CRM (Customer Relationship Marketing) in hospitality.

Database marketing

The process of building, maintaining, and using company's own customer database and other database (products, suppliers, resellers) for the purpose of contacting and transacting with customers. Database marketing is the most sophisticated selling process in the marketing world today. It is the basis for direct marketing and ultimately relationship marketing. Database marketing is often referred to as direct marketing. The term target marketing is also often applied, relating to focusing in on a given group of customers or 'segment.' By categorizing customers into various segments that have common needs, database marketing tools can be applied directly to the different segments and deliver a different message and a different solution to each one.

Database systems

A computerized file-keeping system, and the database itself is a repository of computerized data files. In the context of database management, data are stored and organized by fields and records.

A field (sometimes known as an attribute) is the single unit of information, such as the surname of a hotel employee. A record (also called a tuple) is a collection of related fields. Furthermore, a file (also known as a table) has multiple records that are pertained to a specific topic. Lastly, a database comprises all related files. In hospitality, databases support most business functions and applications. An advantage of database systems application to the hospitality industry is the personalization of products and services. The selective capability of a database system makes it easy for the hospitality practitioners to maintain a direct contact with customers.

Daypart

A subsection of the day during which meals in restaurant are served. There once was a time when conventional meal periods defined the service times of restaurants – breakfast, lunch, and dinner. Many restaurants, primarily in the full-service and quick-service segments, specialized in one or two of these meals. Typically, these were combined into either breakfast/lunch or lunch/dinner, with one of the meals being the focus. In contrast to this business model, the one followed by the mid-scale coffee shop restaurant segment often meant serving on a 24-hour schedule, with the three meals blended together into one 'all day' menu. As this trend evolved during the 1980s and 1990s, customers became more and more accustomed to finding restaurants open and ready to serve them, whenever the impulse moved them, in what has become known as different dayparts.

Decentralized guestroom HVAC

Decentralized guestroom HVAC (Heat Ventilation and Air Conditioning) equipment is installed through the exterior wall of the guestroom and consists of an electrically powered unit capable of providing either space cooling only or space cooling and heating. Space cooling is provided using a conventional refrigeration cycle. Space heating may be provided by an electric heat or by reverse operation of the refrigeration cycle for units that are heat pumps. Generally, the units are controlled using controls integral to the units themselves, not a thermostat in the room. Packaged terminal air conditions (PTAC) or packaged terminal heat pumps (PTHP) are terms used to describe types of decentralized guestroom HVAC units. PTHP units may use air or water as heat sources or heat sinks. Water sources for some PTHP units have been groundwater but more common have been water circulated throughout the property with heat removed or added to this as needed.

Decision-making

The process of determining and selecting alternative solutions that can help to achieve intended objectives in hospitality organizations. Making decisions is one of the primary responsibilities of hospitality managers and it can occur at individual, group, and organizational levels. Hospitality managers make two types of decisions that are programmed and non-programmed decisions. The former is repetitive and routine like making shifts in the Food and Beverage department while the latter is novel and unstructured decisions like deciding to open a new hotel brand by a hotel group. To explain how programmed and particularly non-programmed decisions are made, various decision-making models have been proposed such as the rational model, the bounded-rational model, the process model, the political model, and the garbage can model. Each model is based on a different set of assumptions and offers unique insight into decision-making in organizations.

Decision support systems

Interactive systems that enable decision-makers to use databases and models on a computer in order to solve ill-structured problems. Decision support systems (DSS) consist of problem-solving technology containing people, knowledge, software, and hardware to facilitate improved decision-making. Special types of DSS are expert systems, which integrate and use decision rules and weights from domain-specific experts, and group decision support systems (GDSS) involving multiple decision-makers. Analytical models commonly used in DSS are forecasting, simulation, or optimization models. These models are either developed with a general programming language or with a statistical or mathematical standard software package. In hospitality management, DSS frequently occur in form of travel recommendation systems, in order to support customers in their accommodation and/or travel decision-making process, or as management information systems (MIS), in order to support hospitality managers in their business decisions. An ideal DSS allows managers to combine their experience and intuition with the consistent objectivity of a computer-based model.

Deeded timeshare ownership

A type of interest in a timeshare plan in which the owner receives the right to use the accommodations and facilities of the timeshare plan during the term of the timeshare plan together with an ownership interest in the underlying property included in the timeshare plan. At such time as the timeshare plan terminates, the owner of a deeded ownership interest will continue to own an interest in the underlying property as a cotenant along with all other owners of deeded timeshare interests in that underlying property. The purchaser of a deeded ownership interest is conveyed the interest through the execution and delivery of deed of conveyance, such as general warranty deed or quitclaim deed, similar to the conveyance of any other interest in real property. Consequently, a deeded ownership is governed by the same laws and principles applied to traditional real estate transactions, such as mortgage lending and taxing laws and accounting rules. This type of interest is also referred to as a timeshare estate.

Departing the guest

Typically involves at least three members of a hotels staff, front desk, bell, and airport courtesy van driver and/or doorman when a guest is ready to checkout of his/her room at a hotel. The front desk: inquiring about the quality of products and services that have been provided to the guest; the guest returning room keys to the hotel if the hotel is still utilizing hard keys rather than electronic keys and locks; both the guest and the front desk: (a) reviewing a hard copy of the guests folio for completeness and accuracy; (b) the guest determining the method of payment and the front office receiving payment; (c) inquiring of the guest the need for additional reservations; (d) preparing a copy of the folio and related documents for the guest and for the night audit; and (e) the front desk communicating the guests departures to housekeeping and other departments in the hotel if necessary.

Depreciation of fixed assets

The word 'depreciation' has two principal meanings. In contemporary accounting it means an allocation of the cost of an asset over its useful life. In other circumstances, it means a reduction in the value of an asset. Fixed assets, with the exception of land, are subject to depreciation. Depreciation is a measure of the wearing out, consumption or other loss of value of a fixed asset arising from use, the passing of time or obsolescence (being out dated or superseded). Depreciation involves the systematic allocation over time of the historical cost (the purchase price) or other measure of an asset in financial statements. In order to make the allocation it is necessary to estimate not only a historical or current replacement cost but also the asset's useful economic life and its residual value. The purpose of depreciation is to allocate the cost of a tangible operational asset over its useful life.

Destination management company

A liaison between the out-of-town client and all of the services of a destination that the host property does not offer. Destination management companies (DMCs) range from those that provide very specialized services to full-service firms capable of handling all logistics. For instance, some companies provide only ground transportation (such as busses, limos, and vans), while others can handle personally, or can subcontract, everything a client needs. For instance, full-service firms can book entertainment, plan theme parties, coordinate tours and spouse programs, and handle off-site events (including catering) at museums and other local attractions. Full-service firms can also provide personnel. For instance, exhibitors may want to hire local models to work exhibit booths and registration. Many out-of-town clients are willing to pay a local DMC to provide guidance in an unfamiliar area since it is very difficult for a client to judge the quality of services available if he or she has never visited the area.

Destination management systems

Systems assisting destination marketing organizations (DMOs) to collect, coordinate and disseminate computerized information about a particular region. They offer support the reservation function for local tourism attractions, facilities, and products. Most destination management systems (DMSs) developments have been led by public tourist organizations as these are traditionally charged with information provision and marketing. DMSs emerge as major promotion, distribution, and operational tools for both destinations and small- and medium-sized tourism and hospitality enterprises (SMTEs) locally. SMTEs dominate the tourism provision and contribute a considerable proportion of benefits. However, most small hotels find difficult to establish their online presence and to communicate effectively with their clientele. Hence, DMSs emerge as interfaces between destination tourism enterprises (including principals, attractions, transportation, and intermediaries) and the external world (including tour operators, travel agencies, and ultimately consumers).

Destination marketing

Destination marketing aims at creating positive images to promote tourist destinations for social and economic benefits. A destination can be a geographically defined area but it also varies in scope depending on the perceptions of tourists. Depending on travel motivations and destination offerings, people visit destinations for various reasons such as seeking knowledge, getaway, relaxation, urban life, rural and pastoral peace, and authentic and unique experience. Destination marketing promotions can be done at various levels: local, regional, national, and international. In the USA, Convention and visitors bureaus (CVBs) play an important role in planning and developing destination marketing activities. In other countries or regions, government tourist offices design, coordinate, and administer tourism policies that exert influence on how destinations are introduced and promoted to various markets. Both public and private sectors may seek different interests in destination marketing efforts. Local residents' attitudes and support toward tourism development in the area are essential to ensure successful marketing campaigns for the destination.

Destination marketing organization

Organizations that market their geographic areas to travel trade intermediaries, individual and group travelers on behalf of the tourism organizations (hotels, restaurants, attractions, transportation, and auxiliary services) in their destination. Examples of Destination marketing organizations (DMOs) include government agencies at the national, state, territory, region, county, or city levels. There are also private sector DMOs that represent large tourism organizations that own/manage multiple operations such as Disney Worldwide and Ski Country USA that may not be owned by the same corporation or entity. There are also quasi public–private DMOs that are funded with public tax dollars and membership dues that is convention and visitor bureaus (CVB) or tourism authorities.

Developer rights under the purchaser deposit

The laws of some jurisdictions require that all or a portion of the funds or other property received by a developer of a timeshare plan from a purchaser of a timeshare interest in the timeshare plan must be deposited in an escrow account with an independent escrow agent prior to completion of the purchase transaction. These purchasers funds and property are safeguarded in the escrow account and may not be delivered to or accessed by the developer until certain conditions are met or certain events transpire such as (i) the purchaser's right to cancel the purchase contract during any statutorily required cancellation period has expired; (ii) construction of the accommodations and facilities of the timeshare plan have been completed as promised to the purchaser; (iii) the developer can deliver title to or use of the timeshare interest free and clear of any encumbrances or such encumbrances have been subordinated to the rights of the timeshare purchasers in the plan; and (iv) the purchase transaction between the developer and the purchaser has been completed and ownership or use has been transferred to the purchaser.

Deviance

A term generally associated with traditional practice and morality and refers to negative behavior that contravenes accepted norms. In the workplace, deviance involves a departure from formal or informal procedures, standards, codes of conduct, and/or rules and regulations. Examples of workplace deviance include aggression, harassment, insubordination, tardiness, absenteeism, theft, fraud, obscenity, sabotage, and the consumption of drugs or alcohol within the workplace. Deviant behavior can be directed at an organization or at individuals within an organization. In the hospitality sector the reliance on human capital for service delivery means that deviant behavior by employees can result in customer dissatisfaction with the service experience and a reduction in customer loyalty. Consequently, the effects and costs of deviant behavior are magnified within the hospitality industry.

Diffusion of innovation models

The aggregate of the individual adoption process whereby an individual passes from knowledge, to formation of an attitude, decision to adoption or rejection, implementation of the new idea, and confirmation of the decision. It refers to the process and rate at which various groups of individuals adopt an idea or innovation in a given organization or social system. The diffusion effect is the cumulatively increasing degree of influence upon an individual to adopt or reject an innovation, resulting from the activation of peer networks about an innovation in the social system.

Individuals within a social system adopt new concepts and ideas at different times and can be categorized sequentially according to the relative order in which they adopt. Adopter groups are identified as innovators, early adopters, early majority, and laggards or non-adopters.

Dining room turnover

In the foodservice industry turnover refers to how frequently *seats* or *tables* are occupied by new customers in a given time period. *Seat* turnover is the number of times a seat is used by different individuals during a particular meal period or time. *Table* turnover is the number of times a table is used by different parties during a particular meal period or time. For example in a restaurant that has 100 seats, is open for four hours, and serves 200 diners during those four hours, the *seat* turnover would be 200/100 = 2.0 turns per seat. *Table* turnover is equally simple to calculate. If a restaurant has 30 tables, is open for four hours, and serves 90 parties during those four hours, its *table* turnover would be 90/30 = 3 turns per table. These calculations help operators measure how well their restaurants use seating capacity.

Direct billing

An arrangement that allows a guest to purchase hotel services products on credit terms. When an invoice is direct billed it is sent to the office of the controller where it is processed. The department will receive a photocopy of the invoice that was debited to their account, with a document number stamped at the bottom. Only certain businesses are typically set up for direct billing. For example, in the lodging business, many companies or guests may not want to settle their bills at the end of their stay with cash, check, money order, or even credit card. They would apply for a line of credit with the hotel and have established the line. Upon approval, they agree to pay for the charges incurred during their stay and a bill will be sent to them by the hotel at a later date.

Direct costs

Expenses directly related to operations that result in the production of goods or services. These costs may be controllable or non-controllable in nature, but often direct costs are controllable. Direct costs in foodservice operations pertain to items such as food, labor, paper, linens, glassware, essential contractual services, etc. Costs for items such as payroll, marketing, depreciation, taxes and interest, legal fees paid, overhead, and building rent are not considered direct costs. Though these costs are important for unit operations, they are not related directly to production activities. Sometimes costs that are not directly related to operations are referred to collectively as 'overhead costs.' Frequently, direct costs are analyzed to assess the effectiveness of resource utilization in a hospitality organization. A lower percentage of direct costs indicate excessive overhead and thus ineffective resource utilization.

Direct mail marketing

Individualized advertising that is sent through traditional mail. Direct mail marketing is often called database marketing or one-to-one marketing. Direct mail marketing involves segmentation and customization. The individualized component in direct mail marketing is created from knowledge of the consumer that is available in various databases. The consumer data allows the marketing message to be customized to the needs and/or interests of each consumer. Typically, direct marketing consists of the offer, the audience, and the promotion. The offer consists of an appealing product at an appealing price. The audience is comprised of potential or previous customers that have indicated that they are open to receiving such offers. The promotion is the benefit-oriented message sent via a particular media type. In this case, the media is mail.

Disciplinary action

Any management action intended to control, punish, modify, or inhibit undesirable employee behavior. In some countries there are legislative provisions requiring employers to implement or adopt a fair internal grievance and disciplinary procedure (also known as procedural adequacy/fairness), while in others there is none. In hospitality organizations that have a strong human resources management focus, there is usually a formal disciplinary code or procedure to be followed. In cases where employers and employees have negotiated or agreed on a set of principles, there is a high probability that courts and tribunals will deem them to be fair. Additionally, if employees have contributed to shaping the workplace grievance procedure they will be more likely to accept outcomes without recourse to legal representation. Effective disciplinary codes or procedures in the hospitality industry have three overall aims including prompt resolution, fair and reasonable outcomes which consider the interests of all those affected and promotion of harmony within the workplace.

Disconfirmation theory

Disconfirmation theory involves a subjective before and after evaluation of a service consumption. Prior to using a product or service, a consumer has certain expectations about it. These expectations become a basis against which to compare actual performance and experience. After consuming the product or experiencing the service, customers determine how well the product 'measures up' to their initial expectations and decides whether product performance is better than, equal to, or worse than expected. The extent to which perceptions of the performance or experience 'match' expectations determines the type of disconfirmation:

- positive disconfirmation results when perceived performance or experience exceeds expectations;
- negative disconfirmation occurs when expectations are not met by the product or service;
- zero disconfirmation (also known as confirmation) ensues when performance matches expectations.

A substantial proportion of the 'hospitality experience' is comprised of intangible or service-type elements. Therefore, an understanding of this theory is of paramount importance for hospitality managers and front-line workers.

Discrimination

The unfair treatment or denial of normal privileges to persons because of their race, age, nationality, gender, religion, or other factors. In the USA and many other countries, sexual harassment is considered gender-based discrimination. Discrimination in the workplace has not always been unlawful, and it was as recent as 1964 in the USA that a federal statute addressed discrimination. Equal employment opportunity legislation in many countries (including the USA, UK, Australia, and New Zealand) has sought to implement anti-discrimination policies. Those policies can be classified by their following approaches:

- *Anti-discrimination*: An approach that advocates equal opportunities for all people, regardless of identity difference, through the removal of discriminatory process in the workplace.

- *Direct discrimination*: Specific actions that are taken because of identity group membership (e.g. where someone is refused appointment to a position based on gender or race, etc.)
- *Indirect discrimination*: Result from situations where rules or practices disadvantage members of identity groups more than they do the majority group.
- *Equal employment opportunity*: The creation of conditions that allow all workers or potential applicants to have equal chance to seek and obtain employment, promotion and employment benefits.

Discriminatory pricing

Practice of selling goods or services at different prices to different buyers, even though sales costs are the same for all the transactions. A method of setting prices at different levels based on (1) the customers' price elasticity (i.e. charging lower prices to price sensitive customers and asking full prices from inelastic market segments); (2) the quantity of products or services sold (i.e. larger quantities are available at a lower unit price); or (3) geographical location of the customers (i.e. the presence or absence of competitors in the location). Price differentiations are not sustained by a difference in costs or quality but rather are the result of unique characteristics of the customers and the environment. To be successful, price discriminatory approaches must be well comprehended and accepted by the customer.

Dismissal of employees

The termination or discharge of a person from a position or employment. Two major types of employee' dismissals can occur in present times, *wrongful* or *bona fide*. *Wrongful* dismissal includes 'unfair' and 'unlawful' dismissals. Unfair dismissal is the termination of employment deemed to be 'harsh, unjust, or unreasonable' using a number of criteria expressed as questions. For example, was there a valid reason for the termination, was the employee notified, were opportunities granted for employee responses to the reason, and was adequate warning was given to employee to improve performance? Unlawful termination or dismissal is deemed to be so for reasons prescribed in related legislation. Examples include dismissal on grounds of race, gender, political orientation, union membership, 'whistle blowing,' etc. *Bona fide* dismissal refers to the termination of an employee according to the terms of the contract of employment or according to statute, where a valid reason exists to terminate the contract of employment or where it is illegal to continue employing the person, such as a hotel employee who is employed as a bus driver and has lost his driving license.

Distinctive capabilities

Unique and integrative bundles of a hospitality firm's tangible and intangible resources that allows it to perform distinctive tasks or activities. These capabilities emerge over time and are central to the processes of the firm. Distinctive capabilities are derived through a complex interaction of resources and are frequently developed within functional areas or from a specific part of functional areas of the firm. A portfolio of resources and distinctive capabilities serve as a potential source of competitive advantage. Continually rising guest expectations as well as copying of capabilities by competitors makes distinctive capabilities a moving target for hospitality firms. Therefore, hospitality firms have no choice but to continually develop and renew their distinctive capabilities as well as ensure that these capabilities are matched with appropriate competitive methods for strategic intentions to become realized.

Distribution channels

The vehicles (i.e. a chain of intermediaries) utilized to make a product or service available to the consumer. One of the difficulties in discussing distribution channels is the lack of standardized definitions to describe them. The terms may overlap and the industry is not uniform in its nomenclature. Consequently, different terms are used to describe the same concepts. In the hospitality industry, particularly in the lodging sector, the traditional main distribution channels were the call center and travel agencies. The advent of the Internet leads to profound changes in hospitality distribution. New business models were created, as well as online-based reservations networks, which allowed worldwide exposure to products while avoiding intermediaries such as the global distribution system.

Distribution channels in foodservice

A supply chain (distribution channel) is the network of internal and external functions and processes that are associated with procuring, moving, and transforming basic raw materials into a product or service for an end-user. In the restaurant industry this means getting food products from farmers and processors to manufacturers, consolidators, and brokers, who distribute their products to wholesalers and distributors, who in turn deliver the products to individual restaurant operators. An integral part of the supply chain is the flow of information among all members of the distribution network.

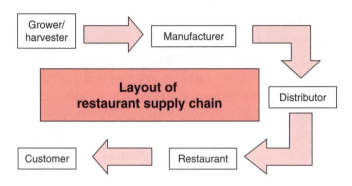

District heating/cooling plants

Heating and/or cooling plants owned and operated by municipalities with large loops running through the downtown part of the city. For example, steam, hot water, and sometimes chilled water from one central plant is run through the city loop and is delivered to many buildings that do not have their own central plants. Instead, each building on the loop relies upon heat or cold from these central plants to provide building services. Using a district plant reduces a hotel's first cost during new construction or when an existing heating or cooling plant requires replacement (see also combined heat and power).

Diversification

Changes in a firm's scope of operations in terms of products/services offered and markets served. More precisely, it refers to a movement away from the original technology used and/or types of customers targeted. The diversification into different realms of business activity is often presented as a means of lowering risk. A growth strategy through concentric diversification into a related industry is considered when the organization has a strong competitive position, but industry attractiveness is low. Diversification of hospitality organizations into the foodservice or restaurant sectors can be viewed as 'concentric' when the customer base is similar and the organization utilizes its proven strengths in the hospitality business to secure the appropriate competitive position in related industries.

Diversity management

The organizational goals, policies, and practices that are put into place in order to help achieve diversity in customers and employees. The globalization of hospitality and tourism enterprises along with changing travel and immigration patterns has resulted in increasingly diverse customer and employee populations within the industry. As a result, today's hospitality managers must be skilled at managing a multi-cultural workforce, responsive to the diversity of their customers, and respectful of the local cultures in which they operate. Research suggests that effectively managing a diverse workforce can lead to many benefits including increased success in global markets; an enhanced ability to meet the needs of diverse customers; the ability to attract increased numbers of high quality employees; increased creativity and higher-quality decision making; increased organizational flexibility and in some instances, reduced costs through lower rates of absenteeism and turnover.

Domain name

The text name corresponding to the numeric IP address of a computer on the Internet. All websites have a web address of the form (e.g. http://www.hilton.com). In this case hilton.com is the domain name. The first part of the address shows that the information is to be transferred using HyperText Transfer Protocol (http), and it is part of the World Wide Web. Domain names always end with the name of a top level domain – in this case .com indicating that this is a commercial site. Other top level domains indicate either a country (e.g. uk for the United Kingdom) or a type of site – .edu for US educational institutions. One can register a domain name through a range of agencies and it is possible to register any domain name one desires, provided nobody else has previously registered it. Domain name registrations are not permanent, and expire after a fixed period of time.

Downsizing

A deliberate reduction in the size of the permanent workforce in response to declining demand, a merger or acquisition, which has resulted in redundancies, increased operational efficiencies, or pressure to reduce labor costs. Downsizing strategies include termination and layoffs – in which employees are forced to leave on a permanent or temporary basis, and enhanced attrition – in which employees are provided with incentives to voluntarily depart. While downsizing can provide the organization with short-term cost savings, it can also result in lost expertise and organizational memory deficits, reductions in loyalty and productivity, work overload and increased stress for those who remain. Increased selection and training costs can also be incurred once business volumes resume. In unionized environments terminations and layoffs are typically based on seniority, but may also be based on position or skill set, particularly in the case of redundancies or skill obsolescence.

Drayage

Delivery of exhibit materials from the dock to an assigned exhibit space, removing empty crates, returning crates at the end of show for re-crating, and delivering materials back to dock for carrier loading. It entails the labor and equipment necessary to move a shipment, including the storage of empty cartons and crates for the duration of the event. Drayage can be as simple as having a hotel bellman unload a car and take exhibit materials to the hotel ballroom or as complex as unloading products and exhibits using specialized labor and equipment, such as dollies or forklifts. Drayage is provided by the official show contractor and often involves minimum time labor calls and/or equipment rentals, thus it can get very expensive.

Duty of care

In Australia and a few other countries of British heritage, the term refers to the employer's duty toward others, as recognized by common law, to take reasonable care for the safety of others usually in the form of: (i) provision of a safe workplace; (ii) provision of a safe system of work; (iii) provision and maintenance of safe plant and equipment; and (iv) provision of competent staff to manage and supervise the business. The duty of care is part of the common law known as tort (the tort of negligence). Negligence is associated with causing another person injury or harm unintentionally but carelessly. Evidence necessary for establishing a breach of the duty of care include: (i) the risk was foreseeable; (ii) there was a reasonably practicably means of avoiding the risk and was preventable; (iii) the person suffered a foreseeable injury; and (iv) the employer owed a duty of care and the failure to eliminate the risk showed a lack of reasonable care.

Ee

Earnings per share

The ratio calculated by dividing the number of ordinary shares in issue by the profit after interest and tax. The earnings per share ratio is considered to be an important measure of corporate performance and is normally required to be shown in the published profit and loss account for a business:

$$\text{Earnings per share} = \frac{\text{Profit after interest and tax}}{\text{Number of ordinary shares in issue}}$$

Alternatively it can be explained as the net profit attributable to each ordinary share in issue. When preference shares have been issued the preference dividend is subtracted from the profit after interest and tax. The more equity increases, in terms of the number of shares issued, the greater the dilution of the earnings per share. Earnings per share tend to reflect the degree of profit stability experienced by organizations.

Economies of scale

A term used to express a firm's ability to reduce the cost of producing one unit of goods or services as the volume of production increases. Mass production and economies of scale were central concepts in the development of modern economic theory. In the hospitality industry economies of scale can originate from different sources. For example, economies of scale can result from the ability to share marketing and sales infrastructure for increasing capacity. A Central Reservation System (CRS) might serve as an example for economies of scale. Economies of scale in the hospitality industry can also result from the utilization of central management teams, acquisition of raw materials and production, and labor utilization. Improving profitability has been a key issue in the hospitality industry, and economies of scale are an important component in that effort.

Economies of scope

The ability to join resources and produce two or more distinct products or services from the same company compared with providing them from two different companies. The result is a lower product cost, as all the products are produced at the same (fixed) cost. In the hospitality industry economies of scope can originate from strategic alliances, joint ventures, or mergers.

For example, a hotel company that forms a strategic alliance with a car rental company. As part of this alliance, the companies use the same Central Reservation System (CRS) to support both hotel and car reservations. Consequently, reservation cost of hotel rooms and rental cars generate a joint reservations system and a general cost reduction in reservations transactions.

Efficiency ratios

Efficiency ratios are asset turnover, accounts receivable turnover, fixed asset turnover, and inventory turnover.

Asset turnover or asset utilization ratio is a key measure of effectiveness, it relates the assets employed in the business to the income or sales revenues generated from the use of those assets. It reflects the intensity with which assets are employed or used, as such, it gives an indication of the productivity of the business. It is calculated as follows: Income (or Turnover/Sales) ÷ Total Assets represented as number of times (e.g. $350,000 ÷ $222,000 = 1.58 = 1.6 times).

Accounts receivable turnover (also called debtor turnover or debtor collection period), measures the length of time it takes for an organization collect the money from its customers. It provides an indication of the efficiency of the accounts receivable (debtors) department. It is calculated as follows and can be presented in two ways: Credits sales ÷ Average debtors (e.g. $100,000 ÷ $23,800 = 4.2016 = 4.2 times).

Fixed asset turnover is similar to asset utilization, but only includes fixed assets. This ratio enables the isolation of short-term assets and liabilities from the overall picture of productivity. It is calculated as follows: Sales revenue ÷ Average fixed assets, represented as number of times (e.g. $350,000 ÷ $196,000 = 1.78 = 1.8 times).

Inventory turnover (stock turnover) measures the average speed by which stock (or inventory) is bought and sold, in other words, how long on average an organization holds stock before selling it. Stock turnover can be expressed in two ways; times per annum or number of days. It is calculated as follows: Cost of sales ÷ Average stock = Stock turnover (e.g. £140,000 ÷ 9635 = 14.5 = 14 times).

Eighty-six

The number '86' is fundamental to the rich foodservice vernacular. The numerical expression was made popular by short-order cooks to inform food servers they were out of a specific dish. Hence, after the last slice of cherry pie was served, the cooks would yell, '86 cherry pie!'. The terms is also applied when customers are asked to leave a bar or restaurant. Typically as the result of behavior associated with intoxication, a manager may tell the bartender to '86' the guest in question. The term has extended to use in other sectors too. The military, for example, uses the term to mean eliminate or destroy ('86 the enemy's headquarters'). It is also evident in contemporary colloquialism where it is used as a slang term to denote the end of a relationship ('My girlfriend just 86'd me').

Eighty-twenty customer pyramid

Developed in the late 1800s by the Italian economist, Vilfredo Pareto, the 80-20 rule or Pareto's principle argues that 20 per cent of a population often account for 80 per cent of an occurrence. In a business context, this means that 80 per cent of a company's business stems from 20 per cent of its customers. Management's task is finding and keeping this lucrative 20 per cent.

The lucrative 20 per cent are sometimes termed 'barnacles', because they tend to stay with a business over their lifetime, while the 80 per cent are sometimes termed 'butterflies' because they tend to give their business to a variety of firms.

Electric power purchasing

Hospitality firms normally purchase their electricity from a local electric utility. Their purchase involves a charge for the electricity itself, measured in kilowatt-hours or kWh, and the peak demand for electricity, measured in kilowatts or kW. Utility rates may vary by season as well as by time of day. These variations reflect the differing costs to produce and delivery electrical energy. One common way that utilities adjust their rates to reflect changing costs is via the fuel clause adjustment – an additional charge or credit on top of the base rate reflecting the costs of fuel (or purchased electricity) to the utility. Normally, hospitality firms are on a 'secondary' electric power rate with electricity supplied at 480 V or less. That is, the meter is set on the customer's side of a transformer that is owned by the utility company.

Electronic commerce

The practice of buying and selling products and services by means of computers, utilizing technologies such as the Web, electronic data interchange, e-mail, electronic fund transfers, and smart cards. E-commerce allows potential customers to select goods and services, review what they have chosen, make necessary modifications, and complete the purchasing process accordingly. Having been accepted as the biggest single transformation that has been happened in the last few generations, e-commerce encompasses all forms of online electronic trading, including business-to-business (B2B) and business-to-consumer (B2C) transactions.

Within the context of hospitality operations, it has become possible to make all arrangements for a trip in a few seconds. Using the Internet as an electronic medium, it gives suppliers (hotels, motels, or holiday villages) intermediaries (travel agencies, global distribution systems (GDSs)), and customers (end users, guests, or visitors) obvious advantages over traditional marketing methods applied in the hospitality industry.

Electronic data interchange

Electronic data interchange (EDI) allows the transfer of data using networks, particularly the Internet. There are various EDI standards approved by the American National Standards Institute (ANSI) (e.g. X12). However, EDI can be expensive and a new cheaper standard AS2 has been developed which enables smaller companies with limited budgets to exploit the benefits of EDI. EDI can be used to provide easy and cheap interaction for business-to-business (B2B) commerce and the secure sharing of data. EDI is becoming increasingly important as an easy mechanism for hospitality companies to buy, sell, and trade information.

Electronic locking systems

Electronic locking systems were created to replace traditional key locks. Electronic locks can be stand-alone systems or online hard-wired systems. In stand-alone systems the lockset in each door has a memory that permits reading of the card when introduced into the lock unit. The lock is powered by a battery and the card is programed at the front desk for a specific room. When the card is introduced into the lock, the memory chip will recognize it as the appropriate 'level' for entry; or deny entry when the card does not carry the proper access code. In the online, hard-wired installation, the card is programed at the front desk and a simultaneous message is transmitted to the lockset in the door to the assigned room. Recently, smartcards have also been used as locking systems. The smartcard has an embedded integrated circuit chip in the card which may be programed for a multiplicity of uses such as a credit or debit card as well as unlocking the guestroom and other facility services (i.e. health club, concierge, or club floor, etc.).

Electronic mail

Most commonly known as e-mail, electronic mail is a networking application that allows users to send and receive mail electronically. E-mail is by far the most popular activity on the Internet. E-mail technology makes it possible to send and receive electronic 'letters' almost instantaneously over the Internet. Because e-mail is asynchronous (a type of two-way communication that occurs with a time delay, allowing participants to respond at their own convenience) it is receiver friendly, as they can deal with it at a time of their choosing, unlike a telephone call, which can be intrusive.

In 1971 Ray Tomlinson, an American computer engineer who worked for BBN, a company hired to build the precursor to the Internet, invented e-mail. He also decided on the now ubiquitous @ as the locator symbol in an e-mail address.

Electronic marketing

Electronic marketing (E-marketing/Web marketing) uses the Internet/World Wide Web (the Web) to market products and services in 'marketspace' – the virtual equivalent of the global marketplace. E-marketing radically changes how hospitality firms operate, requiring a paradigm shift toward dialog with content created by, and for, individuals using information from customers not about them. E-marketing provides low-cost gateways enabling small and non-brand businesses to compete globally alongside brands.

Emotional labor

Inducing or suppressing feelings in order to sustain the outward countenance that produces the proper state of mind in others. Emotional labor has three components; it involves the faking of emotion that is not felt, and/or hiding of emotions that is felt. There are three potential situations regarding the match between emotions felt and emotional display, particularly in work roles. *Emotional harmony* is said to exist in situations where the individual actually feels the emotion required of the display rules and social expectations. *Emotional dissonance* takes place when the emotions displayed for the purposes of the job role are not the emotions felt. *Emotional deviance* occurs when the person displays the emotions felt, but these are not ones that are expected to be displayed.

Employee assistance programs

A confidential counseling and referral scheme that is provided by employers to employees who are experiencing a wide range of personal, emotional, and psychological problems. It is necessary for hospitality organizations to provide employee assistance programs (EAP) as a cost-effective means of reducing staff turnover and keeping employees productive on the job. Organizations that offer an EAP show genuine concern for the wellbeing of their staff by offering this as a part of their benefit package. In an effort to ensure confidentiality of employee issues, an outside contractor would normally be engaged to provide consulting and counseling services.

Employee mentoring

A process of employee development that involves less experienced employees aligning themselves with more senior, experienced employees in order to learn skills. Mentoring is a knowledge transfer approach used to enhance employees' learning of specific tasks or skill-sets. A mentor is a role model and advocate for one or several outstanding performers to sustain their motivation and to realize their abilities to their fullest potential. Mentor pass on their experience, give advice or instruction, and open up career opportunities. Mentoring can be both formal (where a mentor is assigned to an upwardly mobile employee), or informal (where a relationship develops over time). Mentoring is a useful practice in hotel corporate traineeship programs.

(New) Employee orientation

The process used by organizations to introduce new employees to the organization, their job and their work environment. Orientation, or induction, programs generally contain information about safety, the work environment, the new job description, benefits and eligibility, company culture, company history, the organization chart, and other relevant factors. Employee orientation/induction is the beginning of the training and development process of new employees. Whilst job information is essential, it is also just as important for the employee to be socialized into the organization and to be made to feel welcome in those critical first few days/weeks.

Employee participation

The involvement of workers in the work issues that affect them in their jobs. This concept could also be referred to as employee involvement but is not often used. At its simplest, employee participation could be merely being told by supervisors and managers of what is going on (with no opportunity for two-way communication), and at its most complex it could be employee ownership (industrial democracy). Participation can be either direct, where the individual worker is involved, or indirect, where the workers are represented by a nominated person or group.

Employee relations

A term often used interchangeably with industrial relations and human resource management (HRM) to describe particular HRM or industrial relations philosophies and approaches. Some researchers and practitioners suggest a more comprehensive definition of employee relations (ER) that covers all employee communications, employee participation in management decisions, conflict and grievance resolution, trade unions, and collective bargaining. Under this comprehensive definition ER is the process of identifying and responding to all the issues and concerns affecting the employees of an organization.

Employee satisfaction

Employee satisfaction with job-related activities is viewed in the literature as an attitudinal element that relates past events and rewards to current feelings about a job. Research indicates that employee satisfaction is correlated with: loyalty, involvement and engagement on the job, motivation to work, commitment to guest service and the service process, customer satisfaction, high profitability, and many more. However, at this stage many studies are inconclusive as to which causes which. For example, does satisfaction cause engagement or vice versa.

Employee selection techniques

The process of selecting the best qualified candidates that meet the requirements of the job. These requirements – also referred to as the job specification – may include personal competencies, prior work experience, and formal qualifications deemed necessary to be able to competently perform the job. Effective selection processes allow both the candidate and the organization to properly assess the degree to which the candidate fits the job specification and are in keeping with all applicable laws and regulations. Formal selection procedures typically involve several stages of assessment including pre-screening, interviewing, testing, and reference checks. When the selection decision has been made, a formal offer of employment is extended. Only once the offer has been negotiated and formally accepted, the unsuccessful candidates are informed that the job has been filled.

Employer association

A collective association of employers usually organized on an industry basis, to represent the collective interests of a group of employers. Employer associations not only represent their members in industrial issues, but may also be active at an economic and political level. Employer associations tend to be less cohesive than trade unions as their membership is drawn from businesses that also compete commercially with one another. Examples are local, regional, and national hotel associations. Typically, members of local or regional hotel associations are comprised of hospitality organizations but also of firms, which benefit from indirect tourist income. The firms are usually labeled 'allied members'.

Employment

90

The form of the contractual relationship between worker and employer. Employment in the hospitality industry is normally paid but there are significant exceptions. In some countries, including those that are industrialized, there is a high proportion of unpaid labor. This reflects the situation in hospitality where there are a large number of small entrepreneurs with unpaid family members. At least half the employment within the hospitality industry is within SMEs (small- to medium-sized enterprises). However, since the 1970s there has been an expansion of branded chains which has created large multi-site organizations particularly within the fast-food and hotel sectors. In the hospitality industry a small core of skilled full-time permanent employees is supported by a large pool of disposable labor which employers can access in times of demand. Core workers within the industry tend to be sourced from the primary labor market which is characterized by high levels of skill and permanence of employment, whereas peripheral workers are sourced from the secondary labor market which is characterized by less skilled, less valued, and often part-time or casual workers.

Most workers within the industry tend to be young and/or female. Over half of employment in the international hospitality industry is made up of women.

Employment laws

A set of laws related to events that occur in the workplace and that mostly define employees' rights and employers' responsibilities under a given legal system. Employment laws specify the manner in which employers must treat employees, former employees, and applicants for employment. Employment laws vary across the world and are a function of a country's legal, political, and economic system. In the USA employment laws include a wide variety of issues like pension plans, retirement, occupational safety and health regulations, affirmative action, discrimination in the workplace and sexual harassment, etc.

Employment regulations and rules

Employment regulations can either refer to (a) the processes that control and define employment rights and obligations under a country's legal system or (b) the specific company rules that govern employees' rights, responsibilities, and behaviors at a given workplace. As to (a), different countries have different laws and regulations but typically they address such issues as: working conditions, mandatory benefits, wages, overtime, collective bargaining, discrimination and harassment, safety and health, etc.

Empowerment

Generally regarded as a method for promoting greater employee involvement, empowerment is argued to lead to greater organizational success through engaging the employee in the decision-making process. It involves encouraging and authorizing workers to take the initiative to improve operations, reduce costs, and improve product quality and customer service. The focus is on providing employees with opportunities to have greater freedom, autonomy, and self-control over various aspects of their work, whilst at the same time being encouraged to think creatively and take risks to respond quickly to work situations. In service organizations, empowerment is considered a method of improving customer service in which workers have discretion to do what they believe is necessary – within reason – to satisfy the customer, even if this means bending some company rules. Empowerment was first introduced within the hospitality industry as a response to the changing nature of service markets.

Energy management

The use of products, systems, and services to determine the operation characteristics of energy-using equipment and processes so that actual use results in the maximum energy efficiency that is practical. Energy management encompasses decisions about all aspects of an organization's energy usage. It is above all a management discipline, one that should be brought to bear on decisions regarding energy engineering, energy accounting, energy cost control, energy conservation, and energy efficiency. Energy management requires a high degree of competence in the management of capital, the management of technology, and the management of human effort. As with other management disciplines, its objective is not to minimize costs, but rather to maximize value.

Energy management system

A control system (often computerized) designed to regulate the energy consumption of a building by controlling the operation of energy consuming systems, such as the heating, ventilation and air-conditioning (HVAC), lighting, and water heating systems. Energy management systems allow hospitality enterprises to take control of lighting, temperature, and electricity to minimize costs while at the same time maintaining guest comfort. For example, energy management systems can automatically reduce heating in unoccupied hotel rooms until allocation to a guest, at which point they can quickly be returned to an acceptable temperature or when a guest is not in the room, heating and power can automatically be placed into stand-by status to minimize energy usage and cost. Electronically controlled systems allow more precise control to be maintained over temperatures than with the previous mechanical systems.

Enterprise resource planning

A broad set of activities supported by application software that helps a manufacturer or business, manage the important parts of its business, including product planning, parts purchasing, maintaining inventories, interacting with suppliers, providing customer service, and tracking orders. Enterprise resource planning (ERP) software was designed to automate and model the core business functions of an enterprise. It uses data and processes from logistical management, financial, and human resources. The main goal of ERP is to integrate information across the enterprise to eradicate the intricate and costly links between computer systems that do not communicate effectively with each other.

ERP is useful in the hospitality industry because it enables the user to do many functions simultaneously. For instance with a hotel conference center the Conference Coordinator can book a group in for a function via computer, thus informing foodservices whose computer will generate menu in turn informing the Shipping/Receiving department that food would need to be ordered.

Entrepreneurship

Entrepreneurship in the hospitality industry suggests an interest in starting, owning, and operating a profitable independent or franchised operation. Entrepreneurship covers the full range of the hospitality business including, but not limited to, concept; conducting analyses; understanding entrepreneurial potential; financial planning, borrowing, and control; franchising; location and property analysis; and ownership and management.

There are two typologies of entrepreneurs according to personality, background, and behavior: craftsmen entrepreneurs and opportunistic entrepreneurs. These two types of entrepreneurs display many opposite personality qualities in their behavior and orientation. *Craftsmen entrepreneurs* who usually lack formal education in the field, lack depth in managerial experience, and have blue-collar backgrounds. They often enjoy being immersed in operations and doing planning and administrative work. *Opportunistic entrepreneurs* often have a high level of formal education, bring an extensive variety of management experience to a job, and come from middle-class backgrounds.

Entry strategies

Depending on the circumstances, entrepreneurs employ various strategies for entering into the hospitality industry, including (a) acquisition, (b) intrapreneurship (the application of entrepreneurial skills and approaches within an enterprise), (c) purchase of a franchise,

(d) cooperation with a hotel management firm such as Hilton, (e) joining a referral association such as Best Western, or (f) joining a confederation of several businesses to discuss and decide on issues of common interest. Acquisition indicates a high level of ownership and control over the new operation. The other strategies show relatively lower levels of ownership and control and are based primarily on exploiting brand name and marketing resources of well-established business entities. It should be noted, however, that intrapreneurship incorporates all kinds of minor employee-initiated improvements both in products and processes that continue to be in the organization's control and ownership.

Environmental determinism

The view that the physical environment, rather than social conditions, determines culture. Those who believe in this view say that humans are strictly defined by stimulus–response (environment–behavior) and cannot deviate. Within the various strategic management schools of thought, the environmental school offers the least scope for management choice. Drawing upon biology, this school in its most extreme form conceives of the external environment as effectively selecting from the population of firms those which 'fit' and rejecting those which do not. Thus the environment is seen as being dominant and deterministic, with strategy essentially a reactive process whereby the organization is largely passive.

Environmental management

Effective and active measures taken for the protection, conservation, and presentation of the environment, heritage and natural resources for which a government, organization, or individual is responsible. In the hospitality industry facilities managers are often responsible for the overall environmental programs at their enterprises. These programs are aimed at reducing negative environmental impacts of operation. These impacts can be internal involving employees and customers as well as external involving the local, regional, and global environment. Environmental management responsibilities generally include waste minimization, energy conservation and management, management of fresh water resources, wastewater management, hazardous substances, and involvement of staff, customers, and communities in environmental issues. The hospitality industry has moved into environmental management relatively recently, probably because of dual factors. Firstly, it is a common perception that hotels and tourist attractions have a low environmental impact (at least in comparison with heavy industry). Secondly, because of the image of a hotel or tourist attraction as a place of comfort and luxury, managers in these enterprises are often nervous of appearing to be concerned mainly with cutting costs. Thus, for example, asking hotel guests if they wish to reuse their towels or if they would prefer fresh ones may appear to be reducing the level of service.

Environmental management system

A systematic approach for organizations to bring environmental considerations into decision-making and day-to-day operations. It also establishes a framework for tracking, evaluating, and communicating environmental performance. Although environmental management system (EMS) can be different for different types of organizations, depending on their size, products, and the nature of their business, etc., common components include the identification of environmental impact and legal obligations, the development of a plan for management and improvement, the assignment of responsibilities, and the monitoring of performance.

BS7750 (British Standard No. 7750), launched in 1992, was the world's first EMS standard. In 1993, another EMS standard was published by the European Union (EU), called 'Eco-Management and Audit Scheme' (EMAS). Following these two, national EMS standards proliferated, eventually leading to the development of the ISO 14000 standards. In the ISO (International Standards Organization) 14000 series, ISO 14001, commonly known as the most important EMS standard, defines EMS as a management system that includes organizational structure, planning activities, responsibilities, practices, procedures, processes, and resources for developing, implementing, achieving, reviewing, and maintaining environmental policies.

Environmental protection agency

See US Environmental Protection Agency.

Environmental scanning

The employment of systematic methods by an organization to monitor, gather information, and forecast external forces and developments not under the direct control of the organization. Environmental scanning (ES) is an integral part of the strategic management process. It entails a constant examination of the external environment to detect changes that may affect the organization either directly or indirectly. Formal ES begins with the identification of a relevant trend or external forces from the viewpoint of the organization. The selection of the external force to be monitored and analyzed depends on the perspective of the hospitality organization; for example, a domestic chain will have a different focus and set of priorities than a global firm.

E-procurement

Electronic tools that support and expedite the transactional purchasing process. Through e-procurement, buyers search electronic catalogs (e-catalogs) to find needed items, place requisitions, route for approval, and send to suppliers for fulfillment. Some e-procurement tools (but not all) support the back-end invoicing and payment processing. E-procurement streamlines the purchase and delivery processes (e.g. from product ordering to payment by the firm's bank) by integrating them into the Internet for increasing operational efficiencies and creating competitive advantages. Since the Internet is an open shared platform, businesses of any size can gain access to e-procurement, in contrast to expensive and proprietary electronic data interchange procurement systems. E-procurement has the following advantages: one-stop shopping from numerous suppliers; dynamic pricing; increased auditing (i.e. detailed purchasing reports and purchases' authorization control system); just-in-time; automated paperless ordering; chain approved purchases for brand consistency; financial benefits through fast product/supplier search/comparison, purchase aggregation, and streamlined processes.

Equal employment opportunity

In the USA and some other countries, equal employment opportunity (EEO) is defined as employment practices which do not discriminate on the basis of race, color, religion, sex, national origin, handicapping condition, or any other personal characteristic prohibited by the law of the land. In such countries employment decisions are based solely on the individual merit and fitness of applicants and employees related to specific jobs, without regard to race, color, religion, sex, age, national origin, handicapping conditions, marital status, criminal record, and in some countries (i.e. Australia) sexual orientation. EEO is based on a belief in universal human rights and is expressed in the United Nations' Universal Declaration of Human Rights (1948). The aim of EEO legislation is to give legal support to the notion that all people in a society should have equal opportunities to enjoy the benefits of that society, including employment.

Ergonomics

Derived from the Greek ergon (work) and nomos (laws) to denote the science of work, ergonomics (or human factors) is a discipline that nowadays studies how the human body relates to its various environments. It is the application of scientific information concerning humans to the design of objects, systems, and environments for human use. Ergonomists main concern is to ensure that work and leisure products, as well as physical environments are comfortable, safe, and efficient for people to use. Ergonomics is relevant to everything that involves people. All human activities including work, sports, leisure, recreation, tourism, health and safety embody ergonomics principles, if properly designed. Ergonomics is a multidisciplinary field involving numerous professionals such as engineers, designers, computer specialists, physicians, health and safety experts, and specialists in human resources. Ergonomists contribute to the design and evaluation of tasks, jobs, products, environments, and systems in order to make them compatible with the needs, abilities, and limitations of people.

Evaluative attributes

Consumers use three types of attributes to evaluate the quality of goods and services: search, experience, and credence qualities. Search qualities are more tangible attributes that a consumer can easily evaluate before purchasing a product such as color, style, price, fit, feel, and smell. Products high in search qualities include clothing, jewelry, and furniture. Experience qualities are attributes that cannot be judged until after purchase or during consumption such as taste or durability. Restaurant meals and haircuts are examples of experience qualities. The third category of evaluative attributes, credence qualities, includes characteristics that the consumer may not be able to evaluate even after purchase and consumption due to their complexity. For example, few consumers have sufficient knowledge in medical services or mechanical services to be able to judge a medical diagnosis or an engine repair.

Event management

A profession that requires public assembly for the purpose of celebration, education, marketing, and reunion. The event management process includes the research, design, planning, coordination, and evaluation of events. The event management profession descended from the field of public relations. Public relations are a major part of the marketing mix. According to the Public Relations Society of America (PRSA), event management is one of the fastest growing and most important trends in the public relations profession. Event management is a multidisciplinary profession. The elements of most events are basically the same: entertainment, decorations, lighting, sound, special effects, catering and, quite often, transportation. Therefore, employment in the field of events management crosses over into many hospitality positions in hotels, food and beverage, tourism, and meetings and conventions. The most common event markets are association, corporate, casino, cause-related, fairs, festivals, and parades, retail, social, sporting, and tourism.

Event operations manual

Often referred to as 'the bible', it is used during the event to allow management and staff to easily use a master checklist. It is typically a 3-ring binder with a colorful cover for easy identification. It contains all schedules, checklists, task lists, a reference index, contact info for all staff, including the office phone, cell phones, and hotel phone numbers where the staff is housed; contact info for all speakers, officers, and vendors; written procedures for locating lost persons or property; emergency services such as fire, ambulance, etc. It normally includes an event summary including time, action, and location of each activity, a map of the venue, the production schedule, move-in, move-out information, and setup schedule, including date, action, suppliers, and crew list. The Event Operations Manual also contains information on catering services, including catering requirements for staff and crew and security information, including photocopies of all credentials and inspections and incident report forms.

Event program

An organized set of activities designed to meet the goals and objectives of the attendees at an event. It may be as simple as a fundraising dinner with entertainment or as complex as a five-day convention that offers a wide variety of educational sessions, networking opportunities, special events, and organized recreation. Ideas for programing may come from the event producer, previous attendees (if it is a repeat event), sponsors, or the event planner. Once all of the sessions and activities are decided upon, a printed schedule of events will be available giving details of a meeting or convention, including times, places, events, locations of function rooms, speakers, topics, bios, and other pertinent information. Selecting the right speakers, panelists, and other program participants is a key to the success of the meeting as well as the budget.

Event project management

The adaptation of the project management methodology, as developed since the 1950s, to the management of events. The project management methodology has evolved into a formal system which can be described and improved. It includes areas of knowledge, tools, techniques, and processes. Event management, with its intangible outcomes, complexity of stakeholders and changing management environment, represents a further development possibility for project management. The areas of current project management that are found to be useful to event management are as follows:

1. Scope definition – the scope includes the amount of work needed to create the event or festival.
2. Work breakdown structure – arising from defining the scope is the breakdown of all the work into manageable units.
3. Task analysis – once the general areas of work have been defined, the individual tasks that must be completed can be discovered.
4. Scheduling.
5. Responsibility chart – the tasks need to be done by a person or a group of people.
6. Resource analysis, such as equipment, personnel, etc.
7. Risk management.
8. Stakeholder management – for example, the management of sponsors with levels of sponsorship and the sponsor communication plan.

Evoked set

The shortlist of potential products that the consumer has to choose from within the purchasing decision-making process. The evoked set is part of the alternative evaluation stage in consumer buying behavior when alternatives are considered for purchase. It can be viewed as a funneling process beginning with the *total set* of all brands or alternatives available from which a consumer can choose. The total set of available hotels in a large city contains many alternatives, as does the number of pizza or other fast-food alternatives in certain geographic areas. Most consumers would not be aware of every alternative; hence, the total set for a particular consumer would be whittled down to a subset containing only those alternatives of which he or she is aware, or the *awareness set*.

Exchange company

Exchange companies act as brokers between timeshare owners. They give timeshare owners the opportunity to swap their timeshare for another week, in another resort, with confidence that they will experience similar quality. Exchange companies act like a bank so that an owner who does not wish to use the week and/or resort purchased 'banks' the week owned with the exchange company. They are subsequently able to withdraw equivalent weeks at other times and/or at other resorts, which have been deposited by other owners. Exchange companies have mechanisms for matching properties based upon a variety of factors such as size of property, duration of stay, etc., which help to determine the value of different weeks in different resorts. The two principal exchange companies are Interval International (II) and Resort Condominiums International (RCI). They collectively incorporate some 5400 resorts in their schemes. Virtually all timeshare resorts are members of one or other of these organizations. Where the resort is affiliated, a timeshare owner joins the exchange company at the time of purchase.

Executive information systems

A computer-based information system that assists executives to manage information for maintaining and achieving the overall business objectives. An executive information systems (EIS) may or may not have a direct relationship with business decision-making. The system, however, will help executives with the necessary information system support, making them more productive in receiving and selecting the essential information that they need. In the unstructured and loosely defined hospitality context, executives often demand specialized information from a wide variety of resources in unlike formats. An EIS meets such a demand by pulling out, filtering, and processing the essential data from the internal and external data repositories. The EIS will then output the processed information in graphical on-screen displays. Examples of these displays include figures and tables that explain trends, ratios, and statistics. With such information, hospitality executives can set policies, prepare budgetary plans, and compile strategic forecasts easily in a short time.

Executive recruiters/head hunters

Persons who search for and screen many applicants to find the most appropriate candidates (usually three to five candidates) for firms looking to recruit for a top management position. They develop a profile of the ideal candidate that takes into account the unique job requirements and the culture of the hospitality organization through interviews with the client and an ongoing relationship with the client, often offering useful advice on selection matters. Executive recruiters use a variety of methods in screening potential employees including psychological testing, which can be important in service/experience provision situations. Executive recruiters generally do not advertise, instead they approach individuals sourced through research and networks of contacts. Given the level of open cooperation between competitors in the hospitality industry, executive recruiters can, if necessary, keep both parties confidential until much later in the process than would otherwise be the case.

Exhibit prospectus

The exhibit prospectus includes information about attendee demographics and other compelling reasons to exhibit in the show. Information in the prospectus includes: (a) the name and address of the show organizer and the name of the meeting or show; (b) the name and exact titles of key personnel involved with the exhibition including mailing addresses, telephone and fax numbers, and e-mail addresses; (c) goals and objectives of the meeting, exhibit dates, exhibit facility and location, background information on the meeting including a list of previous exhibitors, how many years it has been held, and locations of previous and future meetings; (d) attendee demographics, including titles, and information from the most recent convention including attendance figures, a copy of the program from the previous year; (e) additional marketing opportunities available to exhibitors such as the official newspaper, other publications, availability of attendee mailing labels, hyperlink to show website, sponsorship opportunities, etc.; (f) cost breakdown; and (g) copy of the space contract and well-defined information on space assignment methods. It is essentially a marketing tool sent to exhibitors and potential exhibitors.

Exhibitions

Centralized events, large or small, local or international, focused on an industry or a product area, which bring together a wide range of relevant suppliers and interested customers under one roof. Exhibitions provide unique face-to-face interaction between buyers and sellers and offer educational and networking opportunities for attendees. Exhibiting companies are able to meet with numerous clients and prospects and display their goods and services in the span of just a few days. Finally, exhibitions are deemed cost effective when compared with other marketing media and in terms of providing continuing corporate education and training. Generally speaking, there are two types of exhibitions: trade exhibitions and consumer shows. Trade exhibitions attract representatives from a certain industry or professional group and are generally closed to the public. The attendees learn about new products or services from the exhibiting companies. Consumer shows are open to the general public and attract a local audience. Attendees pay a general admission fee.

Exhibits

Exhibit areas are called *exhibitions* or *tradeshows*. Exhibits are generally called *booths* in the USA and *stands* in Europe. These terms are often used interchangeably. However, exhibit refers to the materials used for display in the booths or stands for the products or services being promoted. Exhibits should be attractive, inviting, and informative to attendees in order to generate a good flow of traffic into the exhibit area. For exhibitors, a tradeshow provides a unique marketing opportunity for targeted customers and potential customers. Exhibits provide a value-added educational opportunity for attendees, allowing them to learn about the latest in products, services, and technology in a hands-on environment. Exhibits also provide a large revenue stream for the organization producing the show, such as associations, corporations, or independent planners.

Expenses

The general term that refers to an outflow of assets that has occurred as a result of activities undertaken to generate revenue. In accrual-based accounting, an expense is recognized at the time it is incurred which may not coincide with the time cash is paid for the expense. In the hospitality industry 'expenses' encompass the whole range of expenditure required to operate a hotel or restaurant business, including the cost of sales (e.g. cost of food and drink items sold), employee wages and salaries, administration, energy, repairs and maintenance, marketing and advertising expense, rent expense, insurance expense, depreciation of assets, etc.

Experience economy

The experience economy suggests that successful businesses in the future will strive to offer a distinct economic offering by 'experientializing' the service or product offering. Mundane transactions become experiences, offering an opportunity for customization and differentiation from the competition. Thus, a product that is a relative commodity may be transformed into an experience that provides the opportunity for increased profits and customer loyalty. One example is coffee. A cup of coffee may be a relatively mundane purchase, but Starbuck's experientializes the coffee purchase and consumption experience, allowing them to charge a great deal more for a cup of coffee than the corner deli.

Expert systems

Expert systems, or knowledge-based systems, are a special type of decision support systems (DSS) that uses knowledge of experts as input information. Essentially, these software applications mimic the logic of the decision processes of human experts. They offer software tools to incorporate inferential and deductive reasoning and heuristic manipulation of data. Expert systems encapsulate and process causal rules that have often been derived inductively from previous experimentation, market research, or experience. Typically, these systems will use the rule base to suggest intelligent advice and explain the basis of its reasoning. Expert systems are commonly used in complex decision situations where objective quantitative information is rare or not available. Ideal expert systems allow combining the experiences and intuition of humans with the consistent objectivity of a computer-based model. In hospitality management, expert systems are most commonly applied to managerial decision problems (e.g. to forecast demand in a yield management system).

Express check-out

A common hotel pre-departure activity that involves producing and distributing guest folios to guests expected to check out. To ease front desk volume during the peak periods of check-out, a hotel might initiate check-out activities before guests are ready to leave. Hotel staff may quietly slip printed folios under the guestroom doors of expected check-outs before 6 a.m., making sure that the guest's folio cannot be seen or reached from outside the room. By completing the express check-out form, the guest is authorizing the front office to transfer his/her outstanding folio balance to the credit card voucher that was created during registration. Once completing the form, the guest deposits the express check-out form at the front desk when departing. After the guest has left, the front office completes the guest's check-out by transferring the outstanding guest folio balance to a previously authorized method of settlement.

External analysis

External analysis focuses on identifying and evaluating trends and events beyond the control of a single hospitality firm, such as increased foreign competition, population shifts, an aging society, and advances in information technology. External analysis helps a hospitality firm reveal key opportunities and threats confronting the organization so that managers can develop strategies to take advantage of the opportunities and avoid or reduce the impact of threats. Empirical studies show that external analysis is fundamental to the competitive development of firms. To be successful, external analysis needs to be an important part of formal planning systems of a firm. The most important outcome of external analysis is identification of events and trends in the external environment and their possible impact on the organization.

Extranet

Private networks that use the Internet protocols and the public telecommunication system to share information, data or operations between trusted partners. Extranets facilitate business-to-business (B2B) communications as they connect external suppliers, vendors, or customers. An extranet can be viewed as the external part of a company's Intranet as it only allows partners to access data and processes. Extranets are firewall and password protected but can be accesses from multiple locations. Extranets can be used widely by hospitality organizations for communications with regular partners. Extranets can be critical for developing and maintaining a network of distributors such as Central Reservation Office, Travel Agencies, Hotel Room Aggregators, Tour Operators, Switch Companies and Global Distribution Systems.

Ff

Facilities engineering

The design, specification, organization, building, construction, and use of machines and equipment in a hotel, foodservice or related area, structure or operation. Facilities generally include all of the installed materials of the property including building construction materials, the completed building itself, heating, ventilation, and air conditioning (HVAC) systems, plumbing and related water-handling systems, pumps, controls, electrical and electronic systems, telephone systems, lighting, waste, and pollution, as well as exterior and interior materials and fittings. The basic goal of the facilities engineering design process is to produce a design of high technical quality which meets requirements in a cost effective and timely manner.

Facilities management

Facility management encompasses multiple disciplines to ensure functionality of the built environment by integrating people, place, process, and technology. The development, design and application of systems to properly maintain, repair and replace all of the elements relating to the physical components of a hospitality structure or operation are key aspects of facility management. Maintenance operations and space management are the primary areas of facility management. Facilities generally include all of the installed materials of the property including building construction materials, the completed building itself, heating, ventilation, and air conditioning (HVAC) systems, plumbing and related water-handling systems, pumps, controls, electrical and electronic systems, telephone systems, lighting, waste and pollution, as well as exterior and interior materials and fittings. Facilities management requires implementation of appropriate computer of manual systems for tracking and prevention, responding to requests for work, for inventory of parts and spares, and for the costs associated with maintenance activities.

Facilities operating and capital expenses

Facilities operating expenses can also be called property operation and maintenance (POM) According to the Uniform System of Accounts for the Lodging Industry, POM consists of 'payroll and related expenses' for the engineering/facilities department and a category of 'other expenses' that consists of purchased supplies and equipment, contract services, waste removal, and other expenses. POM costs typically range from 4 to 6 per cent of total property revenues. Labor and benefits are typically 40–60 per cent of these costs with contract services and supplies being the balance. Capital Expenditures (CapEx) are funds spent to replace furniture, fixtures, and equipment (FF&E), purchase or improve physical assets such as buildings and fixtures, major equipment, vehicles, machinery, or furniture. CapEx may also be called *capital spending* or *capital expense.*

Fairs

A fair can be defined in several ways depending upon the purpose of the event: (1) a gathering held at a specified time and place for the buying and selling of goods (i.e. a market); (2) an exhibition (e.g. of farm products or manufactured goods, usually accompanied by various competitions and entertainments, as in a state fair); and (3) an event, usually for the benefit of a charity or public institution, including entertainment and the sale of goods (also called a bazaar). The most traditional fairs in North America are the numerous county and state fairs which are held annually on the same site, most of which continue to reflect rural and agricultural themes. Some are called 'exhibitions' or 'expositions' reflecting their educational orientation. Most fairs are operated by independent boards or agricultural societies, though many have close links with the host municipality.

Family service

Also called Service à la Française, is a simple method of serving food in which serving dishes are placed on the dining table (on a carrousel in the middle of the table for Chinese service and Chinese dim sum service), allowing guests to select what they wish and to serve themselves. Family service style is predominantly used in Oriental, Middle Eastern, and Mediterranean countries.

Fast casual

A type of restaurant which is similar to a fast food restaurant in that it does not offer full table service, but promises a somewhat higher quality of food and atmosphere. Food here is usually 'hand crafted' as in fine dining, but customers are responsible for some portion of their own limited service. In particular, they wait in line to order and pay in advance, and often carry their own trays to a table. This new hybrid offering has fast service, is casual in style and ambience with generally more complex menu items than the quick service segment, but is offered at a price premium.

Feasibility study

An analysis that is most often conducted by a third party, that indicates whether a project is reasonable, meets the needs of the target market (the group of consumers to which the hospitality operator wants to appeal), and is financially viable, among other things. Such a study is generally conducted only after the concept underlying the hospitality operation is articulated. Moreover, this process of determining where it is feasible to locate a hospitality outlet and what precise form it should take is one of the most critical steps in profitably launching and operating a hospitality business. Properly conducted, a feasibility study pairs the right hospitality operation with a location that will support it. A feasibility study has two major sections: a market survey and a site analysis. A market survey includes evaluating the surrounding community's economics, performing a competitive analysis, and making volume projections. A site analysis includes component analyses of location specifics, traffic patterns, visibility, legal constraints, and utilities.

Federacion de Desarrolladores Turisticos

An association that specifically deals with legislative and educational concerns of Latin American countries regarding the development and conduct of timeshare developers. In a response to these needs the Federacion de Desarrolladores Turisticos (LADETUR) was formed to advance the state of understanding and development of timeshare operations.

LADETUR initiated and funded several initiatives. The first initiative consisted of a review of the legislation affecting the timeshare industry in Latin American countries and the drafting of model legislation based on that review. The second initiative was a market research study of the Latin American timeshare industry and its economic impact in the region. The third initiative will establish the LADETUR Education Institute – a comprehensive educational program aimed at industry staff residing in major timeshare markets throughout Latin American.

Festivals

One of the most frequent and universal forms of cultural celebration, and while many are religious or traditional with long histories, the majority have been created in recent decades. Parades and processions are common elements in festivals, but those that are held on their own also display many celebratory elements. Many of the other major types of event, especially art and entertainment, are frequently found within or as the theme of festivals, and sport and recreational events also commonly add festive elements. Festivity is generally recognized as embodying, gaiety, joyfulness, playfulness, or revelry and liberation from normal moral constraints, but these attitudes and behaviors are not exclusive to formal events. Festivals are closely related to feasts, for example in the ancient custom of feasting at harvest times or in association with religious holidays.

File Transfer Protocol

An application protocol, based on the TCP/IP suite (Transmission Control Protocol/Internet Protocol), which specifies the rules for transferring data files from one computer to another. File Transfer Protocol (FTP) uses the client/server model of communication in which a computer user (a client) requests and is provided a service by another computer (a server). FTP operates among heterogeneous systems and allows users to interact with a remote server without regard for the operating systems in place.

FTP is an authenticated protocol: the user connection to a server requires a user identification and a password; the term *anonymous FTP* represents a way to transfer files by logging in to an FTP server on the Internet as a public guest. Using *anonymous* as user identification and own e-mail address as password, a customer can connect a hotel server and exchange files.

Financial accounting

Financial accounting is concerned with the maintenance of records which track the financial values of transactions made by a business, and the production of periodic statements that provide a summary of the performance and financial position of that business. Financial accounting is based upon double entry bookkeeping. This involves recognizing that any transaction will have an effect on the value of the business to the owners, and the way in which this value is stored. For example, a payment of expenses will both reduce the value of the business to the owner (reduce profit), and reduce its cash balances. Financial accounting records economic transactions as they take place it classifies and aggregates the transactions so that at any moment the accounting database is capable of giving a picture of the financial position.

Financial leverage

The use of debt and/or preferred stocks by a firm in place of common equity to finance its assets. The use of financial leverage tends to raise a hospitality firm's return on equity (ROE) under favorable conditions. On the other hand, the use of financial leverage will raise a hospitality firm's financial risk. Financial risk of a firm is a part of its total risk, in addition to its usual business risk. The higher a hospitality firm's degree of financial leverage (DFL) (percent change in earnings per share or EPS for each percent change in earnings before interests and taxes or EBIT), the greater the fluctuation in its EPS as a result of changes in its EBIT.

Financial risk

The additional risk placed on a firm's common stockholders when the firm is financed either by debt or by preferred stocks. Financial risk may be perceived as the risk of a hospitality firm in addition to its business risk, resulting from its use of financial leverage. Such risk-increasing effect of financial leverage is measured by the difference between the standard deviation of return on equity (ROE) of a financially leveraged hospitality firm or a hospitality firm with debt financing, denoted as $\sigma_{ROE\,(L)}$, and the standard deviation of the ROE of an unlevered all equity or debt-free hospitality firm, denoted as $\sigma_{ROE\,(U)}$.

Fire protection

Various measures taken by a hospitality business to reduce the risk of damage from fire. This includes fire resistant material, fire walls (walls separating parts of a building) and fireproof materials. Fire protection has been a critical concern within the hospitality industry; and especially within the lodging segment, for many years. The effective control of major fire incidents has been the movement within many countries to equip buildings and facilities with automatic fire extinguishment systems (sprinklers), and with full smoke detection and/or rate-of-rise heat detectors. In most developed countries the majority of new lodging units will have an automatic fire extinguishment system, whether it is 20 rooms on a single floor or several hundred rooms in a multi-storied building.

Fire seal

The material placed on the edge of the fire door to stop ingress of smoke during a fire. A fire door in a hotel is closed automatically by a fire system when the threat of a fire is detected. The expandable fire seal is used to seal the gap between the door and frame to prevent smoke and fire, reducing damage to the guestroom from the effect of fire and smoke. When exposed to heat, the fire seal begins a multi-directional expansion and swells up to several times of its original volume to fill any gap, joint, or crevice in a construction where it is applied. The expansion of the seal prevents for flame, heat, smoke, and toxic gases that may be generated in case of fire.

Fire sprinklers

Automated fire sprinklers are a component of a fire protection system designed to protect against single fires in buildings. Until the 1940s, sprinklers were installed almost exclusively in commercial buildings. However, as time went by fire sprinklers became mandatory safety equipment, and today in most countries they are mandatory not only in commercial buildings but in all public buildings such as hospitals, schools, hotels, and others. Sprinkler systems are required to include an automatic water supply that is reliable and adequate to meet the water requirements on a daily basis. The specific type of sprinkler system used is dependent on the types of fire hazard associated with different building types and uses. Standard spray sprinkler models include upright, pendant, or sidewall.

First-in, first-out

This inventory valuation method calculates the value of ending inventory and cost of goods sold (COGS) based on the principle of 'first-in, first-out (FIFO).' In a foodservice establishment, FIFO is a favored rotation method because it helps a kitchen use products before they deteriorate. When using the FIFO method, older products are used first, leaving newer products in inventory. This means that when valuing ending inventory, a manager will use the prices for the most recently purchased items. In contrast, because older products are used first, the value of COGS will be based on the prices of the older products. In times when prices are increasing, this method yields a high value for ending inventory and a low COGS. Since COGS is an expense, a lower COGS means that the operation will show a higher profit.

Fixed charges

All costs that appear below the Income after Undistributed Expenses or Gross Operating Profit line on the profit and loss statement. According to the *Uniform System of Accounts for the Lodging Industry (USALI)*, these costs are captured under six categories: (1) management fees; (2) rent, property taxes, and insurance (both building and contents and liability); (3) interest expense; (4) depreciation and amortization; (5) gain or loss on sale of property; and (6) income taxes. The descriptor 'fixed' describes the charges from the perspective of the property manager, because the costs are the province of ownership and the operator cannot affect their magnitude.

Fixed costs

Fixed costs normally remain constant within a 'relevant range' of activity and a specific period of time (e.g. one year). Examples of fixed costs in hospitality businesses, such as hotels or restaurants, include loan interest, rent, property taxes, insurance, and depreciation; representing the costs of occupying a hotel or restaurant property and referred to as 'fixed charges' in the *Uniform System of Accounts for the Lodging Industry*. Other examples of fixed costs can be marketing, and property operation and maintenance; these costs are regarded as fixed costs when, for example, a (annual) budget is set at a predetermined level. Also, administration expenses cost is, to a large extent, fixed in nature, though some elements such as credit card commission clearly vary with the level of activity.

There are very few examples of costs that are fixed within an unlimited range of activity, which means that fixed costs normally turn into semi-variable costs as the specified range is increased.

Fixed costs in foodservice operations

Restaurant fixed costs typically do not change in the short term. This means that they remain constant over the period of time being analyzed, regardless of changes in the restaurant business volume. As the number of patrons and total revenues change, fixed costs remain relatively constant. As volume and number of patrons change, however, the fixed costs per guest change. Examples of fixed costs include management salaries, rent, and insurance expense. Restaurant fixed costs can be divided into two categories: controllable and uncontrollable. Controllable fixed expenses – management salaries, for example – are considered within management's control since the unit-level manager can determine number of managers and compensation for each manager. Depreciation, which is an uncontrollable fixed cost, is beyond management's purview since it this is predetermined based on number and types of assets (and the depreciation methods used).

Fixed timeshare plan

An arrangement under which an owner receives a timeshare interest together with the right to use the accommodations and facilities at a timeshare property during the same specified period of time each year that the timeshare plan is in existence or for enough years to meet the requirements for regulation as a timeshare product. Depending on the nature of the timeshare plan, the owner of a fixed timeshare interest in a fixed timeshare plan may receive the same accommodation each time of use or may be assigned a different accommodation each time of use; however, the use will occur at the same time of the year.

Flexible firms

Flexible firms (with regards to the utilization of human resources) are organizations that use their workforce with the aim to meet industry demands – seasonal and other. The rationale behind the concept of flexible firms is the increase in the efficiency in managing the workforce and being adaptive to changing environments in order to ensure the organization's longevity. This may include numeric flexibility, such as the ability to increase or decrease the workforce when required; functional flexibility, such as training the workforce to undertake multiple tasks; or outsource sections of the workforce. Although all of these practices have advantages and disadvantages, they may not all be present in an organization at the same time.

Float timeshare plan

An arrangement under which an owner receives a timeshare interest together with the right to reserve the use of accommodations and facilities at a timeshare property during specified periods of time each year that the timeshare plan is in existence, or for enough years to meet the requirements for regulation as a timeshare. The right to make a reservation is grouped according to such variables as season or unit location, with higher demanded times and locations commanding higher prices and more competition among owners for reservations. Depending on the timeshare plan, owners of interests in a floating timeshare plan may receive the same accommodation each time of use or may be assigned a different accommodation each time of use; however, the use may or may not occur at the same time of the year. Floating timeshare plans require rules for governing priority rights in making and confirming reservations and a reservation system to track and process reservations.

Focus groups

A group of individuals brought together to discuss specific issues. The group is usually sized between 10 and 12 participants, although mini-focus groups of 5–7 are common. Participants in a focus group are frequently screened before they are selected to participate. The group is led through a series of topics, questions, and discussions by a moderator that is usually part of the research team. The purpose of using a focus group is exploratory; the focus group provides ideas and insights into a particular subject matter. The group is not used to infer about the population of interest, although focus group members might be representative of the population. The focus group provides ideas and opinions to the organization. A focus group is frequently video taped or observed by other members of the research team, either openly or secretly.

Folio

An account statement in a hotel upon which guest transactions (charges or payments) which affect the balance of their account is recorded. There are four types of folios: (a) guest folio – accounts assigned to individual persons or guestrooms; (b) master folio – accounts assigned to more than one person or guestroom; usually reserved for group accounts; (c) non-guest or semi-permanent folio – accounts assigned to non-guest businesses or agencies with hotel charge purchase privileges; (d) employee folio – accounts assigned to employees with charge purchase privileges. Guest folios can also be 'split', for example a business guest who is getting accommodation expenses paid for him/her. Room and tax charges can be posted to the room folio (A folio) and other charges can be

FOOD CODE (THE) – FOODBORNE ILLNESS

111

posted to the incidental folio (B folio). The accurate and timely processing of all these accounts assists the front office manager in maintaining hard copes of guest's financial transactions with the hotel. These accounts are collectively referred to as the hotel's accounts receivable – what guests owe the hotel. The accounts receivable consist of two categories: the guest ledger and the city ledger.

Food Code (The)

The (US) Food Code is published by the US Food and Drug Administration (FDA). Its purpose is to provide a model for local, state, tribal, and federal regulators for developing or updating their own food safety rules and to be consistent with national food regulatory policy. At the same time it also serves as a reference of best practices for the foodservice industry on how to prevent food borne illness. The overall objective of the Food Code is to protect the public health and to provide food that is safe in foodservice operations. The Code includes recommendations for food handling-methods, employee practices, equipment specifications, building plan reviews, and health inspections. The Food Code is published every four years and reflects the latest food safety knowledge. States may develop their own regulations and local county or city health departments can add requirements. The Food Code is enforced at the local level by health inspectors.

Foodborne illness

Diseases that are transmitted to people through food. When two or more people consume the same food and become ill it is considered an 'outbreak'. The most common foodborne illness pathogens (and their sources) are: *Norwalk-like virus* (shellfish, beef, chicken, pork, salads, dressings, infected worker); *Campylobacter* (raw milk, uncooked chicken, raw hamburger, water); *Salmonella* (undercooked poultry, eggs, or foods containing meats or dairy products); *Clostridium perfringens* (soups, stews, gravies held at warm temperatures); *Giardia lamblia* (contaminated water, infected workers); *Escherichia coli* (contaminated ground beef; unpasteurized juice, milk, or cider; water); *Staphylococcus* (meats, salads containing proteins, sauces, reheated foods); *Shigella* (moist foods, dairy products, salads, water, infected worker); *Listeria* (unwashed vegetables, unpasteurized dairy products, improperly processed meats); *Hepatitis A virus* (infected worker, water, seafood from polluted waters). The US Centers for Disease Control estimate that over 76 million people in the USA are sickened with a foodborne illness each year. Of those cases, over 300,000 require hospitalization and about 5000 result in death. Worldwide the numbers are suspected to be much higher; however, because of variations in reporting methods or lack of reporting altogether, it is difficult to get an accurate estimate of the true magnitude of the problem.

INTERNATIONAL DICTIONARY OF HOSPITALITY MANAGEMENT

Forecasting

Theoretically, the term forecasting means planning for the future, but it is used colloquially in the hospitality industry to mean short-term planning. It is a less formal process than budgeting (planning for a full financial year ahead), being operational in approach and predicting the coming days, weeks, and perhaps months. Budgets in hospitality and tourism firms tend to become outdated quickly due to changes in economic and political circumstances, weather conditions, markets activities, and so on, and hence a more immediate short-term estimate of anticipated volume is required. This then allows the operation to adapt their selling strategies and to plan staffing levels, purchasing, stock movements, and cash flows. It is especially important where departments and/or businesses interrelate such as the impact of tour businesses on flights and holiday accommodation or conference guests on rooms occupied, food and beverage revenues and costs.

Forecasting methods

Some of the simple applications of forecasting include forecasting of revenues to schedule employees; forecasting of revenues to plan food and supply orders; forecasting of revenues to correspond with marketing efforts, etc. Some common methods of forecasting one may observe in the hospitality industry include the *adjustment method* and the *moving average method*. The *Adjustment Method* involves taking some prior interval as a base period and adjusting it with a certain number determined by management. For example, some companies may use the percentage of general inflation in the economy as the adjustment factor. In the *moving average method* an average is calculated every new accounting period by putting in latest value and taking out the oldest value of the previous period. This average is then selected as the basis for forecasting. If necessary, the newly calculated average is again adjusted to reflect managerial knowledge of local operations.

Forecasting rooms availability

The hotel's reservations department is charged with two primary tasks: setting rates and selling rooms. Before successfully accomplishing either of these tasks, the reservations department needs an accurate count of the number of rooms available for sale. Knowing how many rooms are available for sale on a given date is a logical first step for the task of selling rooms. Less clear, however, is the relationship between the number of rooms available for sale and the setting of rates for a given period. This second relationship – the number of rooms available for sale impacts the rate for which the remaining rooms sell – forms the basis for the key objective of any hotel; to maximize revenues through yield management. Availability can be affected by early check-outs, unexpected stayovers, and no-shows. The formula for the calculation of rooms' availability is:

$$\text{Rooms committed} = \text{stayovers} + \text{today's Reservations}$$

Forecasting rooms revenue

There are two approaches to forecasting rooms' revenue available to hotel management. The simplest methods of forecasting rooms' revenue involves an analysis of rooms' revenue from past periods. Dollar and percentage differences are noted and the amount of rooms' revenue for the budget year is predicted. The second method of forecasting rooms' revenue bases the revenue projection on past room sales and average daily rooms rates as follows:

$$FRR = RA \times PO \times ADR$$

where:
FRR is forecasted room revenue;
RA is rooms available (calculated by multiplying the number of rooms in the hotel by the number of days in the year the hotel is operating);
PO is percentage of occupancy (the proportion of rooms sold to rooms available during a designated time period);
ADR is average daily rate (derived by dividing net rooms revenue by the number of rooms sold)

Fractional

A timeshare term that refers to products that divide ownership and use of accommodations and facilities into larger increments of time, such as in 1/6th or 1/12th interests, rather than dividing the year into 1/52nd interests used in traditional timeshare plans. Fractional developers generally distinguish their product on the basis of such factors as purchaser income, a greater focus on the real estate underpinnings of the product, a more extensive amenity package, upscale accommodations, and different sales and marketing practices. The purchaser of a fractional interest is usually in the market for a second home but does not want all of the year-round use, maintenance obligations or high purchase price associated with acquiring and owning a second home. Use of a fractional product can take on many of the characteristics of other timeshare products by allowing the owner to exchange use or reserve different periods of time for use in different years.

Framing

In marketing, framing is a process of selective control over media content or public communication. Framing defines how a certain message is presented so as to allow certain desirable perceptions. Framing occurs in two primary ways. First, the message that a company sends about a product or service is accompanied by images, sounds, or other stimuli associated with the product. These may have a positive or a negative effect on the customer. For example, a hotel company uses rock music in an advertisement, creating a 'frame' for the customer to evaluate the hotel. The rock music has a positive effect on customer who like rock music and a negative effect on those who do not. Framing also includes the choice of language. For example, 'inexpensive', 'economical', and 'cheap' may be synonymous. A hotel might present itself as an 'economy' property rather than a 'cheap' one to avoid the negative connotations of cheapness. Framing also occurs through outside context. Prior exposure to a situation can influence the way that a current situation is perceived. An example is how we perceive the attractiveness of our spouse or significant other which may diminish a bit after viewing pictures of supermodels.

Franchising

An agreement enabling a third party the rights to use the name and image of a company for a fee. A franchisor is the one granting the rights and a franchisee is the one purchasing the rights. The word 'franchising' is derived from the French verb, *franchir*, which means to make free or give liberty to, and often referred to freedom from some restriction, servitude, or slavery. Franchising can be divided into two major categories: business format franchising and product/trade name format franchising. Business format franchising is the preferred format of franchising in the hospitality industry. Product/trade name format franchising, on the other hand, concerns the relationship between a franchisor and a franchisee in which the franchisor grants to the franchisee the right to distribute a product and/or use a trade name. This format is most frequently employed in the soft drink, automobile, and gasoline distribution industries. Examples of franchising in hospitality from before 1940 include such ubiquitous snack and roadside offerings as Howard Johnson's, A&W Root Beer, Dairy Queen, and Tastee Freez. The real growth of restaurant franchising occurred during the 1950s and 1960s with the introduction of *fast-food* restaurants such as Kentucky Fried Chicken, Burger King, and McDonald's.

Free cash flow

Defined as after-tax operating cash flow (OCF) minus additional investments in assets. It is free to distribute to creditors and shareholders because it is no longer needed for working capital or fixed assets investments. Free cash flow (FCF) of a particular period can also be calculated from the financing perspective. It is the increase in debt and stock minus the decrease in debt and stock and minus interest and dividend payments. FCF should be equal to cash flow to creditors and shareholders. The value of a hospitality firm depends on its expected future FCF. A hospitality project's value is determined by the incremental FCF resulting from the project. Other things held constant, higher incremental future FCF leads to higher net present value of the project, and hence higher probability of the project's acceptance.

Frequent guest programs

Any program that rewards guests with points, miles, stamps, or 'punches' that enable the buyer to redeem such rewards for free or discounted merchandise. Frequent guest programs are not the same as loyalty programs. Frequency in itself does not build loyalty; it is loyalty that builds frequency. Frequency can create loyalty if the firm uses the information gathered on frequent visits to focus on the components of The Loyalty Circle; however, if the firm ignores this opportunity, then it ignores the emotional and psychological factors that build real commitment. Without that commitment, customers focus on the 'deal,' not the brand or product relevance. This focus on behavior makes bribing the customer the line of reasoning. Over time, the economics of bribery begin to collapse with greater and greater bribes, eventually eroding the brand image and diminishing product/service differentiation.

Front office accounting

Front office accounting keeps track of financial data in folios for both guests and house accounts or city ledger. Folios provide support documentation for transactions and vouchers detail front office account postings. Front office accounting entails maintenance of the front office ledger. The front office ledger is part of accounts receivable and includes a set of accounts for registered guests (guest ledger) and a set of accounts for non-guests and unsettled guest accounts (city ledger). The front office settles the guest ledger as a part of the front office accounting function. Front office accounting also maintains transfers between folios, cash advances, front office cash sheets, and cash banks.

Front office communications

In addition to memorandums, face-to-face conversations, and electronic communication successful front office communication includes logbooks, information directories, mail and telephone procedures, and interdepartmental exchange of information. The front desk typically keeps a logbook which enables the staff to be aware of important events and decisions that occurred during prior shifts. A logbook is a daily journal which may chronicle unusual events, guest complaints or requests, and other events. The information directory is a tool for the front desk to communicate to guests answers to common questions that might relate to local restaurant recommendations, transportation, directions to local business, shopping, places of worship, banks, ATMs, theaters, stadiums, information about hotel policies such as check-out time and hotel facilities or recreational facilities nearby the property. Telecommunication services provided by a hotel front office for its guests are multiple. They include telephones, voice mailboxes, facsimile, wake-up services, e-mail, and TDD (Telecommunication Device for the Deaf).

Front office ledger

A summary form of information gathered from front office account folios. Information contained in this ledger is from the accounts receivable ledger (money owed to the hotel), which comprises the guest ledger (also known as transient ledger, front office ledger, or rooms ledger) and the city ledger (also known as non-guest ledger). The guest ledger contains account information on guests who are registered at the hotel. The city ledger contains account information on non-guests who have charge privileges. Occasionally, the cashier is requested to transfer an amount from one guest account to another. Transfers also may occur between the guest ledger and the city ledger.

Front office operations

Front office operations consist of many functions that service the guest. The reservation process, which is part of front desk operations, consists of the collection of detailed information about an arriving guest. For walk-in guest, guest information is entered manually into the computer by front desk agent. The check-in is another part of the operations at the front office. Upon check-in the arriving guest is assigned a room and presented with a computer-generated registration card for verification and signature. A form of payment for the room is acquired during check-in as well. Upon departure the guest is provided with a printed copy of his/her folio and can immediately verify whether it is complete and accurate. For a guest account that requires billing, the system is capable of producing a bill to be sent to the guest. Once the guest's account is settled and the postings are considered complete, departed guest information is used to create an electronic guest history record.

Front office organization

The front office is the most visible department in a hotel and the front desk typically occupies a prominent place in the hotel's lobby. Guests come to the front desk to register, to receive room assignments, inquire about available services, facilities, and the city or surrounding area; and to check out. The front office: sells guestrooms; registers guests, assigns guestrooms, processes future room reservations; coordinates guest services; provides information; maintains accurate room status information; manages all guest accounts and credit limits; produces guest account statements; and completes a financial settlement with each guest upon departure. The front desk often serves as the focal point for guest requests regarding housekeeping, engineering, and information. Other services provided by the front office of a hotel handling guest and house mail, messaging services for the guest, and departing the guest from the hotel. Front office cashiers post charges and payments to guest accounts, all of which are later verified during an account auditing procedure. Front desk personnel also may verify outstanding accounts receivable, and produce daily reports for management.

Front office system

Part of the property management system (PMS) that aims to facilitate the interaction between hotel management and the guest. The system controls property management functions for reservations, front desk, cashier, housekeeping, and night audit management. Typical functions include control of room availability, room allocation, yield management, check-in, room status, postings to guest accounts, guest credit audits, advance deposits, guest history, check out, currency exchange, room status, room and tax posting, operational reports, and system set up. As part of the PMS this system is integrated with other systems such as the Food and Beverage or Sales and Catering so that most postings occur automatically. The front office system is very important for customer satisfaction and retention as well as for market analysis, as it retains all information on guest transactions within the property.

Front-of-the house

A hotel or lodging enterprise divisions or departments may be grouped in many ways. One such classification is front-of-the house and back-of-the house. In front-of-the house departments employees have extensive guest contact. The rooms division has many such employees including reservationists; front desk agents; key, mail, information specialists; uniformed services; and other guest services. In addition food and beverage employees have extensive guest contact through restaurants and lounges and are thus part of the front-of-the house. In restaurants the term is used to describe the public areas of a restaurant that are accessible to guests (e.g. dining rooms, bars), hence the areas that are not accessible to customers are considered back-of-the house. Front-of-the house restaurant employees are ones that have guest contact. These employees include food servers, bussers, bartenders, and hosts.

Full-time equivalent

Total full-time equivalents (FTEs) include the number of full-time employees who could have been employed if the reported number of hours worked by part-time employees had been worked by full-time employees and the actual number of full-time employees working at an establishment. By using FTEs, a multi-unit hospitality company can easily compare the number of employees being used across their establishments. Typically, an FTE equates to 40 hours of work per week. The FTE statistic is used to compare one establishment's labor costs with another's. For example, if a restaurant employees 35 full-time employees who work 40 hours/week and 16 part-time employees who each work 15 hours/week, the number of FTEs for that establishment would be calculated as follows:

$$35 + (16 \times 15)/40 = 35 + 240/40 = 35 + 6 = 41 \text{ FTEs}$$

Even though there are a total of 51 employees in the example, there are only 41 FTEs.

Furniture, fixtures, and equipment

Hotels and restaurants are furniture and equipment-intensive forms of commercial real estate. Furniture, fixtures, and equipment (FF&E) selection is generally coordinated with the theme and desired level of a hospitality property. The furniture and equipment component falls between 10 and 20 per cent of the total project cost. FF&E may comprise either fixed attachments to a hospitality facility or moveable items. Permanently installed fixtures may be found in *public areas*: elevators, drinking fountains, signage; in *guestrooms*: built in entertainment centers, bathroom fixtures, track lighting; and *back-of-the house*: kitchen counters, dishwashers, cabinets, walk-in storage units, plumbing fixtures, building mechanical and electrical systems, fixed electronic equipment, and fixed theater seating, as well as other fixtures and equipment mounted for continued use in that site.

Gg

Game theory

Game theory assumes that there are two or more players in a decision-making situation and the aim is to devise a plan that maximizes gains and minimizes losses. It offers a rigorous approach to predict what other players (i.e. hospitality organizations) would do in a well-defined situation and what possible results would be. Game theory offers mathematical techniques for problem solving and competitive decision-making through the use of model buildings game theory which is often referred to as '*the prisoner's dilemma*' can be used in hospitality organizations particularly in decision-making, handling conflicts, competition, cooperation, joint ventures, and strategic alliances between their organization and other companies. By using game theory hospitality firms can systematically examine various combinations of options that can alter the situation in their favor.

Gap model of service quality

The gap model has served as a framework for research in services marketing, including hospitality marketing for over two decades. The model identifies four specific gaps leading to a fifth overall gap between customers' expectations and perceived service, as follows. Gap 1 is the *knowledge gap* which in service quality occurs when management fails to accurately identify customer expectations. Specifically, it is the difference in customer expectations and management's perception of customer expectations. Gap 2 is the *design gap* which is measured by how well the service design specifications match up to management's perception of customer expectations. Gap 3 is the *performance gap* which represents the variation in service design and service delivery. Its extent is a function of many variables involved in the provision of service. Gap 4 is the *communications gap* which is the difference between what is promised to customers, either explicitly or implicitly and what is being delivered. Over-promising is commonly responsible for the communication gap. Gap 5 is the total accumulation of variation in gaps 1 through 4 and represents the *difference between expectations and perceived service*.

General manager

The top executive of a lodging enterprise who ultimately is responsible for the overall profitability and service performance of the operation and all of the enterprises employees. The general manager represents the owner's interests, directs the activities of the departments, and may get

120

involved in the day-to-day operation of individual departments. The general manager must manage effectively including planning, decision-making, organizing, staffing, controlling, directing, and communicating to develop a successful team. Short-term demands on the general manager revolve around the day-to-day operations, issues of quality service, and controlling costs/revenue. In the intermediate term the general manager is responsible for the development and training of qualified subordinates and for implementing systems and programs to improve operational consistency and control. Long-term concerns require general managers to develop strategies for organizational stability consistent with the enterprises' goals and objectives.

General session

A session within a meeting, convention, congress, or conference that is open to all event participants. Often, the general session is designed to appeal to all event attendees. It is also known as a plenary session. General sessions can be held for a variety of purposes, including a keynote speaker, a motivational speaker, or an association business meeting. The organizations that hold general sessions in conjunction with their conventions or conferences may rely on the speakers to attract attendees. Hotel ballrooms, auditoriums in convention centers or civic centers, theaters, or other venues may be used to host general sessions. Theater style seating is most appropriate for these events.

Generic strategies

There are two generic strategies used in hospitality management; marketing-oriented and operations-oriented strategies. These two generic strategies are specifically suited to the hospitality industry because they capture the individualized nature of the customer transaction in service industries and specifically in the hospitality industry. The marketing-oriented generic strategy implies that firms in the hospitality industry need a strategy to ensure repeat purchase by customers. In contrast, operations-oriented strategies are primarily involved in reducing the cost of the product or service and focusing on firm efficiency to attract customers. Regardless of the differences between these two generic strategies, their motto is to achieve the ultimate goal of firms in the hospitality industry, namely to increase the lifetime economic value of the customer to the firm.

Global alliance of timeshare excellence

An industry association whose primary focus is to educate the consumer and to act on behalf of timeshare resort developers concerning legislative issues. As the timeshare industry has expanded into international markets the need has surfaced for an educational and lobbyist voice within international markets. The Global Alliance for Timeshare Excellence (GATE) was established in 1999 by the leaders of timeshare associations in the USA, Canada, Latin America, Europe and the Middle East, Australia, and South Africa to promote the timeshare industry around the world. GATE seeks to serve as a resource to ensure that legislative and regulatory proposals are reasonable and conducive to the industry's business. GATE also seeks to serve as a resource and positive influence to encourage the industry to conduct its business in such a manner as to create positive public perception.

Global distribution systems

A centralized and permanently up-to-date database that is accessible to their subscribers through computing terminals. They provide all kind of tariffs and tourism services to their information subscribers' everyday, allowing the users to reserve, to change, and to cancel reservations, as well as to print tickets and any kind of rights related to services and products. The global distribution systems (GDSs) constitute at the present time the evolution and natural adaptation of the traditional computer reservation systems (CRS) to the market. With the goal of creating an automated system for the capacity administration of their planes, American Airlines and IBM developed a joint program that became the SABRE, considered the first GDS. As of lately GDSs have moved from being airlines CRS to stand alone publicly owned companies that provide 'e' services to both marketing intermediaries (retail travel agents, tour wholesalers, general sales agents, etc.) and to travel principals such as airlines, hotels, tour operators, and rental car companies. They now also deal direct to the consumer using online travel agencies such as Travelocity.com (owned by Sabre) and OneTravel.com (owned by Amadeus).

Globalization

A term that describes a process in which a complex of forces shift the world from a composition of countries, societies, and cultures toward a single world society or culture. Among these forces are the increasing significance of mass production, the development of mass communications, the development of commerce, the increased ease of travel, the increased popularity and use of the Internet, the development of popular culture, and the increasingly widespread use of English as an international language. Given the above, the term globalization refers to the world as the geographical unit of reference and suggests that occurrences in one part of the globe will potentially impact systems in another part.

Glocalization

Glocalization combines the word globalization with localization and refers to the concept that organizations should do business around the world, using methods that are appropriate for that particular country thereby creating a greater balance between global and local dimensions. The premise of glocalization therefore is that a product or service is more likely to succeed when adapted specifically to each locality or culture it is marketed in. The proliferation of McDonald's restaurants worldwide is an example of globalization, while the restaurant chain's menu changes in an attempt to appeal to local palates are an example of glocalization.

Within the context of Information Technology Communications (ICT) and the Internet the phrase 'Think Globally; Act Locally' is used to signify glocalization. This is so as the Internet expands a user's social world to people far away in different continents while at the same time binding users more deeply to the place where they live.

Golf facilities

Golf facilities usually consist of a golf course, practice area, clubhouse, and a golf course maintenance area. The golf course usually includes a layout of two 9-hole segments per 18-hole course, plus optional additional multiples of 9-hole segments. The practice area (range) designed to simulate golf course conditions – from tee, fairway, and bunker perspectives – is for golfers to practice a variety of golf shots. The practice area often includes a putting green and lesson area. The clubhouse often features a golf pro-shop offering supplies, equipment, apparel, accessories, golf car (cart) storage, caddie area, and bag storage, food and beverage outlets such as kitchen(s)/ dining areas, snack bars, and bar/lounge areas, locker rooms with dressing sections as well as shower/health/fitness areas, and often offer adjacent aquatics and tennis programs. The golf course maintenance facility houses equipment and materials used in turf care including vehicles, tractors, mowers, trimmers, chemicals, fertilizers, soil, sand, and rock, a repair and maintenance area, a paint shop, an administrative office, locker room(s), and often times a sod farm.

Golf programs

Private clubs have a variety of golf programs for their members. Most private clubs conduct a variety of golf tournaments each season that typically includes a club championship, invitational tournaments, pro-am events, MGA events, LGA events, member–guest tournaments, men–women events, junior events, etc. Outside golf tournaments (tournaments that are not organized primarily for members and invited guests) are conducted at many private clubs. Some clubs may not allow any outside events, others may only allow a few outside tournaments a year, and certain clubs that are seeking additional revenues may aggressively pursue tournaments. The golf instructional program at a private club is the foundation of the overall golf program. Instruction is a key to getting members to use the golf course and to frequent the club more often. Golf lessons can be in the form of private lessons, group lessons, or clinics. The group lessons or clinics are also divided into age groups (adult and junior), gender (male and female), level (high, average, good, and advanced handicap), and topic (stroke improvement, playing strategy, and rules). Private lessons give members the individual attention that some desire, but at a high cost.

Grease trap

A device designed to capture food oils, fats, and greases, coming from a restaurant and food production facility water drain lines. Grease trap prevents the discharge of grease into a sewer. Grease entering the trap is congealed by the water and settles into a perforated tray. A grease trap works by slowing down the flow of hot greasy water allowing it to cool with the fats and oils separating, solidifying, and rising to the top of the tank. By use of baffles inside the tank, the hardened grease is prevented from passing through the drain line. Food solids settle to the bottom of the trap. The tray must be removed at less than once a week to be cleaned using hot water.

Green globe 21

A global benchmarking and certification program that facilitates sustainable travel and tourism for consumers, companies, and communities. It is based on Agenda 21 and principles for Sustainable Development endorsed by 182 governments at the United Nations Rio de Janeiro Earth Summit in 1992. There are four Green Globe 21 Standards: the Green Globe 21 Company Standard; the Green Globe 21 Standard for Communities; the International Ecotourism Standard; and the Design and Construct Standard. The Green Globe 21 Company Standard is available to operations in 20 different sectors of the travel and tourism industry. The Standards requires an operation or community to achieve a baseline level of environmental and socially sustainable performance before it receives the Green Globe logo without the tick. The operation must also meet all of the requirements of the relevant Green Globe 21 Standard and be independently audited to be allowed to use the Green Globe logo with the tick.

Green power energy purchasing

124

Power that is generated from sources that are considered environmentally friendly. Green power sources include wind, water landfill gas, solar, and others. Green power pricing is an optional service at several utilities, allowing customers the option of purchasing all or part of a buildings energy load from renewable energy technologies. Participating customers usually pay a premium on their electric bill to cover the extra cost of the renewable energy. To date, in the USA more than 300 investor-owned utilities, municipal utilities, and cooperatives have either implemented or announced plans to offer a green pricing option.

Gross operating profit

The current line on the profit and loss statement labeled Income after Undistributed Operating Expenses, under the *Uniform System of Accounts for the Lodging Industry (USALI)*. Gross operating profit (GOP) has long been considered one of the most important measures of the property manager's performance. The level of GOP achieved is determined by management's revenue generating ability; the sales mix the hotel is able to achieve, given its position in the market; and management's acumen in controlling costs. The GOP, when expressed as a percentage of revenue, can be a meaningful measure of property-level management's control of departmental and undistributed operating costs, but may fail to give adequate attention to management's revenue generating responsibilities. Experienced analysts, therefore, measure GOP on both a percentage and a dollars-per-available-room basis when judging the effectiveness of property-level management.

Gross profit and net profit

Profit is determined by deducting expenses related to a period from revenue for the same period. Two fundamental levels of profit are generally referred to in profit and loss statements: gross profit (which is calculated by deducting cost of sales from sales revenue), and net profit (which is calculated by deducting total expenses, from revenue).

The relative size of gross profit and net profit is often determined by referring to gross profit margin and net profit margin. Gross profit margin percentage is determined by dividing gross profit by operating revenue and multiplying by 100. Net profit margin percentage is determined by dividing net profit by revenue and multiplying by 100. The calculation of gross and net profit margins facilitates the comparison of profit levels across different sized hotels. The distinction between net profit and gross profit is highlighted through the following example:

ABC Hotel
Profit statement for the year ended December, 2007

Sales revenue		$45,000
Less: Cost of sales		$10,000
Gross profit		$35,000
Plus: Other revenue		$4200
Net revenue		$39,200
Less: Other expenses		
Employee benefits	$15,000	
Administration	$6000	
Depreciation	$1500	
Other	$2400	$24,900
Net profit		$14,300

Group reservation

A reservation for a block of rooms in a lodging facility. The block of rooms could be for a convention, a meeting, a special event (wedding, party, etc.), a tour group, or various other reasons. A group reservation could be as small as five rooms to several thousands, depending on the size of the lodging facility. By booking rooms in large quantities, the group receives a lower rate. In some cases conventioneers and/or group members are provided with reservation post cards by the marketing and sales department of the hotel. These cards can be presented at check-in show the name of the convention or group and the official dates when the convention or group will convenes at the hotel.

Groups (in organizations)

The building blocks of organizations that are designed to integrate job tasks and people effectively. Groups can comprise any number of people who interact with one another are psychologically aware of one another and who perceive themselves to be a group. In addition to formal groups that are established by organizations, there are also informal groups, created by the members of these groups. Formal groups are constructed by the organization to help with the implementation of plans and the achievement of organizational objectives. For example, within a hotel, employees will be grouped into departments such as housekeeping, banqueting, guest services, etc. However, organizations also comprise informal groups. These are collections of individuals who come together within the workplace as a result of informal interaction to share interests, form identities, and establish informal control.

Guaranteed reservation

A hotel reservation that is guaranteed by a credit card number, cash deposit, or corporate guarantee (if the company making the reservation has direct billing). In exchange for the guaranteed reservation, the hotel can charge the credit card certain fees if the reservation is not kept. When this type of reservation is made by a guest, it requires the hotel room to be held after the normal cancellation time for the property. By guaranteeing the reservation the guest is saying 'I will definitely be there and please hold the room for me no matter how late I am checking in.' When taking a guaranteed reservation, the guest must be notified that he/she has made a guaranteed reservation and has until a specific time to cancel the reservation, after that time he/she will be charged for one night or lose their deposit if he/she cancels after the specified time or does not check-in.

Guéridon service

Also known as 'Service à la Russe'. The actual term 'guéridon' denotes a side table or service trolley (in former times, especially in Russia, a guéridon was a sideboard) which is used in the dining room in front of guests for the service and preparation of foods. Normally guéridon service – also referred to as 'French' service – requires food to be transferred from a serving dish onto the guest's plate on the guéridon, which is then served to the guest. In addition, a guéridon is often used to finish off certain dishes (e.g. to flame (flambé) them), or to prepare certain desserts, or to dress salads, before being portioned and served to the guests.

Guest cycle

The hotel guest cycle consists of four stages, namely: (1) pre-arrival, (2) arrival, (3) occupancy, and (4) departure. Pre-arrival is the stage where the guest chooses the hotel and makes the reservation. Important information is gathered at this stage, which allows the next stage to run smoothly. The arrival stage is when the guest actually arrives and registers at the hotel (check-in). Here the guest verifies the information gathered previously at the reservation stage, confirms method of payment signs the registration card, and collects their key. The occupancy stage deals with security of the guest along with the coordination of guest services to ensure guest satisfaction and try to encourage repeat guests. At this stage the front desk need to keep guest accounts up to date so that the final stage of the cycle runs smoothly. The final stage of the cycle is departure, which is when the guest is ready to check out. The main objective here is to settle the guest account, update room status information, and to create a guest history record.

Guest history

The record of a guest's stay, called the guest history, becomes part of a file that can be used to determine when a guest might visit in the future; the type of accommodation the guests prefers; dining preferences; use of amenities or recreational facilities; and other, more personal data, including home address and telephone number, spouse's and children' names, birthday, and so on. Guest history is used to strategically market new guests with similar characteristics. The guest history can be used by the hotel's sales and marketing department for promotional mailings soliciting repeat business or to target potential guests with similar profiles. Guest history is especially useful at the reservation stage (information already on file) and at the check-in (a guest can be greeted by a well-informed receptionist). It is useful to management as it helps them to gain an insight into guest profiles and trends.

Guest ledger

The guest ledger in a hotel is made up of the balance of all the folios of in-house guests. In accounting terms, the guest ledger is part of the accounts receivable balance on the balance sheet. The front desk collects payment for the guest ledger, once this payment is collected, the balance of the folio is closed out and is removed from the guest ledger.

Guest operated interfaces

Automated devices within a hotel that are operated directly by guests allowing guests to have more control over the services they get. Examples of this include in-room movie systems and fully automated guestroom vending machines. Guests may even be able to review their accounts through the guestroom television being connected to the guest accounting system. Through this system, guests can receive information about events within the hotel and the local area or access airline schedules, local entertainment guides, news, etc. all in the comfort of their own room.

Guest profile

A set of characteristics that define any business-related item, such as an individual customer, a travel agent, source, a company, or a group profile. For example, an individual profile may include characteristics such as first name, last name, title, telephone, addressing information, gender, age, date of birth, nationality, VIP status level, e-mail address, negotiated rate code, comments and preferences, and membership number, if any. A company/travel agent profile may include different characteristics, such as the company name, contact, addressing information, preferred correspondence language, preferred currency, e-mail addresses, industry code, volume of business, and negotiated rate codes. Group profiles are created to handle group events (conventions, meetings, parties, and weddings). Usually, profile data are stored in the data store, by deploying various database management systems-based property management systems (PMS) with reservations and guest history features enabled.

Guest safety

Within hospitality industry, guest safety is a primary concern. Safety focuses on prevention of accidents or injuries. Slips or falls are a major source of injury to guests. These may occur in the parking lot, on the walkways and roadways surrounding the lodging or restaurant facility, in the entryway, lobby, food and beverage service units, public areas, meeting rooms, public restrooms, guestrooms, and guest bathrooms. Serious injuries may also be sustained in falls on stairways and escalators. To prevent accidents and injuries staff should be trained to be more aware of conditions which could cause an accident and resultant injury to a guest, to another employee, or to the general public. In the event of an accident, a report is prepared with full detail as to time, the alleged cause of the incident and the alleged injuries sustained. Witness statements and identification and pictures are obtained, when possible.

Guestroom floor configurations

Three common hotel guestroom floor configurations are: (1) slab configurations, (2) tower configurations, and (3) atrium configurations. In slab configurations, a single-loaded slab, where guestrooms are laid out on single side of a central corridor, is suitable for narrow sites or for taking advantage of views. A double-loaded slab, where rooms are laid out on both sides of a central corridor, offers the most efficient options for elevator cores, exit stairs, and service functions, while offset-slabs offer interior core efficiency and more variety for facades. Tower configurations comprise a central core surrounded by a single-loaded corridor of guestrooms. Their exterior architectural treatment depends on the geometric shape of the plan. In an atrium configuration, first introduced by architect John Portman for the Hyatt Regency Atlanta in 1967, the guestrooms arranged along single-loaded corridors, encircling a multi-story lobby space.

Guestroom occupancy sensors

These devices detect the presence of people in a guestroom and are linked to the heating, refrigeration, and ventilation equipment that services the guest's room. They may also be linked to security and housekeeping functions, but their primary function is as an energy saving device. When the guest is in the room, that guest has the ability to control the room's temperature through a thermostat in the room. There are three types on the market: infrared, ultrasonic, and a combination of both technologies. When the guest leaves, the occupancy sensor sends a signal to the heating and cooling system to move from a 'set point' temperature (i.e. guest selected temperature) to a 'set back' temperature (i.e. a temperature the hotel has selected). This setback temperature is typically only six to eight degrees from the guest's set point temperature. The moment the guest returns, the occupancy sensor notes the return and instantly the set point temperature is reinstated.

HACCP

Hazard Analysis of Critical Control Points (HACCP) is a program developed by the US Food and Drug Administration early in the 1990s for the purpose of eliminating the contamination of food as it is produced, processed, and distributed to consumers. It is designed to be a 'farm-to-fork' approach for ensuring the safety of the food supply. The HACCP program is based on the identification, control, and elimination of food safety hazards through proven scientific methods at critical control points in the process. The general definitions of the terms central to HACCP, according to the National Restaurants Association of the USA, are that hazards include microorganisms that can be grown at any point during the food production process (including storage and those microorganisms or toxins that survive heating); chemicals that can contaminate food, food-contact surfaces, or food-handling utensils; physical objects not intended for consumption that enter food. A critical control point is any operation or process point (such as a preparation step or procedure) where a preventative or control measure can be applied effectively such that it eliminates, removes, or prevents a hazard.

Hands-on learning

Often in the hospitality industry individuals learn by experience, practicing, and displaying certain behaviors. For example a new bartender will learn the mix of cocktail ingredients and then practice how to blend these together whilst a room attendant will practice the various steps involved in making a bed. Many companies now identify key skills for all jobs within their organization to support and target learning. Hilton (UK) for example has defined the technical and behavioral skills (TBS) required for all operations roles and designed learning experiences around these. This is known as behavioral learning and is best suited to skill development. Attitudinal development is better achieved through cognitive learning. In this process learning is stimulated by explanation and understanding of concepts and theories which will then allow the learner to adapt their attitude to a given situation.

Hardware

The physical parts of a computer system, including electrical, electronic, magnetic, optical, and mechanical components. It is divided into machines (computers, displays, disk drives, keyboards) and media (memory devices such as hard drives and any removable/transportable digital memory media, such as magnetic tapes or disks, optical disks, or digital memory card). Hardware components of a computer are organized into two different structures: the central processing unit (CPU) and the peripheral devices. The CPU is built from a control unit that controls the execution of instructions, an arithmetic-logic unit that executes specific instructions, and a primary storage unit for immediate data and program holding. Peripheral devices are used for data and command input, output of information and secondary storage. Hardware devices include palm devices, notebooks and desktop personal computers, mainframe computers, and different specific devices, which contain a processor. Peripherals are divided into input devices (keyboard, mouse, track ball, joystick, graphic tablet, light pen, touch-sensitive screen, bar code reader, optical character recognition devices, voice recognition devices, tills in restaurants, etc.), output devices (display, printer, plotter, microfiche), permanent storage devices (magnetic: hard and floppy disks; optical disks: CD and DVD).

Haute cuisine

Literally 'high (or superior) cooking' in French. A term that refers to the finest food, prepared in an elegant manner. In the French traditional school context, the term is often used to describe the classical French cuisine – *cuisine classique.* Haute cuisine often requires an elaborate and skillful manner of preparing food. Most chefs today define haute cuisine as a culinary practice following a high standard that requires detailed, artistic, and expert preparation and presentation of food.

Health codes

Standards that have been developed to promote food safety and sanitation. Local health department officials enforce these codes during regular unannounced inspections of food-related businesses. The purpose of the inspections is to ensure that operators are following health codes in order to protect the public from practices that could result in foodborne illness. These codes not only regulate food handling, but also include specifications for facilities and equipment. In general, inspectors from local health departments evaluate the procedures for processing and handling food and the temperatures at which products are cooked, cooled, held, stored, and reheated. Health codes are developed by the state, county, or city responsible, depending on the locale. In the USA, the respective codes are generally crafted using the Food and Drug Administration's 'Model Food Code'.

Hearing conservation

Implemented programs in the workplace designed to protect employees against hearing loss precipitated by exposure to high noise levels over an extended period of time. In the USA, the

Occupational Safety and Health Act mandates that employers must have a Hearing Protection Program implemented in any work environment that produces noise levels in excess of 85 decibels (db) over a time weighted average of eight hours. The Hearing Protection Program specifics mandate that employers must measure any worksite thought to produce high noise levels and implement a Hearing Protection Program when the 85 db limit is exceeded. The program (at a minimum) must consist of: (1) audiometric annual examinations to include baseline tests; (2) audiometric evaluation; (3) engineering controls to lessen noise production (when noise levels are above 90 db); (4) the issuance of personal protective equipment; (5) employee training; and (5) record keeping.

Heat detectors

A device that responds to hot smoke and fire gases and is a component of a fire detection system. The three types of heat detectors are rate-of-rise, fixed temperature, and rate compensation. Rate-of-rise detectors react to rapid increases in the temperature, which activates the fire alarm. The actual temperature is not a factor so a slow-burning fire could go undetected unless a fixed temperature heat detector is also used. The fixed temperature detector contains a fusible element that melts rapidly at a set temperature and activates the fire alarm. Rate compensation detectors combine the techniques used for the fixed temperature and rate-of-rise detectors. If the air temperature is rising slowly, less than 40 degrees per minute, the detector will respond when the air temperature matches the rated temperature. If the air temperature is rising quickly, the detector responds based on the temperature rate-of-rise.

Hiring crunch

The hiring crunch in the hospitality industry involves selecting individuals not only on merit but subject to other constraints such as skills availability, competition, and being able to manage high levels of turnover in the workforce. This is a challenge in an industry characterized by skilled labor shortages and a transient workforce. The important point here is to match prospective employees to the organization and the job within the broader hospitality labor market context. Hospitality managers also need to factor in other relatively uncontrollable issues before selection such as staff reliability and commitment. Indeed in the seasonal sector, many small- to medium-sized hospitality firms employ staff using only a few selection criteria with 'availability' being the key. Alternatively, some managers elect to use 'agency' workers during periods of high demand.

Homeowners association

The not for profit organization of a community (planned development or condominium) formed for the purpose of maintaining and improving the property. The officers and directors of an association have a fiduciary relationship to the members who are served by the association. In a timeshare resort, the powers and duties of an association include appropriate maintenance of the resort and proper tracking, and investment of existing funds as collected through maintenance fees and annual member assessments. This means that the homeowners' association is charged with general interior maintenance, exterior maintenance, and upkeep of the resort grounds.

Hospitality distribution terms

Alternative distribution systems (ADS): The terms alternative distribution systems (ADS), Internet distribution systems (IDS), and e-distribution systems, denote the online dispersal and purchase of travel products. They consist of Internet-based reservation networks, which allow information to be instantly available worldwide, bypassing traditional intermediaries such as the global distribution systems (GDS). Travelweb and Hotelbook are examples of ADS.

Brand erosion: A potential decrease in the importance of brand and customer loyalty attributed to the intensive price-based strategies utilized by online third parties.

GDS provider services: Intermediaries between the operators and the switch companies (e.g. Synxis, Lexington). These are reservation companies that allow suppliers to access the GDS via the switch. They perform database update and content management services, which include exchanging information between operators and the switch, distributing rates to travel websites, and updating the hotel's online description.

Competitive information: Information on rates, occupancy, RevPAR, and descriptions of hospitality companies, which is gathered by companies, specialized in providing competitive information (e.g. Travelclick). The information is aggregated and then distributed to members or sold as industry reports.

Connectivity: The ability to make and maintain a connection between different systems. There are different levels of this ability. One-way connectivity means that when an entity books a reservation, the information is automatically placed in the property management systems (PMS). One-and-a-half-way connectivity means that the entity that books the reservation also has the capability to effectuate changes and cancellations in real time. Two-way connectivity implies that in addition to the above, the third party receives rates and availability in real time. As technologies develop, connectivity issues should disappear and hospitality systems should interface.

Destination management systems (DMS): Systems created to cater to the distribution needs of a specific region and/or regional tourism agencies, which include information for hotel, transportation, restaurants, and other tourism operations and attractions in a given geographical area. DMS may be State or privately funded. These systems may also be called Destination Databases, Destination Marketing Systems, or Visitor Information Systems.

Electronic distribution systems (EDS): In hospitality, the EDS involve the electronic dispersal and purchase of travel products, including the GDS, switches, and Internet distribution channels.

GDS provider: A general term that refers to the entity that provides a hospitality company access to the GDS, which may be the GDS themselves, switch companies, or reservation companies. For example, an operator may select the GDS Worldspan to be its sole GDS provider, or contract Pegasus, which provides access to the main GDS (Worldspan, Sabre, Amadeus, and Galileo), or a reservation company, such as Synxis, which uses the Pegasus switch to distribute inventory to the GDS.

Hotel distribution systems (HDS): Hotel distribution system, LLC, normally referred to by the initials HDS, is a venture of Hilton Hotels Corporation; Hyatt Hotels; Marriott Hotels; Resorts and Suites; Six Continents Hotels; Starwood Hotels; and Pegasus. According to Pegasus article, Pegasus Solutions Finalizes Technology Agreement with New Online Hotel Discount Venture HDS (n.d.). HDS plans to provide Internet sites with the ability to sell hotel rooms at net rates via direct connections to hotel central reservations systems.

Links: These are icons that possess the ability to direct an individual from one Web-address to another. There are sites that simply provide links to operators' reservation pages. Examples are travelzoo.com and travelaxe.com. Operationally, these sites function as online advertising tools. Their look, however, is very similar to that of other travel service sites. In order to effectuate a booking, the customer clicks on a link and is directed to the supplier's site or to another intermediary site. They compete in the same markets as Internet distribution channels.

Rate parity: The uniformity of retail rates across different channels of distribution that provide the same product. For example, a standard room for two nights, arrival on January 29 for two people, should be sold at the same price at a proprietary site, at a third-party wholesaler, or through the GDS. If the same product was sold with different restrictions (e.g. non-refundable, non-transferable, or fully prepaid), a different price could be applied to that product without affecting rate parity.

Rate integrity: The trust in the fair price of a hospitality product. It is usually achieved when customers believe they would not find lower prices for a given product through other channels.

Rate transparency: The perfect knowledge of the price for a specific hospitality product, due to the customer's ability to shop for rates across channels. The concept of rate transparency is similar to the concept of perfect information in economic theory.

Rate cannibalization: A dilution in rates due to an increased rate transparency and a lack of rate parity. It occurs when customers shop the same product through different channels and book at the lowest rate encountered, even though they would have booked at higher rates. In other words, there is demand for higher price levels. Rate cannibalization causes a decrease in revenues without increasing demand.

Onward distribution: The dispersal of rates through a variety of distribution channels such as the GDS and Internet sites.

Priority listing: The order in which a website appears in a search engine listing. One of the strategies utilized by suppliers and third-party sites in order to increase booking is to ensure that their sites have priority listing in the travel-related web searches.

Rate erosion: A term mainly used in online distribution to designate the decrease in rates caused by price-based selling strategies.

Seamless connectivity: Occurs when all the links in the distribution channel have access to the same inventory data. In order for this to happen, all systems have to be integrated and the information has to be updated in real time. In other words, there must be a two-way connectivity.

Switch: Electronic devices that enable different systems to communicate. These distribution technologies link the CRS to the other channels, such as the GDS, websites, corporate travel agents, tour operators and wholesalers, representation services, and PMS services. Large corporations may develop their own switch technology to access the GDS, avoiding switch fees (e.g. The Marriott and Priceline). Most hotel companies, however, hire switch companies (e.g. Pegasus and Wizcom), which may also provide related activities such as reservation, representation, and financial services.

Hotel classification

Hotels can be classified by *type* (such as commercial hotels; airport hotels; conference centers; suite or all-suite hotels; residential hotels; casino hotels; resort hotels; bed and breakfast hotels; etc.) by *service levels* (such as budget hotels that provide only 'rooms and a baths' to full-service and premium luxury levels) and by *brand segmentation* that captures elements of what the traveler demands in a hotel, what that demand necessitates in the way of construction, size, décor, service, amenities, personnel, and finally price. The most widely used brand segments usually are among the following eight (1) economy; (2) midscale without food and beverage; (3) midscale with food and beverage; (4) economy extended stay; (5) midscale – or upscale – extended stay; (6) upscale; (7) upper upscale; and (8) premium luxury.

Hotel consortia

Groupings of hotels, mostly independently owned, which share corporate costs such as marketing, while retaining independence of ownership and operations. Small businesses face particular problems in competition with large ones. Consortia can be local groups of hotels to promote a destination, or a group of independent non-competing hotels widely distributed geographically. The largest consortium is REZolutions, with 7700 hotel properties (1.5 million rooms) in 180 countries. This represents 10 per cent of the world's hotel rooms. The organization was formed in 1997 by a merger between Utell International and Anasazi, and is based in Phoenix, Arizona, USA. Europe has 15 out of the 25 of the largest consortia, but the USA's 10 represent 50 per cent of the hotels and almost 75 per cent of the world's hotel rooms. The focus of consortia is marketing, with common reservation systems, quality standards, and logos leading to a unified sales effort without a loss of independent identity.

Hotel fire fighting team

Also known as an emergency response team or alarm response team, is established to verify the cause of fire alarms and respond accordingly. Generally, such a team consists of the duty assistant manager, duty engineer, the security officer nearest to the scene, and the assistant housekeeper. The duty assistant manager is usually the team leader, who is responsible for assessing the situation and directing remedial measures. The leader is normally the only member of staff to make the initial decision to evacuate until fire fighters arrive. Upon confirmation of a real fire, apart from trying to put out and control a small supervised fire, the team will instantly notify the fire department and hotel operators for guest enquiries, and allocate duties as needed to other department heads and staff who report to the command post. In case of evacuation, the team will help hotel guests get to the appointed assembly place and carry out a roll call according to established procedures.

Hotel income statement

Often called a statement of earnings, a profit and loss statement, or a statement of operations. It reports on a period of time and the frequency can be daily, weekly, monthly, quarterly, or annually. The income statement is used to determine profitability, state total sales, and various costs and project trends. The key elements of the income statement are revenue which includes sale of goods and services; investment income; and rental income; expenses which are outflows to produce. On the income statement, revenue minus expenses equals a profit or a loss. If revenues are larger than expenses, a profit will be incurred. If expenses are larger than revenues, a loss will be incurred. Income statements are prepared using a uniform system of accounts.

Hotel leases

At its simplest, the hotel lease involves the owner receiving a fixed rent, usually indexed, over a period of time. The operator would then retain the profits (or losses) remaining after payment of the rent and the owner would be entitled to any capital gains (or losses) accumulating over the length of the lease. Like management contracts, leases separate risks and rewards of the ownership of hotel property from those of its operation. During the lease, the owner is normally responsible for structural repairs and the operator for the furniture, fittings, and equipment (FF&E). In this form, a lease was similar to that of an office building, with the lessee responsible for general maintenance and the owner for major structural repairs.

Hotel management contracts

A means by which a hotel operator runs a hotel on behalf of a third-party owner. In this arrangement the responsibilities and rewards of owning and operating a hotel are divided in accordance with the contract drawn up between the parties. The owner may be an individual, a financial institution, or other corporate body that wishes to own a hotel, usually as a long-term property investment.

Hotel rate structures

Rate structures refer to the rates charged for the room. They are as follows:

- *American plan*: A room rate, which is all-inclusive. This rate includes the room charges as well as three meals per day. Also known as en pension and full board. This is a typical rate structure for a resort hotel.
- *Continental plan*: A rate that includes room charges plus breakfast. The type of breakfast included may vary according to the hotel. Continental breakfast which consists of a beverage, rolls, butter, and jam may be included with a supplemental charge for an English breakfast. Also known as bed and breakfast.
- *Day rate*: A rate which is calculated for a room that will be used for less than an overnight stay.
- *Demi pension*: A rate that includes room charges and two meals per day (usually breakfast and dinner). Also known as Modified American Plan (MAP) and half board. This rate structure may be suitable in a hotel that has a lot of guests who are away most of the day and return in the evening in time for dinner.
- *Double occupancy rate*: A rate that is charged to a room that has more than one guest registered within.
- *En pension*: Same as American plan above.
- *European plan*: A rate that includes room charges only with no meals included. Meals are priced separately. This rate is commonly used by non-resort hotels in the USA.
- *Full board*: Same as for American plan above.

- *Half board*: Same as demi pension above.
- *Modified American Plan*: Same as demi pension above.
- *Rate range*: The range of values between the minimum and maximum rates charged by the hotel. The cost structure can help determine the minimum rate and the competition can help determine the maximum rate.
- *Rate spread*: The difference between the hotel's potential average single rate (PASR) and the potential average double rate (PADR). The PASR is calculated by dividing the single room revenues at rack rate by the number of rooms sold as singles. The PADR is calculated by dividing the double room revenues at rack rate by the number of rooms sold as doubles.
- *Room rate*: The amount that a hotel charges for overnight accommodation is known as the room rate. A standard rate will be designated to each room type and this rate is known as the rack rate.

Hotel rating systems

In most countries, the government ministry or department that is responsible for promoting tourism is responsible for the rating system. In the USA, The Mobil Travel Guide, a division of the Mobil Oil Corporation, uses a star rating system and the American Automobile Association (AAA) utilizes a diamond rating system. Under the diamond system of AAA a hotel applies for evaluation and can receive open to five diamonds, depending on the quality of the services and facilities it provides. In order to be listed in the AAA system, a hotel must meet a minimum of 34 basic operating criteria that include management, public areas, guestroom security, fire protection, housekeeping, maintenance, room décor, room ambiance, and bathroom quality. Once a hotel is approved and included in the AAA system, it is revaluated at least once a year.

Hotel valuation methods

The methods used to value hotel properties can be broken down into three basic categories – those based on conditions in the marketplace at a given point in time (sales comparison), those based on cost to rebuild (replacement cost), and those based on the capitalization of future income flows (income capitalization).

Sales comparison method

Under this method a range of prices should be gathered at which transactions of similar hotels have taken place in the recent past. Clearly these values can only be an indication, since no two hotels are identical. Hotels differ in location, construction, design, fitting out, and so on.

Adjustments are therefore necessary to reflect these differences. Such adjustments are complex and rely on the knowledge and skill of the evaluator. The value derived is generally translated into a value per room that can then be applied to other properties.

Cost of replacement method

This method involves the calculation by professional quantity surveyors of what it would cost to rebuild the same hotel today. This figure is then reduced to recognize the loss of value over time through deterioration and obsolescence. The method depends heavily on the comparability of older hotels and modern building techniques – the greater this time gap, the more problematic the valuation.

Income capitalization methods

These methods are based on the assumption that a hotel has an economic value, which is equivalent to the present value of its future income flows. Thus, the hotel business is valued in the same way as an investment in gilt edged securities or an office generating a rental stream, except that the income flow is less certain and stable, being dependent upon trading conditions rather than contractual payments. The methods involve estimating the future trading profit (income) and cash flow of the hotel and discounting it back to the date of the valuation.

House limit

A credit control mechanism used by the hotel front desk when monitoring guest account folios. At check-in when guests present an acceptable credit card they are given charge privileges. This means that guests have the ability to charge their rooms. The front desk will set a limit to which the guest can charge to their account and this limit is known as the house limit. The front desk regularly checks guest accounts that have been given these charge privileges to ensure that the house limit is not exceeded. The house limit of credit, a credit limit set by an individual hotel, can vary, depending on the amount of projected charges and the length of time allowed for charges to be paid. The credit rating of the individual or corporation in question will play a large part in assigning a credit limit.

Housekeeping

The housekeeping department – one of the largest departments in a hotel – is responsible for cleaning guestrooms, hallways, public areas, the lobby, and practically all areas of a hotel excluding the kitchen. Positions within this department include room attendants (sometimes called maids or housekeepers), housemen, inspectors, lobby attendants, laundry workers. In most hotels the executive housekeeper is in charge of this department.

Housing process

Housing for meetings' attendees can be handled in four different ways. First, is for attendees to arrange their own room accommodations, which does not allow attendees or the organization to take advantage of group rates or other concessions. Second, is when the organization arranges for group rates with the hotel, and attendees respond directly to the hotel with a reservation request which can be done by using a card, a form, the telephone, a fax, or the Internet. The third is when attendees request room accommodations through an organization's in-house housing department which then supplies a housing list to the hotel. The fourth is when a third-party housing bureau, often the local convention and visitor's bureau, manages housing requests from attendees and coordinates the final arrangements with the hotel or hotels involved. All except the first option require the organization to negotiate group room rates and book room blocks with one or more hotel properties.

Human capital

The identification and recognition of persons' abilities, skills, training, education, and experience in their performance of productive labor. This labor contributes to the economic function of an enterprise from both a personal (wage earning) perspective and a management (employee as a resource) perspective. Thus as an employer or user of human capital, an investment in training and education of those providing the labor is required. This investment may take the form of time spent in training, dollars allocated to purchasing, or teaching specific training programs and skills as well as time and resources spent on the identification of the specific skills required for a role or activity. As an employee or supplier of human capital the investment is in time, forgone leisure, or other economic activities in the pursuit of skills or education, as well as the actual (dollars) cost of training. This investment is also reflected in the commitment to maintain those skills once acquired.

Human resource accounting

Human resource accounting (HRA) has been defined by the American Accounting Association as *the process of identifying and measuring data about human resources and communicating this information to interested parties*. HRA involves measuring the costs incurred by organizations in the recruitment, selection, hiring, training, and development of human resources. The process may also involve measuring the economic value of employees to hospitality organizations. Under conventional accounting systems investments in human resources are treated as expenses or operating costs and they are usually written off in the profit and loss account in the current accounting period. However, HRA is based on the premise that the costs associated with the acquisition and training of employees are not merely expenses, but rather the price of acquiring a 'human asset' that will give benefits in future accounting periods. The primary purpose of HRA is to provide better-quality information at a reasonable cost to decision-makers.

Human resource development

A set of organized learning experiences the objective of which is to help employees develop their skills, knowledge, and aptitudes. Human resource development (HRD) includes a variety of schemes such as training, career development, coaching and mentoring, succession planning, tuition reimbursement, organization development, etc. As seen above, HRD can be formal such as taking a class in an educational institution, or informal such as a manger coaching and employee. Initially HRD was seen as primarily being the management of training and development, performance assessment, and career and succession management. However the changes wrought by continuous external change from the mid-1990s onward led to a wave of organizational reengineering which changed that view. HRD is conducted in four stages: needs investigation, design, implementation, and evaluation.

Human resource information systems

A system – most often in the form of one or several databases – that enables organizations to keep track of all employees and their relevant characteristics. These systems include such typical information as: personal details; job title; current and past positions; current and historical salary or wages; benefits selected; career and promotion history; training history; skills' inventory; special qualifications; accidents reporting; disciplinary actions; etc. Some organizations design and develop their own systems, but there are ample consulting firms offering generic computerized human resource information systems (CHRIS).

Human resources management

A contemporary approach to managing employees through a series of principles, policies, and practices that center on the individual employee as an organizational resource and investment. Once called personnel management, human resources management (HRM) considers employees as a key resource to an organization. Several common threads can be identified to give HRM some distinction and meaning. These include employee commitment, strategic integration, and achievement of business goals, all of which can be said to represent the main hallmarks of HRM. Other characteristics include long-term planning horizons, employee flexibility, employee development, unitarist employee relations, teamwork, more individualized contracts of employment and rewards, and the involvement of line managers in HR activities and in developing a nurturing management style.

HVAC equipment and systems

HVAC is an abbreviation for heating, ventilation, and air conditioning. HVAC systems in hospitality buildings serve to provide control of the interior temperature, humidity, air movement, and air quality within the structure. HVAC systems can be comprised of a number of components including boilers, chillers, centralized and decentralized guestroom HVAC units, larger roof mounted packaged terminal air conditions (PTAC) units, air handling units, and cooling towers.

A boiler is a pressure vessel designed to transfer heat (produced by combustion) to a fluid. A chiller is a device that creates chilled water for use in a centralized HVAC system. Centralized and decentralized HVAC units are installed to condition the air in the guestrooms. PTAC units provide space cooling and heating via the operation of a refrigeration system and gas heater or, in some instances, by connections with chilled and hot water supplies. Air handling units consist of heating and cooling coils, filters, and fans. Lastly, a cooling tower is a heat rejection device, which rejects heat to the atmosphere through the cooling of a water stream to a lower temperature.

HVAC loads

Any factors that require the HVAC system to use extra energy for heating or cooling to create comfort in a space are referred to as HVAC loads. HVAC loads can be categorized into transmission and conduction, solar, occupant, infiltration, ventilation, and appliance. Transmission and conduction loads involve the transfer of heat through walls, ceilings, windows, and other structural elements of a building. Solar loads refer to high indoor temperatures generated by sunlight entering a building through windows or heating the exterior surfaces of a building. Occupant loads are heat and moisture generated by the number of people present and what they are doing. Infiltration loads are caused because of the movement of air through window and door frames or open doors and windows. Ventilation loads, very similar to infiltration, are deliberately designed as part of an HVAC system to circulate cool and fresh air throughout a building. Appliance loads refer to all operating appliances inside a space that generate heat or moisture, such as computers, TV, water boilers, etc.

Hypertext Markup Language

A set of rules and commands (called tags) used for encoding text files with formatting and linking information. These documents are stored on World Wide Web servers and retrieved with a Web browser. The HTTP (HyperText Transfer Protocol) protocol manages the communications between a Web browser, client, and a Web server. The address, called URL (Universal Resource Locator) specifies the protocol with which the file must be retrieved, the computer name or Internet Protocol (IP) address, and the full name and path of the file to be retrieved (e.g. http://www.marriott.com/reservations/LookupReservation.htm).

Development and maintenance of HyperText Markup Language (HTML) standards are coordinated by the World Wide Web Consortium (http://www.w3.org).

Incentive travel

Travel provided to employees by companies in an effort to motivate them to increase/improve their performance. Incentive travel is an important tool used to motivate, reward, and recognize employees for outstanding performance, service, and commitment to an organization. This type of travel program intends to yield a positive return on investment, resulting in increased sales, reduction in turnover, improved morale, greater company loyalty, and enhanced customer service. Additionally, incentive travel can be an effective means to influence and create powerful alliances with valued customers. Incentive travel can be organized two ways: (a) *group programs* where participants follow the same itinerary or (b) *individual incentives* where participants choose the program based on established parameters. Most incentive trips take place at desirable or even exotic destinations creating a memorable, 'once-in-a-lifetime' experience. Travel packages such as these typically include first-class accommodations, exclusive transportation, recreational activities, entertainment, cultural opportunities, and sightseeing.

Independent restaurants

Restaurants that have no affiliation with regional, national, or international restaurants or other hospitality corporations. The vast majority of restaurants around the world are independently owned and operated. Independent restaurants can be part of any segment of the industry, from quick service snack bars and coffee shops to the most elegant fine-dining establishments. They are also found throughout the event catering and on-site foodservice segments.

Indirect costs

Expenses that cannot easily be associated with a particular department or area of a foodservice operation. In foodservice establishments located within hotels, casinos, or other retail spaces, indirect costs are allocated based on some other unit of measurement, like square feet, number of guests served over a given time period, or number of employees. Some examples of areas associated with these costs include maintenance, energy or utility usage, insurance, depreciation, administration, and security. Managers of this type of foodservice operation typically have no control over the indirect costs associated with their establishment. The trend in most hospitality operations is to minimize the number of indirect-cost categories and to focus specifically on those cost categories over which unit-level management has the most control. It is also important to note that some costs may be both direct and indirect.

Indoor air quality

Indoor air quality (IAQ) issues involve the exposure of a building's occupants to various air pollutants: particles, gases, and biological organisms, for example mold, and formulation of standards regarding ventilation and health protection. Central goals of formal IAQ movements are: (a) determining required levels of ventilation to sustain acceptable IAQ across a variety of facility designs and (b) assessing the effectiveness of IAQ control technologies in controlling human exposure to indoor pollutants. Ventilation rates and use of indoor pollutant sensors to control rates of ventilation and air recirculation, as well as particle removal technologies are currently in practice. Additional focus is on measuring emission data, determining acceptable levels of exposure for maintenance of occupants' health and comfort, and assessing performance of comparative air-cleaning technologies.

Industrial tribunal

A generic term used in Australia and some other countries to describe various independent bodies and labor/wages boards created in order to prevent and settle legal disputes, fix wages, and conditions of employment and conflict resolution. Associated legislation serves to regulate industrial relations through registration of unions and employer associations. This ensures that employers are compelled to recognize the rights of unions to represent their members and, in turn, unions are compelled to recognize the rights of management.

Industry analysis

A process of assessing the profit potential of the lodging or restaurant industry in a market area. The purpose is to predict the future evolution of the local hospitality industry, to understand its competitors and to use this information to craft a firm-specific competitive strategy. It is a process of first studying the general environment (economic, political, social demographics, technological, and regulatory) to identify broad trends or emerging changes. The next step is to conduct an industry assessment, measuring the attractiveness of the industry and relating any direct or indirect impacts of the general environment. Finally, an industry analysis is completed with an assessment of the competitive set; that is, a careful identification of the demand for the product, the overall market size, and an understanding of the firms that attempt to satisfy it.

Industry life cycle

A theory or model that proposes that hospitality products and services move through four successive stages: creation, growth, maturity, and decline. The time necessary to pass through the each stage varies. The model has been extended to describe individual hotel and restaurant firms and the entire hospitality industry as well, suggesting these businesses follow the same four stages. Creation is the initial stage when the new business or product is introduced to the market. Growth is marked by a rapid increase in size (volume of products sold such as the number of hotel rooms or when additional restaurants built) and maturity reflects a stabilizing of size (sales, number of employees, etc.). The maturity stage may linger for quite awhile; creating a cash cow for the organization after it standardizes and streamlines operations. Decline occurs when the organization begins to shrink in size. Complete decline occurs when efforts to reenergize it fail or are not implemented.

Information system

A computer-based system, which consists of hardware, software, users, data, processes, and procedures that work together to produce useful information that is related to the operation of a business organization. An Information System (IS) can accept data resources as input, and then translates these resources into information as output. Besides, specific instructions are provided for users to follow in order to accomplish an activity. An IS can support both short-term and long-range activities for users in an organization. By using an IS, managers can receive the updated information about the status of their business.

In-house computerized reservation system

A computerized reservation system tracks those reservations reaching the hotel directly from telephone, mail, hotel to hotel, e-mail, cable, and fax. Computerized systems can tightly control room availability data and automatically generate many reservation-related reports including the number of expected arrivals per day, the number of guests choosing to stay over, and the number of guests departing on a particular day. While reservations are being taken, computerized systems can suggest alternative room types or rates, or even nearby hotel properties. They can also display open, closed, and special event dates which may require minimum night requirements. A major function of a computerized reservation system is to provide room availability information. This inventory is adjusted as reservation agents input reservations and reservation modifications or cancellations into the system. In addition, any front desk transaction involving guests who fail to check in, guests who leave early, guests with no reservations who walk-in, will immediately update the computer's room availability. Computerized systems also generate reports that summarize reservations by type room, guest characteristics, and other factors.

Integrated information systems

Integrated information systems (IIS) are essential if modern information and communication technologies are to be used to their full potential within the tourism and hospitality industry. Essentially, systems are integrated if data is defined consistently and means the same in each system. In addition, systems should be able to 'talk to each other', in the sense that it must be possible to conveniently transfer data between them.

The problem of integration is particularly acute within the tourism and hospitality industry because of the number of companies involved, a lack of accepted standards and because of the diffuse, geographically dispersed and autonomous nature of most of these companies particularly the small-to-medium tourist enterprises (SMTEs). Naturally, standards could greatly improve this situation and the wide adoption of XML (Extensible Markup Language) in recent years represents a major step forward here: particularly as a uniform language for data definition and message passing. XML has also been employed as the basis for a number of other significant recent standards developments, including WDSL (Web Services Description Language), the UDDI (Universal Description, Discovery, and Integration) standard services registry, SOAP (Simple Object Access Protocol), and OASIS (a standard framework for trading partner data interchange).

Intelligent agents

Expert or knowledge-based systems embedded in computer-based information systems that work without the assistance of users by making choices. They incorporate capabilities from object-oriented technology and knowledge-based systems, extending both of them. They enable distributed, dynamic and large-scale applications like e-commerce and virtual enterprises. Agents can be divided into four basic forms: personal, application, system-level, and general business activity agents. Personal agents work with users to support presentation, organization, and management of user profiles, requests, and information collections. Application agents are business-to-business e-commerce applications, networked from a large number of application agents. System-level supporting agents provide objects with transparent access to other application objects, transaction processing, permanent object storage, event services, and the like. General business agents perform a large number of general commercial support activities that can be

148

customized to address the needs of a particular business organization such as information search agents, negotiation agents, marketing products and services agents, and legal advising agents.

Interactive systems

Interactive systems enable the provision of customized options and responses to users in a range of public access and self-service applications. Interactivity enables two-way communications and provides the ability to users to interrogate a system foe accessing information or making reservations. Interactive hospitality websites can be used to support customer relationship management, brand building, and to provide multimedia enhancement of information. Interactive digital television is an emerging platform for the delivery of e-travel services, including hospitality products. Options can be presented in interactive telecommunications systems using pre-recorded databases of voice messages, for example for automated hotel switchboards, allowing customers to make selections, to input requisite data, for example account number, and to receive information, using digital phones as input devices. Interactive whiteboards can be used to support presentations allowing users to run computerized applications from the whiteboard, writing on the whiteboard in 'electronic ink' so combining the power of a projector, computer, and whiteboard.

Interactive television

A two-way communication between the TV viewer and service providers. The growth in interactive television (ITV) has been made possible by the spread of digital services through satellite, cable, and terrestrial systems across the world. Digital services provide the opportunity to interact with television programs, from the choice of different commentaries and camera angles to home shopping, including the purchase of travel and tourism products, home voting, games, and also financial transactions. The technology also provides the capability for movies on demand, music, and video games. ITV offers the potential for multimedia presentations and video clips on demand. It can be seen by both individuals and family groups, often for much longer periods of time and in a more relaxed environment. In hospitality services there is demand by clients for Internet connectivity and e-mail, made possible via interactive digital television. It can allow hotel guests to check their account status, local tourism information view hotel and restaurants menus and arrange wake up facilities.

Internal analysis

A process for identifying strengths and weaknesses on which a hospitality firm should base its strategies. A hospitality organization's internal strengths might include financial stability, a particular management capability, and a cost advantage over its major competitors. Internal weaknesses, on the other hand, might be obsolete facilities, high employee turnover, the lack of a certain management capability and high dept cost. A straightforward approach considering strengths and weaknesses is to organize them around the major functions of the hospitality business. Strengths should be judged in relation to their ability to improve a firm's competitive position. Strengths must give a business some kind of competitive advantage. On the other hand, a weakness is something that a firm does poorly that could be a competitive disadvantage. It can also be something that a firm is incapable of doing that its competitors can do.

Internal control

The primary concern of internal control is to safeguard the assets and profits of a business against losses, which occur through error or fraud. The main method of internal control is to install systems where any release of resources or assumption of costs is automatically subjected to checking by more than one person. This key element is known as 'separation of functions', which means allocating different stages in the cycle of a transaction to different personnel. Thus, in a restaurant kitchen, if the chef orders from a supplier, a stores person should physically check the goods in to the business, and accounting personnel should check the invoice. A viable internal control system is essential to allow central management to rely on the figures they receive as being an accurate reflection of what actually has taken place. In many countries the directors of listed companies now have to state in their annual report that they are satisfied with the adequacy of their internal controls.

Internal marketing

Internal marketing is geared toward employees of the firm. In the context of internal marketing, the employee is the 'customer' and the product is the job and its benefits. Internal marketing uses the concept of marketing and applies it to the 'internal customer', the employee, so that the best employee can be acquired and retained to service the 'external' customer. Internal marketing is an important internal function of an organization. Internal marketing leads to greater retention of customer base and eventual higher profits for the organization. Development of appropriate human resource practices and supporting organization culture are essential for the internal marketing to be successful. Effective implementation of internal marketing involves the following steps.

Internal rate of return depreciation method

Also known as the 'discounted rate of return' the internal rate of return (IRR), belongs to the discounted cash flow methods and is the rate that, when used to discount the future cash flows of a project, results in an NPV (see 'net present value NPV method') of zero. Either the 'trial and error' method, or a proper computer algorithm, or the interpolation method (graphic solution), may be used to calculate it. The IRR is usually calculated with a trial and error method, where different rates are applied to the NPV computation of a project. The higher the rate of interest used, the lower the NPV; therefore once a rate of interest (A) has been calculated, which brings the NPV to a positive result, and a different rate of interest (B) has been calculated, which brings the NPV to a negative result, the IRR falls between A and B.

The following example shows the trial and error method.

Table 1 Project to enlarge a hotel's capacity from 150 to 175 rooms outlay of 1 million dollars paid in 20X4.

Trial and error method to obtain the IRR of a project					
	Year 20X5	Year 20X6	Year 20X7	Year 20X8	Year 20X9
Additional cash flow due to the enlargement	230,000	320,000	350,000	400,000	460,000
DCFs using 15% rate of interest	200,000	241,966	230,131	228,701	228,701
NPV = 129,500					
DCFs using 25% rate of interest	184,000	204,800	179,200	163,840	150,733
NPV = −117,400					
DCFs using 20% rate of interest	191,670	222,222	202,546	192,901	184,864
NPV = −5800					
DCFs using 19.766% rate of interest	192,040	223,091	203,736	194,413	186,677
NPV = 0					
IRR: 19.766%					

The formula for the interpolation method is as follows:

$$IRR = A + \frac{a}{(a-b)} \times (B - A)$$

where
A is a discount rate giving a positive NPV;
B is a discount rate giving a negative NPV;
a is the NPV when A is used;
b is the NPV when B is used.

The following example shows the interpolation method.

Table 2 Project to enlarge a hotel's capacity from 150 to 175 rooms outlay of 1 million dollars paid in 20X4.

Interpolation method to obtain the IRR of a project					
	Year 20X5	Year 20X6	Year 20X7	Year 20X8	Year 20X9
Additional cash flow due to the enlargement	230,000	320,000	350,000	400,000	460,000
DCFs with a 15% rate of interest NPV = 129,500	200,000	241,966	230,131	228,701	228,701
DCFs with a 20% rate of interest NPV = −5800	191,670	222,222	202,546	192,901	184,864

$$IRR = 15\% + \frac{129,500}{(5800 + 129,500)} \times (20\% - 15\%) = 19.786\%$$

The IRR is recognized as 'the true interest rate' earned on an investment over its whole economic life. Therefore, this method is used in the decision to proceed with a project or not, comparing its IRR with a given rate of return (minimal return desired or maximum cost of capital applicable to finance the project).

International aspects of financial management

There are several issues that are not present in a domestic operating environment that must be addressed if a hospitality company operates in an international environment. Amongst the most important are currency implications, tax and legal jurisdiction issues, investment appraisal and how these issues impact reporting and performance benchmarking. Currencies pose a particular challenge. In a treasury (cash) sense, the goal is to have the right currency in the right bank account at the right time to meet obligations, whilst managing all other cash reserves to maximize net-of-tax earnings to the shareholder. Taxes differ in each country – indeed in federal countries such as the USA and Germany, taxes vary at a state or county level. The goal in tax management is to achieve an ever lower effective rate of corporate tax – that is to say, to continually drive down the cost of corporate tax. The resultant network of legal entities will represent a corporate governance challenge. Care has to be taken to abide by the laws of each country and in most cases extreme care has to be taken to avoid the impression that the structures are artificial. In making investment decisions that involve a business investing in a foreign country, care also needs to be taken to ensure that the appropriate discount rate is used in investment appraisal. Generally speaking, the techniques noted here continue to apply – they can be summarized as 'Think Local'. Thus the construction costs, the operating profit, and loss should be projected in local currency with explicit assumptions of local inflation.

International hotels environment initiative

A program developed by the international hotel industry for the benefit of all hotels and the environment. The aim is to promote the benefits of environmental management as an integral part of running a successful, efficient hotel business. Focusing exclusively on hotels, the International Hotels Environment Initiative (IHEI) keeps members informed about global environmental trends and provides hotel-specific guidance to assist hoteliers in tackling emerging issues. The IHEI is unique in that it is international, hotel specific and non-profit. Through this initiative, hotels pool resources and experience to produce self-help tools for use by the wider industry. The IHEI is a program of The Prince of Wales International Business Leaders Forum (IBLF) of which HRH The Prince of Wales is President. IHEI represents more than 8000 hotels around the world and over 1 million hotel rooms.

International meeting

1. *International/intercontinental*: A meeting of an organization with multinational membership that is available to meet on more than one continent.
2. *International/continental*: A meeting of an organization with multinational membership that is available to meet on only one continent.
3. *International/regional*: A meeting of an organization with multinational membership that is available to meet in only a given region of one continent.

World meetings are open to all nations and meet worldwide. International meetings require more planning time than domestic meetings, due to the variety of special planning conditions, including the logistics of making long-distance arrangements, budgeting complicated by foreign exchange currency risks, the availability of local services, such as technical support, and shipping and travel time to distant destinations. Some logistical considerations include time differences, language barriers, visas and vaccinations, and currency exchange and restrictions.

Internationalization

The process of expanding a firm's activities beyond the borders of its domestic markets. Historically, the primary motivation for internationalization among firms was the need to become more efficient. Efficiency in the context of the post-industrial revolution era is achieved when a firm becomes larger and thus generates economies of scale. Consequently, many firms searched for and found attractive markets in countries with higher market growth rates, developing consumer consumption, and growing discretionary income. Furthermore, the development of computer technology, communication technology and new means of transportation all served as important enabling forces to internationalization. Today, internationalization has become one of the key preoccupations of firms. As barriers to international trade collapse in many parts of the world, managers become aware of new opportunities in an ever-changing global environment. Hospitality firms can develop an international strategy by using franchising agreements, management contracts, strategic alliances, joint ventures, wholly owned subsidiaries.

Internet

A computer network consisting of millions of hosts from many organizations and countries around the world transporting data across computers. The Internet supports various functions such as the Worldwide Web (WWW), Electronic Mail (e-mail), Usenet, Gopher, Telnet, and File Transfer Protocol (FTP). The Web is similar to a global library with millions of books, directories, records, and movies open all day, every day of the year. The Internet encourages a new marketing approach for hospitality firms and products by supporting customers' involvement, as they benefit by examining in advance hotel facilities, attractions, and events at the destination. The Internet offers hoteliers the ability to show full-color virtual catalogs, provide on-screen reservation forms, offer online customer support, announce, and distribute products easily. It also provides opportunities for extensive e-commerce and distribution as well as for obtaining feedback from potential or actual customers.

Internet channels

The Internet has increased the reach and the efficiency of traditional distribution channels as well as provided new channels through Internet-based reservation networks. For the most part, two major types of players serve the online reservation industry: hospitality companies and third-party travel companies. Different types of Internet channels are described below:

Proprietary sites: A proprietary site is the hospitality company's or the property's Web page. Sales generated through proprietary sites are also called direct sales. In the proprietary site, the reservations are placed through the central reservation system (CRS), and thereby do not incur third-party fees. The reservation booking engine is interfaced with the CRS.

Third-party sites: Third party, or secondary, sites are online retailers and wholesalers. Online wholesalers, also called online merchants, receive discounted rates which are either sold to affiliate websites or posted on the wholesaler's own website (HRN, Expedia, etc.). Online retailers simply reach the final customer.

Third-party sites can access rates and effectuate transactions in a variety of ways. Since the information path determines the reservation cost structure, the sites will be presented next according to how they access rates and availability.

Interval

In timeshare, the specific allotted period time in which each owner/member of a common interest subdivision may, based upon the use rules established by the common interest, use and enjoy the property. Commonly used in dividing timeshare interests (interval ownership) into use periods. Traditional use periods are defined as a one-week (seven nights) period in which the occupant has exclusive rights to occupy a unit or piece of property. Once the intervals have been established the right to occupy specific unit or parcel at a given time is defined by the use rules and reservation system established at the outset of the timeshare or interval ownership plan. Properties utilizing an interval ownership reservation system may include timeshare resorts, second homes, campground interests, or recreational subdivision lots. Interval time periods may be defined by a point-based system.

Intranet

An Intranet disseminates information to employees of an organization using Internet hypertext protocol over private networked computers. It allows employees timely access to confidential company information and other tools (e.g. human resource records, company news) that assist them to be more effective and efficient. It is also used as a communication medium among members of the organization. They are usually WWW based and protected by firewalls and passwords to maintain confidentiality. They are not confined to one location. Like the Internet they can be accessed around the world. The data usually are generated by a firm's property management system (PMS) and is accessible by staff on a need to know basis. In a hotel, the general manager of a property has access to all data on the Intranet; housekeepers have access to room status, marketing staff access to source of sales, average room rates, occupancy rates, and so on.

Inventory

Inventory describes goods to be sold in hospitality operations. In the Food and Beverage department inventory refers to food and beverage products whilst in Rooms Division inventory refers to room capacity. Inventory systems are used to facilitate control of the inventory. In the case of food and beverage, the system is used to order and monitor supplies, control interdepartmental transfers, monitor efficiency, and market trends, by monitoring product sales. In the Rooms Division, the inventory is controlled by the Front Office system. Through this system rooms can be allocated to Tour Operators or other distributors such as online agents. Automated inventory systems allow employees to create invoices, purchase orders, and packing slips and ships with standard inventory and sales-related reports.

Inventory turnover analysis

A ratio used to monitor the efficiency of turnover management. Inventory turnover can be calculated as:

$$\frac{\text{Food cost for the period}}{\text{Average inventory value for the period}} = \text{Inventory turnover for the period}$$

The utility of the inventory turnover statistic is perhaps most obvious when comparing a single operation over time with a number of very similar operations. Even if an operator regularly achieves similar levels of turnover, anomalies may indicate cause for concern.Owing to the related managerial adage and perennial objective of 'slow and old or fresh and fast', inventory turnover analysis can aid operators in identifying problems related to inventory management and can directly help reduce the associated costs. The main caveat here is that more is not always better.

Invitational tournaments

An event, most often a sporting one, restricted to invited participants. The concept of invitational tournaments plays a critical role in making tennis and golf more interesting for the club's sports minded members. A planned invitational tournament instills excitement into the club's sports minded members by creating an atmosphere of social bonding and competitive spirit. An invitational tournament can be conducted on a 'for members-only' basis or it can be open to an outside source such as the PGA tour. On the latter, it is not uncommon for non-equity (alias a corporate owned club) to block off the entire club for a PGA invitational tournament. A great example of this would be the Bay Hill Club invitational tournament that is held each year at the Bay Hill Club in Orlando, Florida. In instances such as this, the club usually makes arrangements for their members to play at other local clubs while the tournament is being held.

ISO 9000

An international set of standards for qualification of global quality assurance and quality control that provides a framework against which organizations can standardize their management of quality. While the vast majority of standards promulgated by the ISO (International Organization for Standardization) are technical in nature, and intended for the use of engineers, two deal with the subject of management systems, ISO 9000, dealing with management of quality and ISO 14000, dealing with management of environmental issues. A significant advantage of having such a framework is that each organization does not have to 'reinvent the wheel'. But the more important benefit of an international standard is that other parties wanting to do business with that organization, particularly customers and prospective customers, can operate with a high level of assurance that quality is uniform and being well managed. This is of particular value where organizations are doing business internationally.

ISO 14000

A series of standards prepared by the International Organization for Standardization (ISO) cover a number of environmental topics. ISO 14001 is the specific certification standard within the ISO 14000 family. It does not set environmental standards, nor does it measure environmental results. Rather, it covers the management systems used to control how an organization deals with environmental issues. To obtain certification, companies are required to set up procedures to identify environmental aspects of all activities so that the impact of those activities can be determined. For the hospitality industry, this would include all supplies and resources used, including water, air and energy, and all waste produced, whether directly or indirectly. Participants then need to document plans to reduce those impacts, and to have a system for continual auditing.

Jj

Job analysis

The process by which individual jobs are analyzed in order to determine the specific responsibilities, working conditions, and requirements of the position. A human resource specialist, the employee, the employee's supervisor, or an external consultant may conduct the job analysis. Methods used for gathering the information used in job analysis include interviews, surveys, observations, and journaling (i.e. having the employee record tasks undertaken as they are performed). Job analysis information supports many important employee resourcing functions such as recruitment, selection, performance evaluation, and pay scales. It can also provide useful information in support of improved job design leading to enhanced employee motivation and organizational effectiveness.

Job description

A written summary of the major duties and responsibilities of the position. Job descriptions typically have several major components: identification information (e.g. title, department, reporting relationships); date last updated; job summary (i.e. a brief statement on the key purposes of the position and its importance to the organization); duties and responsibilities (i.e. a listing of all major functions and areas of accountability along with clearly defined standards of performance); and working conditions (i.e. hours and conditions of work). Job descriptions are used to communicate responsibilities and performance expectations to employees. They are also used to form the basis of job postings.

Job design

Pertains to the way in which specific tasks are combined to form complete jobs as well as the specification of the work environment and reporting relationships. Job design may be regarded as being primarily traditional or non-traditional in nature. Traditional job design is based on the *Principles of Scientific Management* and the work of Frederick Taylor, a noted US industrial engineer, who advocated that operational efficiency is enhanced by breaking down jobs into their simplest components and requiring employees to perform the same narrow tasks over and over again. Traditional job design requires employees to exercise little judgment, and to need few skills and training. In contrast, non-traditional job design embraces the concept of job enrichment, in which autonomous employees are given broad, meaningful jobs, in which they can make use of a variety of skills.

Job posting

A system for informing current and potential employees of available positions within an organization. Based on the information contained within the job description and job specification, a job posting typically includes a brief description of the major duties and responsibilities of the job, along with the minimum required personal competencies, prior work experience, and formal qualifications. Job postings can appear on company bulletin boards and in newsletters and websites and can support both internal and external recruitment strategies. Well-written job postings can serve as an effective pre-screening device, helping potential candidates accurately assess their own appropriateness for the job. Internal job postings have been found to be particularly useful in large hospitality chains for retaining employees interested in relocating.

Job specialization

In hospitality firms, the traditional nature of job specialization (i.e. reservations, reception, wait staff, kitchen staff, housekeeping staff, and so on) means that many workers tend to do a rather limited range of mundane and routine tasks within their jobs leading to poor job satisfaction and lack of motivation. To overcome these problems three job design strategies can be employed: *job enlargement*, *job rotation*, and *job enrichment*. *Job enlargement* is a job design strategy the purpose of which is to increase the number of tasks that an employee does in order to reduce employee boredom and job dissatisfaction. It is a horizontal expansion of the job and leads to an increase in job scope. This approach can be seen in the front office area of a hotel where employees are given a range of tasks across specializations (reception, reservations, communications, and guest services). In *Job rotation* employees are either assigned to different jobs or different tasks on a temporary basis or periodically transferred among lateral jobs involving different tasks. Some hospitality firms use cross-training as a job rotation mechanism. *Job enrichment* appears to be most effective in increasing worker motivation and satisfaction. Rather than focusing on skills and variety, this approach provides staff with more authority, responsibility, and decision-making over their work. In hotel terms, this could equate with empowering front-line staff to take responsibility for delivering best-practice service to guests.

Job specification

A description of the employee's characteristics such as knowledge and skills, required to competently perform a given job. A job specification is often included as part of the job description. It identifies the personal competencies, prior work experience, and formal qualifications considered essential in carrying out the responsibilities outlined in the job description. Personal competencies are typically designated as knowledge, skills, and attitudes. Prior work experience typically pertains to similar jobs done elsewhere, or prerequisite types of experience. Formal qualifications relate to education and/or certification requirements. In determining what requirements to specify, every effort should be made to identify what is a required minimum, recognizing that employees can be trained and developed once on the job. In addition, it is important to keep in mind that the focus between these three areas (knowledge, skills, and attitudes) will vary depending on the nature of the job.

Key control

The process of controlling keys for security purposes to ensure that all keys are accounted for at all times. In the past, the concept of key control usually related to a metal key. Today, most hotels in the developed countries have moved away from metal keys and use electronic guestroom access cards. However, there are sufficient metal keys in many other countries, in small hotels and in the 'back-of-the-house' operations to give special consideration to this area of security controls. Good security practices requires that keys should not have any identification of the property or the room of the facility controlled by the key. Coding has been successfully used to assist in such control.

Kitchen fire suppression system

Kitchen fire suppression systems are designed to prevent fires from spreading to the duct system and ultimately the rest of the building. A kitchen fire suppression system is incorporated into the hood design and designed to sense fires in the foodservice equipment under the hood. When a fryer or char broiler ignites, the suppression system discharges a fire suppressant from the duct area on the cooking appliance involved. The original suppression systems used a dry chemical agent; however, wet chemicals were introduced in the early 1980s. In 1994 the Underwriter's Laboratory in the USA adopted UL 300, Fire Testing of Fire Extinguishing Systems for Protection of Restaurant Cooking Areas because of new equipment and new frying oils. Wet chemical extinguishing systems, using an increased amount of extinguishing agent, were effective for the hotter fires.

Knowledge management

The process through which organizations generate value from their intellectual and knowledge-based assets. It is a concept in which an enterprise gathers, organizes, shares, and analyzes the knowledge of individuals and groups across the organization in ways that directly affect performance. Knowledge management can be described as a process that helps organizations find, select, organize, disseminate and transfer important information, and expertise necessary for activities such as problem solving, dynamic learning, strategic planning, and decision-making. It is basically about helping people communicate and share information. Knowledge management envisions getting the right information, in the right context, to the right person, at the right time, for the right business purpose.

LI

Labor costs

Labor costs include wages paid to hourly employees, salaries paid to management and supervisory staff, and employee benefits for all employees. In the USA, average labor cost is typically 25–40 per cent. Employee benefits represent another significant component of labor costs for a hospitality operation. In addition to wages and salaries paid to employees, companies must pay federal and state taxes on all wages earned by these employees. Also, many employees receive additional benefits, which can include, but are not limited to, health insurance, vacation/sick pay, employee meals, and uniforms.

Labor turnover

A ratio that calculates the relationship of the number of workers that had to be replaced in a given time period to the average number of workers. There are three ways to calculate labor turnover. The first, as advocated by the United States Department of Labor, is as follows:

$$\frac{\text{Number of employee separations during the period}}{\text{Total number of employees at the midpoint of the period}} \times 100 = \text{Turnover rate}$$

This method is considered inadequate because it assumes that employee separations will occur at equal intervals throughout the period of measurement.

The second method allows for the often subjective determination between the 'desired turnover' of undesirable employees and the 'undesired turnover' of desirable employees. This approach treats the resulting statistic as the *undesired turnover statistic*. The calculation is performed as follows:

$$\frac{\text{Number of separations} - \text{desired separations}}{\text{Average number of employees during the period}} \times 100 = \text{Undesired turnover rate}$$

This calculation appropriately takes the average number of employees during the period (as shown in the denominator). In essence, however, this method is useful only for managers who wish to justify some elements of the turnover problem.

The final method is the easiest and offers the greatest utility. The calculation is:

$$\frac{\text{Number of employees separations during the period}}{\text{Average number of employees during the period}} \times 100 = \text{Turnover rate}$$

This statistic is not subject to interpretation and also allows for intra- and inter-unit analysis (in the case of multi-unit onsite operations).

Laddering techniques

In-depth interviewing and analysis methods used to elicit the salient characteristics that customers seek when they make a choice to purchase a product. It is a qualitative research technique that researchers and managers can use to understand the underlying reasons for people's behaviors. Understanding the relationship between a hospitality product's attributes and customers' desired benefits can provide hospitality marketers with information useful in targeting advertising and customer segmentation.

The 'laddering' interview technique can be used to examine the 'ends', or values in the 'means-end-chain', that hospitality customers hope to fulfill when they make a choice to visit a hospitality operation. The central concepts of the means-end chain model are two linkages: the linkage of values and desired consequences and the linkage between consequences and product attributes. Laddering can also identify the categories that customers group the 'ends' in. The laddering interview consists of two steps: (1) eliciting salient characteristics and (2) probing to reveal the means-end structure.

Late arrival

Any hotel guest arriving after a designated hour of the day, typically 6:00 p.m., is considered a late arrival. At that time a guest who did not guarantee his/her reservation may have it canceled. With out a guarantee payment, the hotel may not hold the room for the guest and may not have a room available when the guest arrives. Most large hotel chains in the USA and other countries do not allow non-guaranteed reservations. Some reservations require advance payment of one or all room nights. This is done in an effort to ensure payment of rooms that do no show, as well as to ensure better ability to fully book all hotel rooms.

Layout and design for food and beverage

Foodservice facilities are unique in that the design of the 'factory' is part of the product. Guests enjoy the physical elements of their dining experience as well as the food and service they receive, while the part of the design that they do not see is integral to the successful execution of their requests. Foodservice operations are almost all divided into two distinct physical components: the front–of-the house, or those areas that a guest or customer sees; and the back-of-the house, or those areas that are limited to employees. The design challenge for each component is to create a functional setting while at the same time expressing the unique personality of the operation.

When determining the size of the front-of-the house, it is common practice to allocate a fixed amount of space per seat, which varies depending on the type of experience desired. For fast food restaurants, it is not uncommon to allocate about 1 m^2 (10 ft^2) per seat to front of house areas, whereas a fine dining restaurant might allow as much as 2.5 m^2 (25 ft^2) per seat. This allocation is often adjusted to accommodate additional features such as a bar, a retail area, or demonstration cooking stations.

Leadership

The process of influencing the behavior of others by inspiring, influencing, and motivating them whereas management is about controlling and coordinating processes. Often leadership is assumed to be synonymous with management or management style. However, although the terms may be used interchangeably within popular management literature, there is a fundamental difference. Although traditionally the hospitality sector has been typified by an autocratic, task-centered approach to leadership, there is growing support for a more human relations approach, especially one that recognizes the importance of job satisfaction and employee motivation in delivery of good service. This is especially important within flatter organizational hierarchies and dynamic work environments where close supervision is no longer possible.

Leadership in Energy and Environmental Design

The Leadership in Energy and Environmental Design (LEED) Green Building Rating System is a voluntary, consensus-based national standard for developing high performance, sustainable buildings. Members of the US Green Building Council, representing all segments of the building industry, developed LEED and contribute to its improvement. LEED standards are currently available for new construction and major renovation projects. LEED was created to: (a) establish a common standard defining a 'green building'; (b) promote integrated, whole building design practices; (c) recognize environmental leadership in the building industry; (d) stimulate green competition; and (e) raise consumer awareness of green building benefits. LEED provides a framework for assessing building performance and meeting sustainability goals. Based on well-founded scientific standards, LEED emphasizes state of the art strategies for sustainable site development, water savings, energy efficiency, materials selection, and indoor environmental quality.

Learning environments in meetings and conventions

164

The concept of lifelong learning has a major impact on meetings and conventions. In order to facilitate their learning, the space in which the meeting is held needs to be conducive to information sharing and not set up barriers to communication. The learning environment should be comfortable and inviting. A room should be setup in consideration of the type of communication that will be used for the meeting. Other considerations are the acoustics, the ceiling height, the wall décor and/or coloring, lighting, windows, drapes, mirrors, audiovisual capabilities, and light and temperature controls. When interaction is desired, the group must be kept small. Distance between attendees affects interaction, and the outcomes are affected by culture. Some cultures are more comfortable up close and personal; others are more comfortable with more distance between them. Sight lines are important, if attendees cannot see the speaker or the stage they tend to disconnect. Sight can be obstructed by columns, shape of the room, or a too tall centerpiece.

Learning organization

An in which people at all levels, individually and collectively, are continually increasing their capacity to improve organizational actions through better knowledge and understanding. Learning in organizations takes place in three levels: individual, team or group, and organizational level. Individual learning is a precondition for organizational learning, but it does not guarantee organizational learning. An organization learns through actions and interactions that take place between people who generally work in teams. Organizational learning increases greater capacity for organizational adaptation to changing internal and external environmental demands, a fuller utilization of the members' abilities and motivation, and higher level of job and personal satisfaction by organizational members. A learning organization can be achievable in the hospitality industry by systematic problem solving, experimentation with new approaches, learning from one's own experiences and mistakes, learning from the experiences and best practices of others, and transferring knowledge quickly and efficiently throughout the organization.

Legacy system

A computer system or application program which continues to be used because of the prohibitive cost of replacing or redesigning it, despite its poor competitiveness and compatibility with modern equivalents. The implication is that the system is large, monolithic and difficult to modify. Legacy systems are critical information systems that significantly resist evolution to meet new and constantly changing business requirements and cost is a major factor. However, the cost of maintaining a legacy system may eventually outweigh the cost of replacing the software and hardware. Many legacy systems used in the hospitality business today still rely on distributed networking and serial port interfaces for communication between applications. Besides being slow and unreliable, these old technologies require custom development for almost every application that uses them. Furthermore, these systems cannot benefit from the advances of new web-based applications, mobile and wireless communications, which have made storing and transferring data between systems much more efficient, faster and reliable.

Legionnaire's disease

Also known as Legionellosis, is a form of pneumonia called Legionnaire's disease and is attributed to a bacterium named Legionella. The first indication of the disease was noted in the Bellevue Stratford Hotel, which was hosting a convention of the Pennsylvania Department of the American Legion. Guests or 'Legionnaires' succumbed to the illness after breathing in droplets of air and water that contained the Legionella bacteria. Follow-up determined that the bacterium thrived in contaminated water found in the cooling tower in the hotel's air-conditioning system. Subsequently, the bacterium has been found to be somewhat widespread and has also been found in potable water systems and in some water features as well. Multiple venues in hotels exist as breeding grounds for these bacteria: air-conditioning cooling towers, whirlpool spas, showers, and other plumbing systems. Legionellosis is not passed from person to person, nor is there evidence of infection from auto or home air-conditioning units.

Les Clefs d'Or

Literally, means keys of gold in French, the crossed gold keys are the international symbol of the organization. The keys displayed on a concierge's uniform lapels assure travelers they are dealing with a seasoned professional, one who is dedicated to serving the guests' every need. In October 1929, three of the more prominent concierges met in Paris to exchange service tips and ideas. They found that, together they could more effectively network and enhance guest services throughout their cities. As a result, many countries created national concierge societies. The 'Union Internationale des Concierges d'Hotels "Les Clefs d'Or" ' (UICH) is the international organization that represents the hotel concierge occupation throughout the world.

Life cycle costing

Also called total cost of ownership analysis, is a technique designed to systematically consider the full financial costs to an organization of a particular purchasing decision over the whole time

166

period that the purchase, or its alternatives, will be relevant. It is especially valuable where the operating, maintenance, training, and disposal costs (or salvage value) of one purchase choice are different from another. Reliability is another particularly complex but important factor in evaluating the overall cost of any purchase; the costs and implications of reliability issues to continuity of an organization's mission are often poorly understood. Tax and inflation ramifications also need to be considered.

Life cycle costing can also aid in the evaluation of service contracts and the best selection of consumable supplies. In the hospitality industry, life cycle costing can be profitably applied to mundane purchases (e.g. light bulbs) just as readily as to complex purchases (e.g. outsourcing the housekeeping or laundry function).

Lifelong learning

People who participate in seminars, training sessions, workshops, and other learning activities outside of a traditional classroom are examples of life-long learners. They want an opportunity to increase their knowledge and skills while sharing their experiences and expertise. The philosophy of lifelong learning as essential at all levels of staff and throughout an individual's career is increasingly popular in modern hospitality organizations. For example, the Club Managers Association of America (CMAA) provides learning and development programs for all levels of management from entry to senior management. Managers work toward professional qualification with the Certified Club Manager (CCM) designation. In the UK, the government has supported the philosophy of lifelong learning by setting up an organization called Learndirect whereby individuals and businesses are given advice and support to promote the continuous development of skills at all levels.

Life Safety Code

The life Safety Code began its existence in the USA in 1913 when a special committee for the National Fire Protection Association (NFPA) saw fit to develop standards governing the design of buildings for the effective, efficient, and safe egress of occupants during times of emergencies. It has been in almost constant revision since that time with a new edition appearing approximately every two years during recent times. NFPA 101 is the designation for which the life Safety Code is otherwise known. The general content of the code covers anything that could possibly impact the safe evacuation of a building during a fire emergency or panic situation and therefore is explicit in its standards for the construction, maintenance, and protection of exits and exit pathways. The code recognizes that for people to safely survive fire or panic situations they must first be able to get to an exit. Therefore the code will mandate such things as sprinkler systems and firewalls that serve to protect the property as well.

Lighting equipment and systems

Lighting equipment consists of lamps, fixtures, and controls. Selection of the appropriate elements of equipment and integration of these into a lighting system that operates harmoniously with the interior design as well as with the lighting needs for various tasks results in a pleasant visual environment that can be operated in an efficient manner. Lighting also serves to advertise the hospitality product via lighting of the building exterior and the lighting found in signage. Lamps are the component of a lighting system that produces light. Two broad categories of lamps are incandescent and discharge lamps. Incandescent lamps produce light by means of an element heated to incandescence by the passage of an electric current. Discharge lamps product light, directly or indirectly, by an electric discharge through a gas, a metal vapor, or a mixture of several gases.

Limited menus

A menu which is typically limited in one of two senses. It may be limited in the number of menu choices offered or in the number of ways a menu ingredient is prepared/served. In the first instance the term refers to the number of menu items a restaurant has for its guest to choose from. The most limited menus in terms of choices are thought by most to be offered at quick-service restaurants. 'Variety' in this setting is provided by the numerous condiments and toppings that can be applied to each order. Limited menus reduce the need for equipment, personnel, and extensive inventories. Cost control and quality control are much easier than in a restaurant with extensive menu offerings. However, limited menus appeal to a narrow segment of the market.

Line pricing

Line pricing can be practiced only by large organizations with a wide array of products offered within various product lines. It is commonly noted in the hotel industry. For example, when a hotel organization has a portfolio of hotel lines, it can set the price for each hotel line (brand) differently to match the target customers' needs and expectations. Such a pricing practice must also match the services offered by that specific hotel line. In this scenario, one may find the same hotel company practicing different pricing strategies to meet the different needs of each hotel line. As is obvious, hospitality companies that specialize in single line of products cannot practice this strategy.

Liquidity ratios

Ratios that measure how well a business is able to meet its short-term obligations. In other words, liquidity ratios represent the ability of a business to pay obligations that are expected to become due with the next year or operating cycle. The two main liquidity ratios are the 'current' and 'acid test' ratios.

The current ratio is also known as the working capital ratio. In accounting, current assets less current liabilities equal working capital. In ratio analysis, the current ratio is calculated as follows:

$$\text{Current ratio} = \frac{\text{Current Assets}}{\text{Current Liabilities}}$$

The other liquidity ratio is the acid test ratio. It is also known as the 'quick' or 'liquid' ratio, and is calculated as follows:

$$\text{Acid-test ratio} = \frac{\text{Cash} + \text{Marketable securities} + \text{Accounts receivable (quick assets)}}{\text{Current liabilities}}$$

Quick assets are those that are either cash or 'near' cash. Such assets are considered as 'quick' as they can normally be rapidly or 'quickly' converted into cash.

Local area network

A communication network, which links computers together within an office, a hotel, a university, or other organization. It can be contrasted with a wide area network (WAN), where the computers to be linked are further apart – for instance, all the hotels in a chain might be linked by a WAN. Each computer in a local area network (LAN) is fitted with a network card, and cables link the computers to each other and to at least one server. It is also possible to link the computers using Wireless Technology, linking the machines by radio and removing the need for cables to connect them. A File Server is used to store software and data files which are shared by users at the various computers. A property management system often uses a LAN, to share information between different departments of the hotel.

Lock-off

The concept of a lock-off is basically adjacent units in a vacation ownership facility that can function as independent living units that contain separate bedrooms, kitchen facilities, dining space, living quarters, and frequently balcony facilities. Many vacation ownership (timeshare) resorts have 'lock-off' units consisting of two bedrooms and two bathrooms, three bedrooms and three bathrooms, or even four bedrooms and four bathrooms that by design can function as two discrete units. This offers the owner the ultimate in flexibility in using their villa. The flexibility comes in three basic forms whereby the owner may occupy the living room and one or two bedrooms while another uses the remaining and physically separate villa space. The first option allows the owner to spend two separate weeks in a year at their home resort by electing to choose the main portion of the unit during one week, while using the other week stay in the lock-off. The second choice occurs when the owner chooses to spend one week at their home resort and exchange the other section of the villa. The last option occurs when the owner arranges two separate exchanges for a single maintenance fee.

Lock-out/tag-out

A US OSHA (Occupational Safety and Health Administration) mandated program (29 CFR 1910.147) that is designed to protect employees from the uncontrolled release of hazardous energy. The term lock-out means using a lock and a device that, when in use, makes it impossible to activate a switch, circuit breaker, etc., that would energize or set a machine/process in motion endangering an employee working on the machine/process. It takes into account the total energy system sources, such as electrical, mechanical, hydraulic, pneumatic, kinetic, and chemical. Locking out to a 'Zero Energy State' is a planned approach for service and maintenance safety. It takes into account the total energy of a system, and eliminates the possibility of sudden or unexpected release of that energy during such service or maintenance functions. OSHA requires that an employer have a written lock-out/tag-out program, the proper tools, an equipment inventory, and employee training.

Locus of control

A theoretical construct with it's foundations in the field of psychology; locus of control is designed to assess a person's perceived control over his or her own behavior regarding subsequent events. In other words, who or what is responsible for what happens. The classification internal locus indicates that a person feels in control of events. This person feels in control of his/her own destiny and often excels in educational or vocational settings. External locus indicates that others are perceived to have that control. Persons with this view their fate based upon luck rather than effort in determining whether they succeed or fail. Employees with an internal locus of control are more likely to believe that they can influence their own performance and therefore are more likely to be satisfied in their work. Locus of control varies across cultures, with employees in Far Eastern countries more likely to have an external locus than Western countries.

Loyalty Circle (The)

The Loyalty Circle© is a way to create customer loyalty. The three main functions on the circle are process, value, and communication. With different points along the circle, there are places where the customer might exit the circle and hence the relationship. The goal of companies is to keep the customer in the circle by executing equally well the three functions of the circle. On one side of The Loyalty Circle© is the process, which is 'how the service works.' It involves all activities from both the customer's perspective and the service provider's perspective. A second component of The Loyalty Circle© is value creation. Value creation is subdivided into two parts: value added and value recovery. Value-added and value-recovery strategies are designed specifically to enhance customer perceptions of the rewards and costs associated with present and future service transactions. The final component of The Loyalty Circle© is communication. It involves all areas of how the company communicates with its customers.

Mm

Maintenance fee

In timeshare properties, the amount established (or 'levied') by an owners association against owners of a common-interest subdivision for maintenance, improvements, upkeep, and management of the association's property. Assessments are generally levied to each owner/member in proportion to the ownership interest, or combined ownership interest of each owner. The manner in which the assessment will be levied will be determined upon the declaration of the common-interest owners association. Methods used to determine the proportional assessment to owners include equal assessment of fees levied against owners of each interval or unit and assessment based upon the size of the unit owned and the number of units or intervals owned. Maintenance fees are generally assessed and collected on an annual basis at the beginning of each fiscal year. Some common-interest resorts, particularly in resort locations where maintenance costs are prohibitive, allow for quarterly or semi-annual payment of the fees.

Maintenance management

A key and possibly the most important managerial responsibility of the facilities area is the on-going maintenance of building systems and equipment, the building itself, recreational facilities, and areas such as the grounds and parking facilities. Maintenance activities in lodging properties can be thought of as involving preventive and predictive activities, scheduled activities, emergency and breakdown activities, and guestroom maintenance. Preventive maintenance (often abbreviated PM) is a systemized approach for maintaining the equipment in a lodging facility. Predictive maintenance entails monitoring engineering systems in order to forecast when and where system failure will arise, and inspecting, repairing, or replacing the system before that breakdown occurs. Scheduled maintenance requires advanced planning and preparation and is initiated by a formal work order. Emergency maintenance is crisis oriented and requires immediate attention by the engineering department. Breakdown maintenance, like emergency maintenance, is crisis oriented and occurs when a piece of equipment or a structural component of the facility completely fails. Guestroom maintenance is a critical maintenance activity that focuses on PM although emergency maintenance may be required on occasion. Guestroom maintenance includes checking and repairing furniture, fixtures, and equipment; inspecting plumbing for leaks; checking the condition of the floor coverings and walls; and inspecting exterior windows.

Management accounting

Management accounting is used internally in a hospitality firm and consists of a selection of methods and techniques that can be used to monitor and improve the profitability of the business. Systematic management reporting provides regular financial information covering short-time periods (week or month) and which is analyzed to reflect the management of profit-generating centers within a business (such as room, food and beverage departments in a hotel) and permit a close control of those units. It includes decision-making techniques such as models to determine optimum levels of output (e.g. room occupancy and numbers of guests), and understanding how profit varies in relation to changes in a given level of turnover (cost–volume–profit). Much of the data is drawn from the financial accounting system, but techniques such as the 'balanced score card' bring in comparative data from outside and non-accounting performance indicators.

Management contract

A type of contract in the lodging industry which stipulates that the operator of a hotel is acting fully and completely as an agent of the owner and for the owner, and assumes full responsibility for operating and managing the hotel. Such operators can be individuals or a third-party management company. Employees of such hotels are employees of the owner. Generally any losses resulting from lawsuits or judgments against a hotel operating with management contract must be absorbed by the owner. Similarly, the final financial result of the operation, be it a profit or a loss, is recorded on the owner's account, not the operator's account. For fulfilling the role of manager of the hotel on behalf of the owner, the operator receives certain fees. The management company provides the management talent, standardized training programs, and name recognition. Generally the key factors in the selection of a management company include cost, market strengths, lender reputation, efficiency of operations, and flexibility in contract terms and negotiation.

Management development

From a personal perspective, management development (MD) can be defined as those activities that are undertaken by managers to learn new and/or improve their professional skills. From an organizational perspective, MD can be defined as all learning experiences provided by an organization for the purpose of supplying the organization with a team of competent and highly skilled managers. MD activities may include in-house and external training, formal education, mentoring, succession planning, and others. In most instances, MD in the hospitality industry is reserved for the larger companies, with smaller independent properties relying on buying-in well-developed managers and leaders through selective recruitment.

Management information systems

A management information system (MIS) consists of people and equipment and contains procedures to gather, sort, analyze, evaluate, and distribute timely and accurate information needed for managerial decision-making. Fundamental elements of MIS functions include collecting, storing, and processing of data and then allowing managers to select various formats for presenting such data. Once data are stored and processed into a suitable format, managers can access and analyze the data for decision-making. Organizations typically process both text (such as reports) and numbers (such as counts).

An effective MIS provides query functions for quick information retrieval on a video display terminal and delivers printed forms or reports to alert the manager when an unexpected situation – either positive or negative – has developed. An MIS is important for effective decision-making in all aspects of management: organization, human resources, strategy, customer service, and operations. In the hospitality industry, the main sources of an MIS are information collected by the firm on a regular basis as a routine part of business activities (internal data) and market research information from an organization's environment (external data) both stored in a database format. More advanced systems also provide features to forecast the future state of the economy and market demand for hospitality/tourism products. By analyzing complex marketing data, disseminating information, and providing decision support features for hospitality/tourism managers, an MIS contributes to the improvement of managerial performance.

Management of change

Managing change in hospitality organizations can be defined as reshaping of strategy, structure, and culture of an organization over time by external forces or through using internal mechanisms. The characteristics of change in hospitality organizations can be categorized along the following two dimensions: radical versus incremental change and planned versus emergent change. Several potential barriers and resistance to change in hospitality firms may include financial difficulties, cost of the change, fear of losing the existing customers, time limitation, priority of other businesses, and lack of skills and cooperation, and internal politics. The abilities, skills, experience of managers, and active support and coordination from other management levels are the key factors in overcoming the barriers and resistance to change in hospitality organizations. To effectively manage the change in a hospitality firm it is recommended that the firm should develop a dynamic and responsive organizational structure and culture where change is seen as the norm and is accepted as part of the normal process of organizational evaluation.

Management proficiency ratio

A set of key measures for evaluating management goals and objectives. Ideally, a manager would have input into selecting the goals and objectives to be achieved, the ratios (measures) to be used for evaluation, be given the appropriate power by the organization to facilitate achievement, and be held responsible for such achievement. The ratio should be set as objective (based on counts and timed events) instead of subjective (based on feelings and impressions). The management proficiency ratio may include ratio analysis, formulas, guidelines, and rules of thumb to help, analyze, and evaluate any business-related problem. Finally, quantitative methods (mathematical and statistical techniques for solving managerial planning and decision-making) may be used for forecasting and validity testing. An array of these types of measures is used in creating a management proficiency ratio.

Management styles

The way a manager uses their authority to coordinate and organize the efforts of staff and the ability to direct and guide using systems and procedures toward the achievement of organizational goals. This can be achieved through a combination of factors that are internal to the individual, such as national culture, personal values, and personality and external factors such as explicit and implicit organizational rules and procedures, and how these are interpreted by the manager. The work of Douglas McGregor concentrated on the manager's assumptions about human behavior and placed them into two categories: those that managed according to what he referred to as 'theory X' and those that managed according to 'theory Y'. Theory X managers assume that employees have an inherent dislike of work and are therefore lazy and shiftless. As a result, the manager adopts a style of management, which emphasizes control to the point of coercion, with little room for empowerment, delegation, or trust. Conversely, theory Y managers believe that employees view work as natural and motivating. Unlike theory X, which assumes that the goals of the individual and the goals of the organization are mutually exclusive, theory Y managers see their role as creating the conditions under which these goals can be integrated. The contingency theory perspective argues that there is no universally applicable model of management. Rather, the most useful style of management is contingent on and consistent with such factors as the type of environment in which the organization is functioning, the type of task employees are carrying out, and the attributes of those employees.

Manager on duty

In hotels, during the absence of the general manager, an assistant is typically identified as the manager on duty. The manager-on-duty fields concerns, questions, and issues that may arise from guests and employees. Since hotels operate 24 hours 365 days a year, it is essential that the hotel staff have a person who they can go to with issues or concerns at all times particularly when their department supervisor or manager may not be available. Because of its central location and focal point in a hotel or lodging enterprise often the manager on duty is an assistant who is located at the front desk or reception of the hotel. The key demands facing the manager on duty are in large part short term. They include day-to-day operational issues of quality service and controlling costs and revenue. The manager on duty, like all operations managers is under tremendous pressure to produce short-term positive results.

Marginal costs

The cost of the last unit produced. There are often considerable differences between the average cost (calculated as the total cost divided by the volume) and the marginal cost. Marginal cost is an important concept in economic analysis. The optimal production volume is achieved when marginal cost equals the price of the product. The marginal cost is then normally much higher than the average cost which implies that the volume of the optimal result will not be the volume that minimizes the average cost. Marginal cost is the theoretical basis for contribution margin pricing whereas average cost is the basis for full cost pricing. Depending on the level of analysis, marginal cost may also include fixed costs.

Market penetration

As one component of a core set of growth strategies, a market penetration strategy seeks to *increase sales of existing products or services to existing markets*. Although this seems like a simple concept, variants of this definition are used by both marketing academics and practitioners. How a market penetration strategy is ultimately defined, applied, and measured depends on how the user of the concept defines its elements – existing products, existing markets, strategic outcomes – in terms of sales or some other desired result. In the strictest sense, market penetration involves existing products that are not modified in any way. Thus, a product that is in some way changed or improved, whether through different packaging or some other feature enhancement, counts as a new product.

If this new product is sold to existing markets, the firm is using a product development strategy as opposed to a market penetration strategy. However, for practical management purposes, the definition of 'existing products or services' can vary widely. It might include only unmodified products or products that are modified somewhat to replace an existing product offering. Existing products might also include those in a product line or portfolio. Finally, market penetration can also be achieved by employing distribution strategies. Starbucks Coffee Company is widely recognized as a leader in growth via market penetration. In October 2004, the company had opened its 8569th store worldwide. By comparison, whereas one can find a Starbucks for every 15,000 residents in the company's home state of Washington, there is a Dunkin' Donuts store for every 7500 residents in the latter company's home state of Massachusetts.

Market saturation

The point at which current market demand no longer supports additional units of supply – the market (actual and potential buyers) is effectively glutted. In product markets, saturation is achieved when there are no new buyers for a marketer's existing product offering. For example, if there are only 10 restaurants in a particular geographic area, and a marketer of coffee machines has already sold machines to nine of them, with the final potential buyer unwilling to purchase, the market is saturated.

In service industries, market saturation similarly occurs when a market can no longer support an additional outlet or service provider without harming the sales of existing firms serving that market. Although the major cause of this type of market saturation is clustering of providers – too many stores located too closely together and chasing too few customers – this is often only part of the story. Changing buyer preferences, lack of innovation in the product or service mix, and intensifying competition can accelerate the effects of market saturation.

Market segment profit analysis

In order to improve financial performance, hotel companies often target multiple customer segments by expanding their product and services which is likely to result in an increase in a property's support costs. A property's overhead costs (see *Undistributed operating expenses*) are likely to increase with both customer and product-service variety. Hotels that focus on one or two well-defined customer segments, and maintain a narrow product mix, are likely to have lower support costs than those properties that offer many products to a diverse guest population. It is widely recognized that 'revenue-enhancing' techniques are important in the present-day hotel market, but even more important are analytical methods that help managers determine what segments of the business are making the most substantial profit contribution to the bottom line. Therefore, from a hotel company standpoint, the main benefit of market segment profit analysis accounting is the provision of financial information for planning and decision-making, rather than as a control mechanism.

Market segmentation

The process of dividing larger, more heterogenous markets into smaller, more homogenous markets based on specific characteristics and wants of the buyers. Market segments can be described in myriad ways. Common bases for segmentation include *geographic* (e.g. from nation to neighborhood), *demographic* (e.g. age, education, income, occupation, gender, and ethnicity), *psychographic* (e.g. lifestyle as reflected in activities, interests, and opinions), and *behavioral* (e.g. product usage or media usage).

The segmentation approach can be priori versus posteriori and forward versus backward. *A priori* approach is one where the segments are chosen before the data is analyzed (i.e. male/female, non-users/first-time users/repeat users, etc.). *A posteriori* approach is one where the segments are determined by the data rather than by the researcher. This *Forward* segmentation approach includes grouping consumer characteristics based on their similarity in demographics, personality, attitude, and benefits sought followed by discriminating groups by consumer response (i.e. chosen product or service). *Backward* approach, on the other hand, involves grouping consumer response based on their similarity in choice of products and services followed by discriminating groups by consumer characteristics. In recent marketing literature, one-to-one marketing (or mass customization) and the characteristics of post-modern consumers have been debated as factors posing challenges to the segmentation practices. Advances in information technology and computerization now allow companies to track customers individually and customize marketing efforts. This practice, so called one-to-one marketing, mass customization, or database marketing, does not eliminate or preclude market segmentation.

Market share

The percentage of total market output produced by a single firm. The market share is a useful indicator that helps identify the various positions (according to inventory, sales, or revenues) of one company toward its direct or indirect competitors. In sales, market share is expressed as the total sales of a firm divided by the sales of the market it serves. The calculation can be a broad industry scope or a set of companies similar in product offerings, category, geographical location, or target markets. Unlike consumer goods, for which global market shares are calculated on a total potential market, the hotel industry uses the inventory of the number of available rooms as a basis for its fair market share calculation. Market share is a common business concept and is therefore a powerful indicator to use when presenting the company's performance to owners or head offices. It is often used in public relations to communicate positive results to journalists or potential customers. The simplicity of the concept makes it easy for employees to understand. It motivates them to aim at and fight together for higher market positions.

Marketing

The process of planning and communicating the attributes of a service or product in an effort to get consumers to purchase that service or product. Important in this definition is that marketing involves a planning process that begins before the product or service is created. In addition to the development of an idea, product, or service, marketing includes the development of pricing, promotion, and distribution plans. Finally, it is important to note that the exchanges must be satisfactory to both the customer and the organization. Marketing activities are ongoing and include continuous research about customers, their preferences, and lifestyles. Marketing requites a long-term view of business whereby chant is expected, accepted, and adapted to. Adaptations necessitate cooperation among the organization's constituents, such as managers and other employees, intermediaries, and complementary businesses.

Marketing concept

A philosophy that espouses the idea that a business should be intuitively aware of its customers' needs and wants and practice a management style that revolves around these items. The four bases of the marketing concept are (1) customer orientation, (2) integrated company effort, (3) profit or goal orientation, and (4) social responsibility. The philosophy implies that a firm's success is dependent upon its ability to understand its customers, deliver value to its customers, have employees that are customer oriented, and be more effective and efficient than its competitors. The customer focus must extend beyond marketing personnel to all employees and managers in an organization. The result of a business that practices the marketing concept is that the business will yield favorable results and benefit from long-term profitability.

Marketing information system

A routine, planned, gathering, sorting, storage, and retrieval system for market information relevant to the operation of a particular business. A marketing information system is intended to bring together disparate items of data into a coherent body of information. Marketing information system is more than a system of data collection or a set of information technologies, it is an interacting structure of people, equipment, and procedures used to make accurate and timely decisions regarding the planning implementation and control of marketing activities. It is suggested that whilst the marketing information system varies in its degree of sophistication, a fully fledged one should have four main constituent parts: the internal reporting systems, marketing research system, marketing intelligence system and marketing models, the methods (and technologies) of collection, storing, retrieving, and processing data.

Marketing research

The systematic process of collecting and analyzing information in an attempt to reduce the uncertainty surrounding marketing decisions. The execution of marketing research is done in five steps as follows. The first step is to *define the problem*. The researcher determines the problem from the marketing manager's perspective and then translates in into a research problem. Once the research problem has been defined, the second step is to *plan the research*. The third step in the marketing research process is to *collect the data*. The decisions made during this step involve choosing a data collection method, designing data collection forms, and determining the sampling plan. The primary data collection methods are observation, experiments, and surveys. The fourth step in the research process is to *analyze the data* using either descriptive or inferential analysis. The fifth step is to *prepare the final report*. The final report should summarize the activities performed in the previous steps in a clear and concise format using visual aids where applicable.

Mark-up in menu pricing

In menu pricing, 'mark-up' refers to the traditional way operators price individual menu items above the variable costs associated with that item. Some menu items may have a higher food cost, such as those with considerable quantities of meat, while others have a higher direct labor component. The price charged is rationalized as a means of returning an amount that reflects a fair return for the time, effort, and risk involved. While it is necessary to price above cost in order to produce a profit, the amount of the mark-up depends on whether the item is a commodity or a specialty good and whether the price is demand driven or market driven.

If an operator chooses to add a substantial mark-up, it is critical that the operation be on the leading edge in terms of food quality, taste, freshness, and plate presentation.

Mass customization

A technique used by product manufacturers and service providers to resolve the 'cost versus variety' dilemma in a way that allows them to achieve acceptable economies of scale (and hence lower costs), for example through the use of standardized products or platforms, while providing a considerable degree of customization (and hence differentiation), of their product or service to the individual customer or market segment.

Examples in the service industries include checkbook printing, special meal orders on airlines, and the choice of in-room amenities offered to arriving hotel guests. In general, mass customization is more difficult to achieve in the services industries than in the manufacturing industries: indeed, how does one apply the equivalent term 'built to order' to a stay in a hotel room, or a flight from one city to another? Mass customization, while generally requiring substantial investments in technology, allows companies to customize products to meet the needs of relatively small customer groups (microsegmentation) at a cost far lower than that of true customization.

m-commerce

Any transaction with a monetary value that is conducted over a wireless telecommunication network. Fueled by wireless communication technologies converging portability and networking, m-commerce is creating several new business models (e.g. m-gambling, m-advertising, m-payments, m-music, m-banking, m-education). Equipped with micro-browsers and other mobile applications, the new mobiles offer the Internet at any place, any device, and at any time and 'always on'. m-commerce involves a number of players in a chain of value-adding activities that terminate with the customer. Infrastructure and service players include mobile transport companies (e.g. AT&T, DoCoMo, Vodaphone); mobile services and delivery support (e.g. WAP, i-mode), security, the service platform and payment systems; mobile interface and applications. Secondly, players involved with content creation and aggregation, packaging firms, and mobile portals (e.g. Vizzavi).

Media markets

The area and persons receiving media messages via media outlets such as television, radio, and newspaper are commonly referred to as media markets. Media messages come in many forms such as motion pictures, sound recordings, books, newspapers, magazines, and the Internet. In regard to marketing, these messages are in the form of advertising within the various media outlets. Media markets are frequently discussed in regard to advertising and programing because media markets identify the persons that can be reached by an advertisement or program. An organization that wishes to deliver (communicate) a message (advertisement) to a particular group of people about a new product will purchase advertising in specific media markets that reach the target market. In marketing, media outlets are commonly referred to as communication channels. Media markets are an important concept in marketing because these markets often provide the communication link between marketers and consumers.

Meeting

A formal or informal gathering of people to share information. Different types of meetings include the following:

- *Colloquium*: An academic meeting where one or more content specialists speak about a topic and answer questions.
- *Conference*: An event used by an organization to meet and exchange views, convey a message, open a debate, or give publicity to an area of opinion on a specific subject and an assembly of individuals to discuss items of mutual interest or engage in professional development by learning.

- *Convention*: A general and formal meeting of a legislative body or social or economic group to provide information on a particular situation and to establish consent on policies among the participants.
- *Congress*: The European term for a convention.
- *Panel discussion*: Three or more subject area specialists each give a brief presentation after which the audience has the opportunity to ask questions of the panelists.
- *Structured panel*: Eight to ten questions are prepared and distributed in advance to selected attendees and following each presentation, attendees ask questions of the panelists from the list. Presenters have prepared answers, eliminating the potential for misinformation.
- *Round tables*: Tables seating 10–12 attendees are placed at round tables throughout the room. A key topic and an expert in that area are assigned to each table and the experts lead the discussion.
- *Seminar*: A lecture, presentation, and discussion under the guidance of an expert discussion leader allowing participants to share experiences in a particular field.
- *Symposium*: Experts discuss a particular subject and express opinions or a meeting of a number of experts in a particular field where research papers are presented and discussed by content specialists that then make recommendations.
- *Workshop*: A training session in which participants develop skills and knowledge in a given field, an event designed to stimulate intensive discussion, and compensate for diverging views in a particular discipline or subject, an informal public session of free discussion organized to take place between formal plenary sessions on a subject chosen by the participants, or on a special problem suggested by the organizers.

Meeting/event history

Meeting/event histories are critical to planning. Meeting/event histories are accurate, detailed records about the meeting. They are useful to the planning organization and the hotel or venue under consideration. Before a hotel responds to a request for a proposal, the sales manager will ask for a history of past meetings. Data generally collected includes attendee demographics, including age, political preferences, religious preferences, geographic differences, educational levels, gender, music tastes, food tastes, and recreation preferences. Historical data of the meeting itself include the objectives for the meeting, location, and sites of the previous three to five years, the length of previous meetings, actual guestroom usage (pick up), arrival and departure patterns, occupancy mix, no-show factor, affiliated or ancillary business, for example hospitality suite revenues, use of recreational facilities, outlet activity, actual meeting attendance numbers versus anticipated, actual meal function numbers versus guarantees and projections, attendance, registration patterns; detailed information about all food and beverage events; pre/post-meeting events scheduled; sleeping room information and the number and size of general sessions and break-out, concurrent sessions exhibit sales, spouse/guest events, rebates, assessments, commissions.

Meeting/event planner

An individual whose primary responsibility is to coordinate all the details to produce a meeting. The term meeting or event planner may be used generically to refer to people who plan a variety of events, including meetings, exhibitions, seminars, conferences, and conventions. Regardless of the type of event, however, there are many tasks that a planner would have to complete in order for the event to be successful. The planner, either alone or as part of a team, determines the objective of the meeting, decides on a location, conducts site inspections, contracts with the hotel(s) and/or convention center, plans the educational program, books speakers, arranges transportation, plans events, parties and banquets, contracts with suppliers, such as audio-visual, florists, photographers, and manages on-site operations. Evaluations of the meeting are also the responsibility of the planner. The meeting/event planner is responsible for the meeting/event budget.

Meeting/event profile

The meeting/event profile contains the history of the meeting/event including facts and details regarding previous meetings, including receptions, banquets, dinners, audio-visual requirements, and recreational activities such as golf, tennis, health club, spa, etc. The profile also contains information on other sponsored functions that piggyback with the event. Information that should be included is the anticipated use of foodservice outlets such as room service, cocktail lounges, and snack outlets and the spending habits of attendees based on prior years' histories. The specific profile of the attendees as well as who is paying the bill is vital information. The meeting/event profile should contain the length and time of stay as well as the arrival and departure patterns. Other information included is the space pattern (guestroom nights, meeting room, and exhibit requirements), transportation needs, and information on outside vendors for equipment, decorations, and services not supplied by or used from the property.

Meeting/event timeline

The chronological list of details and procedures essential to planning a meeting or an event. This list typically begins with the present and outlines each function necessary to finalize all details of an event. The first step for planning any event is typically the development of objectives and goals while the last step would be the evaluation of the event. While there is no standard timeline formula, it is suggested to list each function and determine the necessary time needed to complete the task as it is placed in chronological order. Some meetings may take years to plan, for example a large convention or a trade show which would have to be made years in advance of the actual meeting because the number of venues that could host the events is limited. Corporate meetings, on the other hand, tend to be planned in a relatively short period of time, sometimes with only a few weeks notice.

Menu mix

Also referred to as sales mix, menu mix is the ranking of each menu item by customer preference (popularity) by meal period. It has a direct impact on the overall food cost percentage that will be produced at the end of the month and on the profit generated by the operation. The objective of sales-mix analysis is to identify specific menu items that contribute to a restaurant's profit, cost, and revenue objectives. Major contributors become featured items on the menu (using menu-psychology techniques). This also works in the reverse in 'hiding' items that do not contribute to cost and revenue objectives. Menu-mix optimization is assessed using a variety of menu-engineering techniques. The simplest of these take into account the popularity and food cost of each item relative to all other items within the menu-item category (e.g. entrées).

Menu pricing

Pricing is a complicated process that cannot be reduced to a single quantitative formula for marking up raw food cost. While food cost percentage and gross profit return are important considerations, the pricing process is more subjective and enigmatic. Pricing decisions are affected by the clientele, the amount of business the restaurant will generate, its location, the meal period, and even the menu item itself. If the price is perceived as too high, it may not be selected. If the price is too low, it could be viewed as low quality by the customer and also not be selected. The consumer sometimes uses price as a gauge of quality. In the broadest of terms, menu pricing can be viewed as either market driven or demand driven. The appropriate categorization depends on the uniqueness and monopolistic aspects of the item and the restaurant. Prices that are market driven must be responsive to competition (e.g. items that are common). Demand-driven prices are the operator's response to customers who want items for which there are few if any alternatives in the marketplace. Examples include items featuring specialty meats or rare produce.

Menu psychology

The psychology of menu design uses the layout and format of the menu to call attention to particular menu items a restaurant prepares best and wants to sell more of than other menu items for reasons including profitability, check average, and ease of preparation, or because the item is a specialty of the restaurant. The concept of menu psychology was developed from merchandising techniques used by retail grocery and department stores when setting up counter or window displays. When used properly, menu psychology will help the restaurant operator achieve sales, cost, and profit objectives more directly than a menu designed without such techniques. These techniques include distinctive font sizes and styles, and the incorporation of graphics, illustrations, and dot matrix screens as 'eye magnets'. Eye magnets employ any of several techniques used to 'draw the eye' of the customer to particular items.

Merchandising

The selection and display of goods in a retail outlet. An increasing number of hospitality businesses are creating product ranges using their logo, name, or reputation. Whilst these will bring in additional revenue, it is likely that the promotional benefits of spreading the organization's name are actually more valuable. Destination and boutique hotels in many parts of the world offer a range of items for guests to purchase. These range from embossed dressing gowns, clothing, and tableware to beauty products and local delicacies. In-house leisure facilities are also an excellent merchandising opportunity. When analyzing a merchandising strategy one must assess how customers perceive the product range, offer, and ultimately the brands. Good quality and effective merchandising is essential to create the right shopping environment so as to positively affect customers' buying decisions.

MICE

An acronym for group business organizations whose market segments are comprised of *M*eetings, *I*ncentives, *C*onventions, and *E*xhibitions. Four major parties are generally involved in the group business travel industry consumption cycle: (1) the individual participant in the event, (2) the sponsor of the event (the association or corporation), (3) the intermediary (the meeting planner, travel agent, or convention and visitors bureau), and (4) the venue (the hotel, convention/exhibition center, or municipal facility). Although the letters of four segments of the group business industry are used for the acronym MICE, the industry is usually subdivided into four primary market segments: (1) *meetings and conventions*, the two primary entities that hold meetings and conventions are associations and corporations; (2) *incentive travel*, a motivational tool to reward employees for the achievement of outstanding accomplishments; (3) *exhibitions* that permit manufacturers and service providers to directly reach a target audience that would otherwise be difficult and expensive to contact, and (4) *trade fairs* which constitute a marketplace for commercial suppliers of products or services that are of interest to a specific profession or market segment.

Midscale restaurants

The term midscale refers to both pricing and service components of a restaurant. This market niche has also gone by the terms *coffee shop*, *limited service*, or *family restaurants*. Pricing is midscale because menu items are generally priced above the QSR (quick service restaurants) level but below the Casual Theme segment. Service falls between traditional full service and the low-cost fast food/quick service offerings. Midscale/family coffee shops are typified by a strong identification with breakfast and lunch menu offerings (see Dayparts), often serving these items in a 24 hour/7 day-a-week operating environment. Menu selection can be quite broad, primarily to appeal to a general population of consumers ranging from young to old, traveler to local, business to leisure, and everything in between. For the midscale company, pricing pressure comes from being compared with the lower-priced QSR players, and service pressure comes from the full-serve Casual Theme restaurants.

Mini-vacation

Discounted or free vacation accommodations offered as an inducement to the recipients to experience a vacation ownership resort with the understanding that acceptance of the accommodations will require the recipients to participate in a sales presentation of the host vacation ownership resort. Mini-vacations may also be offered as discounted or free accommodations in hotels in the general vicinity of the host vacation ownership resort with the understanding that acceptance of the accommodations will require the recipients to participate in a sales presentation at the host vacation ownership resort. Mini-vacations may, in addition to the accommodations being offered, be packaged with other ancillary benefits and services to be enjoyed by the recipients during their use of the accommodations. Such ancillary benefits may include rental car use, meals, attraction tickets, attendance to sporting events and activities, etc.

Minimum wage

The minimum rate a worker can legally be paid. More positively, the existence of a legal minimum wage set by statute or labor tribunal determinations, attempts to protect employees from falling below the 'poverty line' in many developed economies. However, appropriate levels for minimum wages are largely a matter of political opinion. Interestingly despite these 'safety nets', hospitality employees remain some of the lowest paid workers internationally. Employers usually justify low wages by citing high fixed costs and a high ratio of labor to total costs (because of the labor intense nature of the industry). In some cases this is justified as they can account for around 50 per cent of total costs, particularly in 'luxury' enterprises. Some managers also consider that many of their workers are more than recompensed for their efforts by additional income provided through customer tipping.

Mise en place

French phrase meaning '*setting in place*' which means the setting out the ingredients and equipment required for the preparation of dishes on the menu in a restaurant or foodservice enterprise. In foodservice organizations, employees are often found to be spending too much time searching for things they need to perform their daily activities. In addition, employees may also be searching for food items that have been misplaced in storage areas. Most managers and employees agree that smallwares are often misplaced, for example. To minimize wasteful spending of employees' time searching for misplaced things, foodservice professionals are trained to practice mise en place – keeping everything where it belongs to the extent possible. Typically in foodservice organizations, employees who close a unit at the end of the day are not expected to return the next day to open the place. In those circumstances, mise en place is very essential so that everyone opening in the morning knows where everything has been placed the night before.

Model Timeshare Act

In 1983, the American Land Development Association adopted a Model Timeshare Act that became the basis for subsequent state legislation. Its provisions were designed to curb scam artists while providing a framework within which reputable developers could operate. In 1994, the American Resort Development Association adopted a Model Vacation Club Act that recognized vacation clubs as a distinct product type and proposed a separate regulatory framework for them. Like the Model Timeshare Act, the Model Vacation Act was designed to protect consumers without imposing unreasonable limitations on legitimate developers and marketers. The Model Timeshare Act has been superseded by the ARDA's Model Vacation Club Act, and a version adopted by the National Conference of Commissioners on Uniform State Laws.

Model Vacation Club Act

The Model Vacation Club Act was adopted by the American Resort Development Association (ARDA) on November 15, 1994. In January 2001, the State Legislative Committee of ARDA formed a task force to revise and update the 1994 Model Vacation Club Act. The task force, nearing completion on the project, has recommended adoption by the State Legislative Committee of guiding principles to be used by legislatures to develop legislation instead of specific proposed language. The Act is a proposed model act developed by the ARDA for the purpose of providing legislatures with recommended provisions for developing or amending timeshare legislation for their particular area in with respect to regulation of timeshare plans, including multi-site timeshare plans. The areas of recommended regulation include applicable definitions, scope and exemptions, subordination and financial assurances, management and assessments, reservation systems, purchaser disclosures, cancellation rights, escrow requirements, and agency governance.

Moments of Truth

The interaction that occurs between a service provider and the guest is one of the key elements of service that define a guest's service experience. Richard Normann, of the Service Management Group, developed the term 'Moment of Truth' for any moment when an employee and customer have contact in a service operation and the guest determines his or her impression of the service quality. During a service encounter, the employee and guest both exhibit behavioral cues that allow them to form impressions and choose their reactions. A positive Moment of Truth occurs when the service provider has the ability to monitor the guest's behavioral cues and react in a way that promotes guest satisfaction along with delivering the service. In order to develop positive Moments of Truth, service operations support the staff members that have direct customer contact. By turning the organizational structure upside down, the employee with direct guest contact will be empowered to react appropriately to the customer's behavioral cues.

Motivation

The process by which people seek to achieve certain goals, which in turn satisfy a need. The word motivation is used to describe the things that motivate people, the process through which a goal satisfies a need, and the social process by which a manager seeks to influence the performance of a subordinate to increase productivity. Motivation is a key aspect of hospitality management and one of the mechanisms for tackling the high levels of labor turnover within the industry in developed countries.

The academic discussion of motivation has been dominated by a dichotomy between the study of the things that motivate – content theories – and the process by which people are motivated – process theories. Content theories of motivation focus on identifying the things or situations to which employees aspire as a way of describing motivation. The main examples of content theories are Maslow's Hierarchy of Needs and Herzberg's Two Factor Theory. Process theories of motivation seek to explain the reason why people might be motivated and the individual differences evident in people's choices of goals and behaviors, rather than identifying the things that are motivators. Examples are theories such as Equity Theory, Expectancy Theory, and Goal-Setting Theory all of which seek to describe the cognitive processes that people follow in evaluating motivational drives.

Multi-branding

Multi-branding is based on the process of differentiation by offering independent, unconnected brands that maximize a company's impact on the market and increase its market share. Several hospitality companies have resorted to multi-branding to correspond to the various market segments and niches. For example, Choice Hotels has eight different brands that include Comfort Inn, Quality Inn, Clarion, and Econolodge. Similarly, Starwood Hotels and Resorts offer Westin, Sheraton, St. Regis, and W, which concentrate upon well-defined and diverse market segments. In the restaurant business, Darden Restaurants operates Red Lobster, Olive Garden, Bahama Breeze, Smokey Bones, and Season's 52, each catering to distinct market segments.

Multimedia

A number of diverse technologies that allow visual and audio media to be taken and combined in new ways for the purpose of communicating. Multimedia can be defined as any combination of two or more of the following: text, graphics, sound, animation, video which are integrated together and can be delivered in various formats including standalone (PC, CD-ROM, DVD) and networks (WWW, ISDN, cable, cellular, wireless). Multimedia is currently used in the hospitality sector to enhance the in-room guest experience, for training of staff, and for communicating internally and externally. More adventurous multimedia applications, such as virtual reality, are yet to be fully exploited the hospitality sector.

Multi-site timeshare plan

A timeshare plan, also referred to as 'vacation club', that connects more than one timeshare property together through a central reservation system such that the owner of a deeded timeshare interest or a right-to-use timeshare interest at one of the properties in the plan, or the owner of a right-to-use interest in the plan as a whole that is not tied to a specific timeshare property, has the right to reserve and use the accommodations and facilities at any of the properties that are part of the plan pursuant to the terms and conditions of the reservation system. Unlike exchange programs, membership and participation in the multi-site timeshare plan is mandatory, and the owner cannot use a timeshare period without accessing the reservation system. Many multi-site timeshare plans provide for a 'home resort' priority reservation right that allows owners of a deeded timeshare interest or a right-to-use timeshare interest at one of the timeshare properties to have a priority right to reserve and use an accommodation at the timeshare property of ownership before the owners of other timeshare properties that are part of the plan can make a reservation at that property. Multi-site timeshare plans are sometimes referred to as 'vacation clubs'.

Multi-skilling

A term given to instilling competence for a task or activity in trainees through training. Multi-skilling is the process of training workers in a number of skills in an effort to broaden the skill set of the worker. Multi-skilling is usually based on two principles: (1) competency within the workplace (i.e. the ability of a single individual to assess and rectify problems as they occur day to day), almost regardless of the nature of the problem and (2) the full utilization of capabilities (i.e. the only limitations on who does what, how, and when are the skills that an individual has or can acquire), the time available to perform any new or additional tasks, and the requirements of safety. In a hotel, staff put through a multi-skilling program can regularly be redeployed across two or more work areas such as housekeeping and bar.

Musculoskeletal disorders

Injuries of the muscles, nerves, tendons, ligaments, joints, cartilage, or spinal discs. Other expressions used to describe musculoskeletal disorders (MSDs) include repetitive strain injuries (RSIs), cumulative trauma disorders, overuse injuries, and repetitive motion disorders. Some common MSDs are back pain and carpal tunnel syndrome (wrist pain). MSDs are not typically the result of any instantaneous or acute event (such as a slip, trip, or fall) but reflect a more gradual or chronic development. MSD-type injuries are not only very painful for the victim; they are also difficult and very expensive to treat. MSDs account for nearly 70 million physician office visits in the USA annually and an estimated 130 million total healthcare encounters including outpatient, hospital, and emergency room visits.

Nn

Net present value method

The underlying concept of net present value (NPV) is that if cash to be received in the future were received now, the cash could be invested to earn interest (return), or it would not be necessary to borrow money now and to pay interest (cost of capital). In addition a future cash flow bears the risk of not being paid by the debtor (risk) and finally the nominal value of a cash flow will correspond to a lower purchasing value in the future than now, according to the general price increase (inflation). NPV determines the sum of future cash inflows related to a project, after having discounted them by an appropriate rate of interest; it then deducts the initial cash outflow. The NPV method also allows a sensitive analysis to be carried out where the estimated selling price, cost of capital, life of the project, initial cost, operating costs, sales volume, and the estimated level of risk can be varied in order to observe their effects on the NPV.

The formula for NPV is as follows:

$$NPV = \sum_{t=1}^{n} \frac{C_t}{(1+r)^t} - C_0$$

where
t is the time of the cash flow;
n is the total time of the project;
r is the discount rate;
C_t is the net cash flow (the amount of cash) at time t;
C_0 is the capital outlay at the beginning of the investment time ($t = 0$).

Net profit/income ratio

The key measure of operational performance, showing the amount of profit generated from sales in percentage terms. There are many variations of this ratio but the key ratio is usually presented Profit before Interest and Tax (PBIT) divided by Sales Revenue expressed as a percentage.

$$\text{Net profit ratio} = \text{PBIT} \div \text{Sales} \times 100$$
$$\text{e.g. } \$16{,}875 \div 135{,}000 = 14.22\%$$

This ratio reflects performance after all expenses have been taken into account including prime costs/cost of sale and other expenses such as wages and salaries, overheads, insurance. It excludes interest and taxation as these are arguably not within managerial control and are the result of financial and treasury decisions. This ratio is also known as net income to revenue ratio and net operating margin. This ratio forms a key part of the return on capital employed (see ROI – Return on investment) and combines with asset turnover to deliver overall company performance.

Night audit

During the night audit, financial activities are used to review and check the accuracy and reliability of the hotel's front office financial transactions. The night audit occurs during the last shift that begins at night and ends in the early morning, called the grave yard shift. A special desk clerk called the night auditor performs the night audit.

The night audit function can be described in a series of steps that encompass the night audit. The basic steps of the night audit are as follows:

- Complete outstanding posting and reconcile front desk discrepancies.
- Reconcile departmental activities.
- Verify room rates and post-room and tax.
- Prepare cash receipts for deposit.
- End the day by clearing out the day's activities and backing up the system.
- Prepare the night audit reports.

One report in particular, called the Manager's Daily Report or just the Daily, is a snapshot or financial picture all hotel revenue and operation for the previous day.

No-show

This refers to people who have made a reservation with the hotel but fail to show up on the day of arrival or have not cancelled the reservation. No-shows create a problem for the hotel in that it makes it difficult for them to maximize their occupancy. It represents a loss of revenue for the hotel. However, guests who have guaranteed their reservation (either by paying a deposit or giving credit card information) and failed to show up on the day of arrival will be charged for the first night of the reservation. Most hotels calculate the percentage of no-shows to help make decisions on when (or if) to sell rooms to walk-in guests particularly in busy periods. Various types of travelers – corporate, group, or pleasure – have varying no-show rates.

Non-controllable expenses

Costs that cannot be changed in the short term. Some fixed costs are considered non-controllable since management staff is not able to effect change in them during the short term. Conversely all non-controllable expenses are fixed costs. Examples of non-controllable expenses in restaurants and foodservice enterprises include rent, mortgage interest, depreciation and amortization, insurance, license fees, legal and accounting fees, and taxes. Although these amounts may change over time, the management staff of a foodservice operation usually is not responsible for negotiating new rates or making changes to these numbers; hence, they are considered non-controllable. Non-controllable expenses may include direct and indirect expenses.

Nouvelle cuisine

A French term meaning 'new cookery' which is a culinary movement that owed its momentum to two food critics, Gault and Millau, in the early 1970s. Practitioners of nouvelle cuisine revised much of the classical food preparation methods by doing away with complicated preparations, overly rich sauces which masked the true flavor of food, rigid recipe formulae, and pretentious and elaborate rituals and service arrangements.

To counter the rigidity and obsolescence of some of classical cuisine's repertoire and to counter an increasing use of processed foods, nouvelle practitioners embraced authenticity and simplicity in preparation and cooking methods; freshness of ingredients; lightness and use of natural flavors; greatly reduced use of fat; doing away with flour-based sauces; use of rapid cooking methods, natural flavorings, grilling, steaming, and slow cooking; doing away with elaborate garnishing; and use of natural juices, stocks, and essences to make sauces.

Oo

Occupancy costs

All the costs of occupying a physical area. For many foodservice establishments, the most significant cost is rent. If a foodservice operation owns its own facility, however, these costs include property taxes, mortgage expenses, and property insurance expenses. In the USA, the average occupancy costs are 4–10 per cent of total revenues. According to Deloitte & Touche – a large international consulting and financial advisory firms – each of the following should be categorized under occupancy costs on the income statement:

- Rent (including leases of land, buildings, and equipment)
- Property taxes and property insurance (prorated accordingly if paid in lump sums)
- Real estate taxes (including those assessed by a state, county, or city government)
- Personal property taxes (such as those payable by the restaurant operator)
- Other municipal taxes (such as charges for use of sewers)
- Insurance on building and contents (including insurance against damage or destruction)

Occupancy management formula

The goal of a hotel's management is to achieve 100 per cent occupancy. Management achieves this by monitoring the occupancy of the hotel for each date by using the occupancy management formula. The occupancy management formula includes confirmed reservations, guaranteed reservations, no-show factor for these two types of reservations, predicted stayovers, predicted understays, and predicted walk-ins to determine the number of additional room reservations need to achieve 100 percent occupancy. The total number of rooms available: minus the confirmed reservation times the no-show factor; minus guaranteed reservations times the no-show factor; minus predicted stayovers; plus predicted understays; minus predicted walk-ins is equal to the number of additional room reservations needed to achieve 100 percent occupancy.

Occupancy percentage

Computed daily, occupancy percentage is the number of hotel rooms sold divided by the number of rooms available multiplied by 100. Occupancy percentage historically revealed the success of a hotel's staff in attracting guests to a hotel. Investors have utilize occupancy percentage to determine the potential gross income of a hotel by multiplying the occupancy percentage times the number of available hotel rooms times the average daily rate which provides revenue per day. Variations might occur on a daily basis and this must be factored into any weekly, monthly, and annual projection of gross revenue from room sales. A variation is the multiple occupancy percentage, which determines the average number of guests per room sold or occupied. This ratio is particularly useful in forecasting food and beverage revenue and operating requirements such as the clean linen requirements. The multiple occupancy percent is calculated by determining the number of rooms occupied by more than one guest divided by the number of rooms occupied.

Occupancy, types of

Occupancy of a hotel is comprised of walk-ins, reservations, stayovers, understays, and no-show reservations. The objective of the hotel's management is to attain 100 percent occupancy. Careful monitoring and tracking of the types of occupancy permits hotel management to more accurately predict occupancy and effectively use management tools such as the occupancy management formula. The front office manager can obtain the data for this formula by reviewing the property management system reservation module, which lists the groups, corporate clients, and individual guests who have made reservations for a specific time period. Also, the front office manager can check the tourism activity in the area, business events planned in other hotels, and other special events happening locally.

Occupational Safety and Health

The discipline concerned with protecting employees from harm while on the job. All industrialized countries have statues and regulations aimed to protect the health and safety of working people. For example, in the USA, the US Congress in 1970 passed the Occupational and Safety Health Act to ensure worker and workplace safety. Their goal was to make sure employers provide their workers a place of employment free from recognized hazards to safety and health, such as exposure to toxic chemicals, excessive noise levels, mechanical dangers, heat or cold stress, or unsanitary conditions. In Australia and other countries of British heritage most occupational health and safety legislation has incorporated elements drawn from the common law of 'torts' that all persons owe a duty of care to others requiring employers to implement and maintain a safe working environment for employees and others.

Occupational Safety and Health Act

The US Occupational Safety and Health Act (OSHA), Code of Federal Regulations (CFR), 29 part 1900, was passed into law by the US Federal government in 1970. Its purpose is to promote worker safety and health in the USA by regulating workplace conditions and training requirements.

The act includes numerous regulations that employers and employees are required to follow. The Federal program instituted the formation of OSHA (Occupational Safety and Health Administration), which is charged with overseeing employer compliance to current OSHA regulations, the issuance of citations for employer failures to comply, monitoring the occurrence of workplace accidents for the purpose of identifying opportunities for new regulations, and providing advice, guidance, and training for employers on how to provide a safe work environment. OSHA enforces its standards through a program of compliance officer inspections. These officers will visit an employer for one of the three following reasons: (1) accidents involving fatalities or the hospitalization of three or more employees; (2) employee complaints about workplace conditions; and (3) an ongoing program of inspecting various industries.

Off-premise contact

Off-premise contacts (OPC) or 'outside property contacts' are terms used to describe those whose job it is to invite potential resort owners to visit the timeshare resort. These employees use selling techniques in order to get potential buyers to purchase vacation ownerships. Typically, these are agents employed to generate potential sales leads from specified target groups. The OPC with potential owners is chiefly concerned with generating visitors to tour the resort with the aim of generating sales of timeshare slots. The resort pays the OPC a commission for each qualified prospect making a tour of the property.

On change status

The status of a hotel room which indicates that the room is dirty and needs to be cleaned by the housekeeping staff. At check-out along with settling the guest account, the front desk agent must change the status of the guest-room from occupied to on change, or a room from which the guest has checked out but is not ready for the next arrival or is ready for cleaning, and notify the housekeeping department of the departure. With an integrated property management system, departure notification may be forwarded to housekeeping automatically. Because the room is not available until housekeeping is finished with it, the on change status is typically for a short of a time as possible. Thus, an effective interaction between the front office and housekeeping is critical. Housekeeping and the front office must inform each other of changes in a room's status.

On-line booking

The revolutionary development of the Internet in the past 15 years has meant a paradigm shift in the way central reservations are regarded. Prior to that, it was assumed that the wave of the future was to have ever larger central reservation networks. The largest companies controlled access to the inventory. The Internet has meant that the smallest bed and breakfast operation can now have a global presence alongside the largest names in the industry. For the larger operators it has meant a reduced cost for customers trying to access their central reservation system. The growth in Internet bookings (particularly in the USA where estimates quote increases from US$276 million in 1996 to US$8.9 billion in 2002), is due to a number of issues: more people on-line; secure transaction systems for payment on the Internet; and increased competition between on-line travel sites. Airline reservations are the most common travel arrangements made online by either business travelers or their administrative assistants.

On-site foodservice

Sometimes referred to as contract catering or non-commercial foodservice, on-site foodservice comprises food outlets in business and industry, schools, universities and colleges, hospitals, skilled-nursing centers, eldercare centers, correctional facilities, recreational facilities such as stadiums and national parks, and childcare centers. Today, the on-site segment represents some $230 billion in global revenue. Its complexity is evident in the sophistication of board plans offered by many colleges, and its similarity to traditional foodservice outlets is apparent in cafes found commonly in the corporate headquarters of companies such as Motorola and Microsoft. The high quality of food and service found in leading healthcare institutions, where foodservice often includes 24-hour room service, contradicts the outdated perception of bland, and boring dishes. Indeed, the streamlined production systems, progressive management development programs, and aggressive brand management approaches used by many managed service companies to whom many firms outsource their on-site needs, underscore the evolution of on-site foodservice and its growing presence in the foodservice industry.

Operating cash flow

The cash flow resulting from a firm's day-to-day operation activities of production and sales. Before-tax operating cash flow, often referred to as earnings before interests, taxes, depreciation, and amortization (EBITDA) by financial analysts, is an important measure of the operating performance of a hospitality firm. In particular, since the management has no control over a hospitality firm's fixed charges and financing costs, EBITDA is an appropriate performance measure for hospitality management. After-tax operating cash flow can be calculated as:

$$\text{Operating cash flow} = \text{Earnings before interests and taxes} + \text{Depreciation and amortization} - \text{Taxes}$$

Operating cash flow is an important concept in hospitality financial management because it shows whether a hospitality firm is generating enough cash flows from its business operations to cover its cash outflows. A negative operating cash flow often signals trouble for the hospitality firm.

Operating leverage

The extent to which costs are fixed within a firm's operations. A hospitality firm with higher percentage of fixed costs is said to have a higher degree of operating leverage (DOL). Operating leverage may also be perceived as the responsiveness of a hospitality firm's earnings before interests and taxes (EBIT), and hence its return on equity (ROE), to fluctuations in firm sales. The DOL is defined as the percentage change in a firm's EBIT resulting from a given percentage change in its sales.

$$\text{DOL} = \frac{\text{Percentage change in EBIT}}{\text{Percentage change in sales}}$$

The higher a hospitality firm's DOL, the greater the fluctuation in its EBIT as a result of changes in its sales. All else remaining equal, the higher a hospitality firm's operating leverage, the greater the firm's business risks.

Operating ratios

Ratios calculated from a set of accounts, which throw light on the profit making activities of a hospitality firm for a period of time. They are utilized to evaluate the success of the various departments of a hospitality firm and are compared against proper standards such as budgeted percentages. Any significant difference between actual and budgeted labor cost percentages must be carefully investigated, since payroll and related expenses represent the largest single expense category. In addition, operating ratios are compared against corresponding historical ratios and industry averages. A key to operating ration that measures success in the lodging industry is ratio analysis. Ratio analysis is a mathematical expression of a relationship between two numbers. It is useful because: it determines the lodging enterprises ability to meet its short-term obligations; it determines the lodging enterprises ability to generate profits, and it determines the lodging enterprises ability to meet its long-term obligations. To be useful, a ratio must be compared against some standard of which there are typically four: comparison with a past period; comparison with an industry average; comparison with a budgeted ratio; and comparison with similar and close competitors.

Operating system

A set of software products that jointly control system resources and the multitude of processes which use these resources on a computer system. In simpler terms this is a computer's primary software program that controls all its basic operations. It may provide scheduling, debugging, input/output control, system accounting, compilation, storage assignment, data management, and related services. Most popular operating systems, generally, as in hospitality, today are Windows Unix and Linux. Operating system software is consisted from three levels of services: kernel, library, and application-level services. The roles of operating systems include hiding details of hardware by creating abstractions, managing resources, and providing a pleasant user interface. Resources enable the execution of fundamental computer functions: storing programs in computer memory, executing instructions, accepting data, and presenting results.

Organization structure and design

If organizations are to successfully implement their chosen strategy, it is essential that they devise an appropriate organization structure and design. The appropriateness of any organization structure and design is dependent upon a number of key factors: the chosen strategy, the nature of the external environment, and the organizational culture. Organization design addresses three key elements: the degree of centralization versus devolution, organizational configurations, and resource allocation and control processes.

Structural options include 'the simple structure', 'the functional structure' (or 'unitary (U) form'), 'the multidivisional structure' (or 'M-form'). The most complex organizational structure is the 'matrix structure' which is essentially a combination of structures such as product and geographical divisions or functional and divisional structures. Furthermore, organizational structure is often reflected in the 'informal' structure that refers to the power, control, influence, and knowledge flow that are not officially recognized by the members of the organization, particularly top management.

Organization Timeshare Europe

The official trade body representing the timeshare industry within Europe. Some of Europe's operators also term this sector as 'resort ownership', 'vacation ownership', or 'holiday ownership'. In principle all these terms refer to timeshare arrangements, but are attempting to find alternative to the somewhat negative image of timeshare. The Organization Timeshare Europe (OTE) was formed in 1998 as the result of pooling the resources of the various national trade bodies throughout Europe. OTE's purpose is to support the pace and quality of growth of the sector. It promotes best practice across the industry and aims to raise a positive profile of timeshare organizations with customers and communities within which operations take place. The OTE has a major lobbying role with the European Union and undertakes pan-European research for the industry.

Organizational climate

Organizational culture is sometimes measured by organizational climate. Climate is the employee's perception of the atmosphere of the internal environment. Organizational climate is important because the employee's perception of the organization's services is the basis for the development of their attitudes toward it. Their attitudes in turn affect their behavior. Climate is concerned with the entire organization and all major subunits within it. Morale is an important part of organizational climate. Morale is a state of mind based on attitudes and satisfaction with the organization and can be affected by:

- *Structure*: The degree of constraint on members, that is, the number of rules, regulations, and procedures.
- *Responsibility*: The degree of control over one's own job.
- *Rewards*: The degree of being rewarded for one's efforts and being punished appropriately.
- *Warmth*: The degree of satisfaction with human relations.
- *Support*: The degree of being helped by others and cooperation.
- *Organizational identity and loyalty*:The degree to which employees identify with the organization and their loyalty to it.
- *Risk*: The degree to which risk taking is encouraged.

Organizational culture

Organizational culture consists of intangible attributes of an organization such as attitudes, values, beliefs, norms, and customs. Organizational culture is exhibited in the style and character and reflected in the way things are done by employees of that organization. It includes the following dimensions:

- *Observed behavioral regularities* when people interact, such as organizational rituals and ceremonies and the language commonly used.
- *The norms* shared by working groups throughout the organization, such as 'Ladies and Gentlemen serving Ladies and Gentlemen', from Ritz-Carlton.
- *The dominant values* held by an organization such as 'service quality' or 'price leadership'.
- *The philosophy* that guides and organization's policy toward employees and customers.
- *The rules* of the game for getting along in the organization, or the 'ropes' that a newcomer must learn in order to become an accepted member.
- *The feeling or climate* conveyed in an organization by the physical layout under way in which its members interact with customers or other outsiders.

No dimension by itself represents the culture of the organization. Taken together, however, they reflect and give meaning to the concept of organizational culture.

Organizational structures, types of

Structure is important in all organizations including hospitality organizations because it reduces ambiguity and clarifies task and role expectations. It also has an undeniable impact on the attitudes and behavior of organizational members and thus productivity. The structure of individual firms varies; some are simple with only a few levels of hierarchy. These are commonly known as 'flat' organizations. Others are more complex and have a 'taller' structure with many hierarchical levels. Additionally, some hybrid organizations display characteristics of both extremes. Flat structures are also sometimes known as 'organic' and are said to have improved communication, imperceptible chain of command, and extensive delegation of responsibility. These organizations often perform better in dynamic business environments because they respond quickly to these trading shifts. The hospitality industry tends to be dominated by this type of small-to medium-sized organization. On the other hand, larger taller organizations have the opposite characteristics. This type is also known as a 'mechanistic' structure. The chain of command is clear, managerial decision-making tends to be slower and there is limited employee empowerment (or delegation of responsibility).

Outsourcing

Outsourcing takes place when a business appoints a third party to carry out functions that were previously performed within the firm. The boundaries are blurred between outsourcing, subcontracting, working with a partner, even with simply purchasing. The principal distinction is that outsourcing implies transfer of ownership of that process.

Hospitality organizations often outsource their legal, finance, and marketing functions as well as use a certain degree of outsourcing for housekeeping, catering, and procurement. This allows them to fluctuate resources according to demand and to hire skills for as long as they are required. Outsourcing allows the firm to build skills quickly, often to catch up or overtake the competition. The hotel industry makes great use of outsourcing on the supply side – hotel management companies depend on the willingness of hotel owners to outsource the management of their hotels to them. Outsourcing of business processes such as laundry services, security services, and limousine services has become more common. A number of facilities services are commonly outsourced. These include landscape care, snow removal, window washing, pest control, elevator maintenance, and many capital project activities. Some reasons for outsourcing of these services involve cost, equipment, special skills, and licensing.

Overbooking

A situation where the hotel has accepted more reservations than there are rooms available. Hotels practice overbooking to overcome the changeable number of arrivals that may occur on any given day due to no-shows, cancellations, and understays. One of the front desk goals is to achieve as high an occupancy rate as possible and practicing overbooking is a way to try to achieve this. Care has to be taken however, to make sure that one does not end up having to turn away ('walk') a guest as this creates poor guest relations and is not good for repeat business. The financial loss due to no-shows can be substantial. In a hotel that typically has 100 confirmed reservations (not guaranteed with a credit card) and experiences a 5 per cent no-show rate, five rooms per night would remain unsold. With an average room rate of $70, these five rooms would cost the hotel $350 in revenue or $127,750 in a year.

Overstay

This refers to guests who stay in the hotel beyond the date of departure that they had originally indicated. Overstays need to be carefully monitored by the front desk as the rooms may be pre-blocked for other expected guests. A way of trying to avoid this problem is by verifying at check-in when the actual departure date of the guest is. In the modern hotel is not uncommon for the guest to initial the departure date on the registration paperwork to confirm the number of nights for which the lodging is required. Minimizing this is critical when a hotel in near full occupancy, however, overstays can represent extra revenue for the hotel when it is not operating at full occupancy. Electronic locking systems provide the front office with another tool to prevent overstays in that the key can be programmed with the number of nights the guest has access to the room.

Overtrading

Revenue expansion without sufficient working capital can easily overstretch the financial resources of the business. This position is called overtrading and is a common feature of growth businesses that fail, not because of insufficient product profitability, but due to insufficient liquidity to purchase current assets such as inventories. The *working capital ratio* measures the relationship between working capital and sales as a percentage.

$$\text{Working capital ratio} = \frac{\text{Inventory} + \text{Receivables} - \text{Payables}}{\text{Sales}} \times 100$$

The faster a company expands in terms of investment, the more working capital it will require. Therefore, a company that borrows long-term and invests in short-term assets such as cash and stocks is creating liquidity for the business that can create a buffer against risk in times of financial distress. Similarly using cash to purchase long-term assets will reduce the liquidity of the business and other forms of longer-term financing should be considered such as equity, loans, or leasing.

Pp

Pay and benefits

Pay is simply the consideration arising from a contract of employment (as opposed to a contract for services associated with subcontracting) to give somebody a particular amount of money for work done for goods or services provided. Benefits are similarly defined as a regular payment made to somebody qualified to receive it. Total pay and benefits are also known collectively as a 'remuneration compensation package' and this includes wage and non-wage payments such as bonuses and fringe benefits such as health insurance, pension fund, sickness benefits, etc. Both definitions are understandably similar and draw attention to a number of key issues. First, there is a suggestion of equity or a fair exchange of something for something else with each outcome having benefit for both parties (money and goods and services provided); second, a notion of 'worth' attached to qualifications.

PBX

An abbreviation for private branch exchange. A PBX is a telephone system within an enterprise that switches calls between enterprise users on local lines while allowing all users to share a certain number of external phone lines. The main purpose of a PBX is to save the cost of requiring a line for each user to the telephone company's central office.

The PBX is owned and operated by the enterprise rather than the telephone company (which may be a supplier or service provider). Private branch exchanges used analog technology originally. A PBX includes telephone trunk (multiple phone) lines that terminate at the PBX; a computer with memory that manages the switching of the calls within the PBX and in and out of it; the network of lines within the PBX; usually a console or switchboard for a human operator.

Perceived risk

The extent of possible consequences versus uncertainty or likelihood that it will occur and is part of the decision-making process in purchasing a product or a service. Perceived risk is classified into four categories: (1) financial, (2) performance, (3) physical, and (4) social/psychological. Before purchasing the product, the customer will often consider the risk or likelihood of any negative impact buying the product will produce and compare this to the benefit expected. Generally, effective marketing and advertising can reduce the perceived risk and uncertainty of a customer.

However, a customer will perceive or believe what the risk will be based upon many other factors, including sociological and psychological reasons. Often the perceived risk is greater when it comes to purchasing a service rather than a product due to the intangible characteristics of a service.

Perceptual mapping

An easy way to illustrate how competing products are rated, relative to each other, is by generating a perceptual map, using multi-dimensional scaling (MDS) techniques. This technique is most appropriately used for two types of research questions. First, MDS and perceptual mapping can help us identify previously unrecognized issues or attributes of a product or service that lead to customer behaviors. Second, MDS and perceptual mapping can help compare how a product performs against a competitors' products. It can also help to identify which combination of features and/or benefits are most preferred by one's customers. The end result of the analysis – the perceptual map – provides a graphic illustration of how the competitors or options compare against each other. The technique is often used in marketing to understand how one's product is positioned against the competition. It is particularly useful to reposition a product to a new target market.

Performance evaluation

The process by which employees receive formal feedback on their job performance. Conducted by the employee's immediate supervisor, they are typically held within the first three to six months of employment (particularly if a probationary period has been established), and thereafter on an annual basis. Performance criteria, on which the evaluation is ideally based, are often included as part of the employee's job description or communicated as part of the employee's initial orientation. Such criteria can include both outcome measures (e.g. sales, costs, customer satisfaction ratings) and process measures (e.g. effective team player). In completing this form, the supervisor may rely on his or her own observations, solicit input from others with whom the employee interacts (e.g. peers, subordinates, customers), and/or draw on operational data.

Performance indicators

Indicators that measure the efficiency and effectiveness of an employee's work. Managers and employees at all levels in the hospitality industry need to have a clear view of work-related objectives/goals. These objectives/goals are assessed and wherever possible measured as outputs or performance using performance indicators as a tool for appraisal. Performance reviews, assessments, evaluations, ratings, and appraisals are all terms that refer to the task of assessing the progress of workforce. Performance indicators serve similar purpose such as:

- To assess the quality of job performance.
- To provide feedback to employees regarding job performance.
- To plan future performance goals and objectives.
- To establish a better knowledge of the employee so as to understand what motivates him or her.

Performance indicators seek to establish objective measures against which such behaviors may be assessed.

Performance measurement

Performance measurement is utilized for different reasons: to monitor activities in business units and through time, for diagnosing problems and taking corrective action, to facilitate continuous improvement in key areas, and to promote behavior in ways that would help sustain competitive advantage. Overall, performance measurement is considered to be an integral part of the management processes to identify the poor performing areas or opportunities so that better plans can be developed. Traditionally, performance measures were mainly financial, profit, return on investment, residual income figures, and their ratios are the most commonly used indicators both in manufacturing and the hospitality industry.

Performance measures in foodservice/restaurants

A periodic analysis of a restaurant's financial performance is vital to effective management. Such an examination may uncover undesirable trends or indicate serious issues underlying the data. Moreover, analyzing key performance measures allows operators to gauge a given restaurant's operational health over time and against that of other similarly positioned units. Variance analysis for each income statement line item is a good starting point; also, sales per seat (for a given period) and daily seat turnover (customers ÷ seats ÷ days in the year) are key indicators. Gross profit per seat and net profit per seat are also useful. Other macro measures include RevPASH (revenue per available seat hour) and average check. Finally, productivity analysis is among the best performance measures when it includes multiple input and output variables. Critical inputs include major expense categories and constraint factors (e.g. number of seats), while necessary outputs include revenue, profit, and – where appropriate – guest satisfaction.

Permission marketing

The term 'permission marketing' (also referred to as 'permission-based marketing' or 'opt-in marketing') describes marketing actions taken with the express consent of the customer, for example through the use of e-mails. The customer's permission increases the likelihood both that the e-mail will actually reach the customer (and not, e.g. be eliminated by a spam filter) and, because message content reflects interests expressed by the customer (e.g. in a customer profile previously established), will ultimately result in a sale. Thus, permission marketing can be described as a method which addresses both legal (e.g. privacy) issues and marketing criteria. Permission marketing can be described as marketing which is driven by customer 'pull' rather than by company 'push'. Although permission marketing can apply to direct ('snail') mail and telemarketing, its primary use is in internet-based marketing.

Perpetual inventory

A survey or record of an operator's goods and supplies in stock that is ongoing and kept continually up to date. It can be tracked manually or with a computerized inventory management system. With a manual system, a bin card, which is placed on the front of the shelf, contains the name of the item, how it is packaged, and, the item number. As items are removed from inventory and inventory is depleted, the date, the number of the item, and initials are recorded on the bin card. The final column on the bin card keeps a running total of the items as they are issued for use or are replenished. When using a computerized inventory management system, as stock is received the items and their quantities are entered into the system. As items are sold, the quantities of each item are automatically subtracted from the amount in storage.

Personal selling principles

A set of eight principles that professional sales representatives (sales reps) follow which guide their actions:

1. *Prospecting and qualifying*: This step includes the work done to uncover potential customers (*prospecting*) who may have the need and the ability to enter a contract and to pay for the product or service (*qualifying*) that the sales rep offers.
2. *Pre-approach*: The pre-approach requires the sales rep to gather as much information about the customer, including the 'decision-maker' in the household or firm, before setting up a meeting with the customer.

3. *Approach*: The approach step occurs when the initial contact is made with the customer.
4. *Presentation/demonstration*: This step occurs when the sales rep meets with the customer to present the actual product.
5. *Negotiation*: The negotiation step occurs once a formal proposal is made. Most sales involve some discussion or alteration to the original proposal.
6. *Overcoming objections*: The customer often raises objections or questions during the approach, presentation/demonstration, or negotiation phases of a sale. The experienced sales rep will use a variety of techniques to undercover, and then overcome or address, each objection.
7. *Closing*: A typical proposal for services is 'closed' when the customer says 'yes' and signs the proposal, thereby creating a contract.
8. *Follow-up/account maintenance*: Truly professional sales reps know that it is important to follow-up with the customer shortly after the sale is completed, both to address any lingering doubts or 'buyer's remorse' that the customer may experience as well as to uncover any misunderstandings.

Personalization

A term related to several different approaches toward increasing customer loyalty through understanding needs or goals of each individual customer. This helps to find, design or obtain the perception of services or products that efficiently and with knowledge address these needs and goals. Personalization is supported through different customer interfaces: the Internet, brick and mortar, call centers, and various voice/telephony services using automatic speech recognition and text to speech or dual-tone multi-frequency. The goals of personalization are: to make a website easier to use, increase sales, create a one-to-one experience, improve customer service, save customers' time, increase customer loyalty, attract a broader audience, achieve cost savings, target advertising, and build a community. Personalization is user or system initiated and can facilitate the work (enabling access to information content, accommodating work goals and individual differences) or address social requirements (eliciting an emotional response and expressing identity).

Persuasion

The deliberate effort to change the attitudes of one or more people. Attitudes are evaluations of people, objects, or ideas. Attitudes are important to hospitality marketers because marketers assume that consumer attitudes affect consumer behaviors. Thus, marketers design advertising and promotional campaigns to change consumers' attitudes toward their product and service offerings in the hope that the altered attitudes will result in greater sales and profits. When trying to change attitudes, marketers typically rely on either a hard sell or a soft sell to persuade consumers. Hard selling pursues a *central route to persuasion*. Central route persuasion occurs when a consumer thinks carefully about the information intended to change his or her attitude, and is then persuaded because of the strengths of the arguments. Soft selling pursues a *peripheral route to persuasion*. Peripheral route persuasion occurs when consumers are persuaded as a result of superficial cues in the persuasive message.

Petty cash fund

A limited amount of cash that is kept on hand at the place of business to use for small purchases. The fund is usually established to cover small purchases incurred over a short-time period (a week or two). Initially, a specific, limited amount (e.g. $200) of funds are removed from the operation's bank account and kept at the establishment. Over the course of the short-time period, funds may be removed from petty cash to purchase small items and the receipts are kept when money is removed from the fund. At the end of the time period, a manager or bookkeeper collects the receipts and replenishes the missing cash from the fund using money from the bank account. The receipts are used to adjust cost of goods sold (COGS) and other balance sheet accounts appropriately before the next cycle begins. A given amount (e.g. $200) should remain in the fund at all times (cash + receipts).

PGA of America

Founded in 1916 and with more than 27,000 members across 41 geographic sections, the PGA (Professional Golfers' Association) of America claims the title as the world's largest working sports organization. The PGA of America, with headquarters in Palm Beach Gardens, Florida (not to be confused with the PGA tour – an organization comprised of golfers who compete in golf tournaments professionally) conducts four major golf events including the Ryder Cup Matches, the PGA Championship, the Senior PGA Championship, and the PGA Grand Slam of Golf. The PGA of America conducts scores of programs to promote golf to people of all skill levels and backgrounds at its PGA Golf Club in Florida and across the USA. PGA Professionals, who comprise the association's membership, work in the golf industry providing golf instruction, retail, and facility management.

Physical inventory

A physical inventory involves the manual counting of each item in stock on a regular basis. For accounting purposes, an inventory is usually conducted at the end of each calendar month or, if using the period system, at the end of each four-week period. The ending inventory numbers are then used to calculate the cost of goods sold on an income statement; these calculations are then used for related processes such as inventory-turnover analysis. Some operators take inventory on a weekly basis and may even count high-cost or very select items on a daily basis. Inventory sheets are most effective when organized by storage area, that is freezer, walk-in refrigerator, etc. Many operations use a computer software program that calculates the value of the ending inventory after the purchase unit counts have been entered into the system. To be accurate, unit costs must be updated in the computer with each change in price from the supplier.

Plate service and silver service

Plate service is a type of service in which the food is plated in the kitchen and served to the guest on the plate. This is often referred to as 'American' service or Service L'assiette. For silver service the food is first presented on serving dishes, which may or may not be silver nowadays, to the guest and is then portioned and transferred from a serving dish onto the plate in front of the guest by using a service spoon and fork, which is commonly referred to as the service gear. This style is also known as 'Russian' service if the portioning is performed by the food server or 'English' service if the maitre d'hotel assists. Often, however, a combination of the two techniques can be used. The main food item, for example meat, can be portioned onto a plate in the kitchen and served using the plate service method and the accompaniment can then be served at the table using the silver service technique.

Pluralism and unitarism

In hospitality, unitarism refers to the concept of the hospitality organization as one entity, with 'everyone serving the customer' is common. Similarly, sections in texts on human resource management sometimes treat the hospitality workface as a homogenous entity, without recognition of the diversity of needs and wants of the individual or the organization culture of the workgroup. Pluralism is a pragmatic, effective alternative to the unitarist approach. The approach sees conflicts of interest and disagreements between managers and workers, and workgroups with each other, as normal and inescapable. Realistic managers accept that conflict will occur and that a greater propensity for conflict exists rather than a harmonious organizational situation (unitary perspective); and anticipate and resolve these conflicts by securing agreed procedures for settling disputes.

There are two additional perspectives which are pluralist in nature. The first is known as 'interactionist' and the second, 'radical pluralist'. Interactionists recognize conflict but view

210

it as inevitable and potentially beneficial because changes will result. Radical pluralists view organizations chiefly as political entities. As such, conflict is inevitable because of the never-ending struggle between management, workers and shareholders.

Point-of-purchase promotion

Also known as point-of-sale (P-O-S) advertising, point-of-purchase promotion (P-O-P) refers to promotional displays positioned in the distribution channel (usually at retail) where buyers actually purchase or make the decision to purchase a product or service. Common P-O-P displays are tabletop tent cards in restaurants, shelf 'talker' signs attached to store shelves to promote packaged goods, and cardboard cutouts of brand symbols or characters at end-of-aisle displays (see the table below for more P-O-P display examples). P-O-P displays can serve a number of purposes: to build store traffic, attract attention to a specific brand, advertise a brand, or cue recall of brand advertising the buyer may have seen elsewhere. Ultimately, though, the main goal of P-O-P displays, like that of most promotions, is to boost immediate sales. P-O-P examples include banners, brochures, counter displays, end-of aisle displays, floor-stand displays, grocery bag advertisements, grocery cart advertisements, magnets, neon beverage signs, P-O-P coupon checkout machines, shelf coupon dispensers, shelf talkers, tabletop tent cards, video consoles, wall posters, window clings, and window signage. P-O-P promotion has also found utility in recruiting line employees. Many foodservice operations, particularly in the quick service restaurants and fast-casual segments, use a variety of P-O-P materials to inform customers that job opening exist.

Point of sales terminal

A computerized replacement for a cash register that has the ability to record and track customer orders, process credit and debit cards, connect to other systems in a network, and manage inventory. In a point of sale (POS) system, a computerized cash register system replaces stand-alone cash registers. While a cash register performs the single purpose of reporting how much income is received, a POS system can report additional information such as profit, how much inventory is on the shelf, which products should be ordered, and how many individual menu items were sold for a specified period. POS systems can be used at any point where a sales transaction can occur such as a restaurant or a bar. Hotel integrated property management systems, feature electronic POS systems (EPOS), which are equipped with a cash register and can retain and communicate data. EPOS systems can be linked directly to the main hotel computer system and a transaction at the restaurant can instantly debited on the room bill. The hardware included in a

POS system usually includes computer terminals, cash drawers, barcode scanners, receipt printers (including remote location printers), touch-screen monitors, credit card readers, and pole displays. 211

Point spread and price point

According to this pricing strategy, companies prefer to maintain a certain point-spread distance above and below the competition. If the competitor above raises prices, then a hospitality firm may try to maintain the price distance by raising prices proportionately. Point-spread strategy is common across all segments of the hospitality industry. In the hotel industry, the price points vary geographically. Price points for major metropolitan companies differ from medium- and smaller-size cities. Similarly, price points for downtown properties vary from the rural and suburban properties. Various segments of the hotel industry try to identify the appropriate price points for their segment and try to match the pricing strategies. In the restaurant industry, some companies try to identify the price points that their customers do not like to cross. This phenomenon is common where buffet pricing or *prix fixe* is practiced. Customers resist price increases under those conditions and set 'price points.'

Points system

A system used in the timeshare industry that employs points as a unit of use measurement to value or define the rights of a timeshare owner to reserve accommodations in a timeshare resort or resorts. Points may also be used both as a unit of use measurement and as an expression of the percentage ownership interest in the timeshare plan owned by the owner. In a point system, points are assigned to each timeshare interest or accommodation based on such factors as accommodation type, location, and time of year. The timeshare owner purchases points in the system, or is assigned points based on the timeshare interest owned, which are then used to reserve and use the accommodations of the timeshare plan in accordance with the values assigned to the accommodations. The point system may be established to permit reservation and use of accommodation types different then the type purchased and for larger increments of time or for as little as a day.

Portal

A website or service that offers a broad array of resources and services, such as search engines, e-mail lists, and forums for a number of content providers who usually are located elsewhere and maintained by other parties. Portals vary according to their users and services: (1) public portals are generally available and bring together information from various sources (e.g. Yahoo);

(2) enterprise portals give employees access to organization-specific information and applications; (3) marketplace portals are trading platforms that connect sellers and buyers; and (4) specialized portals (e.g. www.visiteuropeancities.info) offer an access path to specific information and applications for travelers. In addition to fulfilling customers' actual needs, portals provide a platform for hospitality managers and other tourism organizations to bundle information from their websites in order to allow joint marketing initiatives.

Portion control

For each recipe produced in an operation, a precise serving size is included to ensure consistency in quality from those who are using the recipes. Portion control is used to regulate serving size and can be implemented by using the appropriate weighing and measuring tools. This can be accomplished for food portions through the use of scales to weigh, or scoops, ladles, and other volumetric measuring tools such as measuring cups or measuring spoons. Similarly for beverages, the use of measured pouring devices, jiggers, and shot glasses will help accomplish this outcome. Portion control ensures that each guest receives the same amount of product each time or that the amounts used in production will be consistent. In the short term, poor portion control may lead to increased cost of goods in cases where portion sizes exceed those specified in the standardized recipes.

Portion cost

The cost of goods purchased and consumed in preparing and delivering a given menu item to customers. It is determined through recipe costing, which is an extension of recipe standardization. Portion cost calculations are fundamental to all pricing activities. Operators calculate portion cost by summing the cost of each ingredient in a standardized recipe and dividing this by the number of portions that the recipe produces. For example, if the cost of a recipe's ingredients totals $120 and the recipe produces 80 portions, then the portion cost is $1.50. Factors that affect portion cost include improper portion control (overly large portions lower profit while portions that are insensitive to customer preferences diminish customer satisfaction) and shrinkage (employee theft or incompetence depletes ingredient stocks).

Positioning

A strategy aimed to separate a particular brand from its competitors by associating that brand with a particular set of customer needs. Positioning helps establish a product's or service's identity within the eyes of the purchaser. It is based on customer perception acknowledging that perception is reality. As a fundamental concept in marketing, it is intertwined with another basic marketing concept, differentiation. Differentiation is the creation of tangible or intangible differences between a company's product or service and its competition. Positioning is useful in three general instances. First, positioning is critical in establishing a new service or product image. A company must distinguish this new product from the services/products to which it will be compared. Second, positioning is important for maintaining and reinforcing an established image in the consumer's mind. Finally, positioning can be used to reposition a product/service in the consumer's mind. Repositioning is necessary when the current product/service position is no longer competitively sustainable or profitable.

Power

The capacity for one individual or group to exert influence over another and to produce results or outcomes consistent with the former's interests and objectives. Power is one of the key aspects of leadership. There are five types of power: *legitimate power*, where the individual's power comes from their position within the organizational hierarchy; *reward power*, when the individual has control over both tangible and intangible rewards; *coercive power*, the opposite of reward power, is where the leader has the power to punish for non-conformance or poor performance; *charismatic or referent power*, where power derives from the regard in which the leader is held by followers, and their desire to maintain a positive relationship with the leader; and finally, *expert power*, where the leader's power is a function of their specialist knowledge or experience.

Pre-convention meeting

Briefings that are usually held 24–48 hours in advance of the beginning of a meeting, to reconfirm and review meeting logistics and discuss the fine points and any last minute changes. The purpose of the pre-convention meeting is to meet and establish rapport with the entire facility team and to clear up any procedural questions. For small meetings, a brief meeting with the convention service manager and/or catering manager may be sufficient to go over room setups and other requirements. A larger meeting will require key staff from each department. Often official contractors and other suppliers are included as well. All function sheets, banquet event orders, and other instructions are reviewed in these meeting. The meeting format involves introductions of the meeting staff with the facility staff.

Precosting

Precosting or precontrol uses forecasts, standards, and budgets to predict cost activity so that appropriate steps can be taken to prevent losses. This term is used less often today than it was

214

25 years ago. It may also be referred to as 'precontrol' and it implies 'preplanning.' It takes a 'proactive' approach to cost control instead of a 'reactive' after-the-fact response. It also relates to planned production and scheduling. It relies on historical sales and production records as the basis for forecasting sales and production quantities. Thus, the primary concern with any related precosting activity is use of accurate data and quantitatively based forecasting information. Moreover, precosting is dependent on management's ability to ensure related production systems are in place and are maintained throughout the production process.

Pre/post-meeting tours

A program offered by a meeting organizer to provide for educational, recreational, and/or sightseeing tours in conjunction with a planned meeting or event. Many organizations offer their attendees the opportunity to explore the destination where they are holding a meeting by arranging pre- and post-meeting tours. Attendees can combine leisure travel with their business travel. The destination is happy to promote these programs because they mean additional room nights and revenues for the hospitality enterprises. Some organizations arrange their own tours while others may employ a tour company or destination management company that specializes in arranging tours. Tours are often priced on a per person basis with a minimum number required to make the program viable. Tours may last one day or several days. They may target families as a way to encourage attendees to bring their families with them to a meeting.

Prestige pricing

High-end resorts, tourism attractions, and fine dining restaurants usually adopt this pricing strategy. It is based on the belief that consumers associate high prices with high quality and low prices with low quality. Restaurants that maintain a large inventory of wines follow this strategy to reflect the image of the valuable and prestigious wine collection. This strategy has limited appeal and limited usage for many mid-price and low-end hospitality firms. High-end resorts, cruise lines, exclusive tour operators, etc. follow this strategy to offer additional psychological benefits of exclusivity.

Preventive maintenance

The process of checking, testing, making comparisons to performance standards, and replacing low-cost items with the objective of preventing premature device or facility component failures. At a minimum, preventive maintenance starts with the manufacturer's scheduled recommendations for device or component safety checks, efficiency testing, and the general wear–tear of devices and components. In addition, routine maintenance reports of repeated device failure and repairs may indicate required changes in the preventive maintenance schedule to minimize future failures. The automation of preventive maintenance provides the building management personnel with a powerful full featured preventive maintenance system. Such systems establish preventive maintenance performance frequencies including seasonal, specific calendar dates, high/low performance values, consideration for outages, and facility down days and weekends. Automation of the preventive maintenance function creates tasks and routines including a library of preventive maintenance procedures; conversion of job plan/job standard into preventive maintenance routine, seasonal activation of preventive maintenance work; fixed and float preventive maintenance reset capability; tasking on-demand; and preventive maintenance performance route definition.

Price bundling

Price bundling takes place when a hospitality/tourism company wraps several products with one price. It is most commonly noted in the tourism industry. For example, a tour operator may wrap travel, hotel accommodations, food, entertainment, and sightseeing services with one charge. By charging one set price for several bundled services, tour operators may gain economies of scale. Bundled services are also prevalent in the hotel industry. It is very common for high-end hotels to offer weekend packages to include lodging, dining, and entertainment in town. Similarly, even planners may prefer to offer bundled services to improve their revenues. From the customers' perspective, price bundling is an additional service at a reduced price. Bundled products minimize the search efforts for various sources of services. Typically, business travelers prefer bundled services to economize the search process.

Price customization

The practice of charging different prices on identical products to different people. Price customization is a technique used in yield management which is a system used in hotels, airlines, and restaurants to optimize revenues depending upon demand, competition, timing, and capacity. The process of yield management includes understanding and anticipating customer (guest) behavior by using price customization (multiple pricing) in order to maximize revenues. The key to multiple prices is that each price must represent a different product and that those who have a high reservation price will not be able to buy a lower priced product. An important aspect of price customization is how to keep those with high reservation prices from buying less expensive products. This occurs through what is known as fences. In choosing fences, it is important that 'the fence' makes sense to the consumer. That is, the customer must believe that the rate she/he is paying is based on his or her choices, not on greed by the firm. For instance, the consumer needs to think 'I need to pay more because having flexibility is more important than price.' Or, 'I am paying more because I cannot decide exactly what I want to do.'

Price discrimination

A pricing action may be judged as a case of price discrimination when a seller charges competing buyers different prices for 'commodities' of like grade and quality. Also named as segmented pricing or revenue management, discriminatory prices might be direct, or indirect in the form of allowances (e.g. payments for advertising or other services). Price discrimination is not illegal per se, and it is widely practiced as a profit-maximizing pricing approach. For differential pricing to be deemed discriminatory and illegal, it must substantially lessen competition in commerce or be intended to injure, destroy, or prevent competition among buyers. For example, airline passengers and hotel guests are likely to pay different prices for the same seat or hotel room as the customer right next to them. This revenue-managed approach to differential pricing is made possible because demand for a perishable, fixed-capacity inventory (seats on a plane or rooms in a hotel) is often time variable – typically, customers who buy closer to the use date (e.g. business travelers) are less price sensitive.

Price earnings ratio

A ratio intended to measure the relative value of a security based upon the current market conditions. It is calculated as follows:

$$\text{Price/Earnings} = \frac{\text{Current market price per share}}{\text{Earning per share}}$$

This ratio can be seen as the number of years that it would take, at the current share price and rate of earnings, for the earnings from the share to cover the price of the share, and is, therefore, in effect a capitalization factor. The ratio indicates how much an investor is prepared to pay for the business earnings and is one of the most common methods of share valuation. Typically, price earnings ratios for the hospitality firms tend to be lower than averages for other industry sectors reflecting the relative risk of the business, the stability of earnings, perceived earnings trend, and the perceived potential growth of the share price.

Primary and secondary electric power rates

Secondary electric power rates are power rates with electricity supplied at 480 V or less. That is, the meter is set on the customer's side of a transformer that is owned by the utility company. Most hotels use this type of power. Primary power customers take power from a utility meter that is in the line before the customer owned transformer. Primary power may be supplied at voltages in excess of 480 V and up to in excess of 13,400 V. The primary power customer pays a lower kilowatt hour rate than secondary power customers do, but primary customers must pay for the transformer or pay for a replacement if the existing one fails. Primary power can be a dramatic energy savings for hotels that can qualify for the rate; usually only very large full service properties, large convention centers, or resort properties. A majority of hotels are secondary power customers.

Prime costs

Prime costs are the most significant cost for any operation. In a foodservice operation, these costs include raw materials (food and beverage) and labor costs. The associated labor costs include labor payroll (salaried and hourly), payroll taxes, and employee benefits. In the USA, these costs typically constitute 50–70 per cent of total revenues. Managers generally spend more time trying to manage prime costs than any other costs because they comprise such a large portion of total costs. The majority of prime costs are variable, which means that managers have some ability to control their totals in the short term. The prime costs indicator is also used often in comparing restaurants within a given segment as a barometer of unit- and corporate-level managers' operational prowess. This measure also affords operators the latitude to trade labor efficiencies realized through the use of food ingredients requiring less handing (such par-cooked meats or shredded cheese) with increased food costs in their efforts to minimize overall prime costs.

Private Club Advisor

A monthly business newsletter, that produces timely information specific to the private club industry. The Private Club Advisor (PCA) has a circulation of 16,000 readers that comprise private club chief operating officers (general managers), club officers, private club owners, and club members. The foci of the PCA is to (a) update these club executives on trends and issues of great importance and (b) improving the transfer of information between policy makers (e.g. law makers, government officials, etcetera) and management so that these club managers can properly implement policies. The PCA plus is a bimonthly newsletter targeted toward top-level executive members of private clubs and specifically focuses on issues surrounding daily club operations.

Private club dining types

As the private club product evolved over time, the type of club service offerings changed in direct accordance to member wishes. In particular, one area of the private clubs industry that has witnessed the most dramatic change in member desires is that of foodservice operations. In particular, the type of dining facilities has evolved from a formal dining experience to that of an informal dining experience. This is not to say that all private club have disbanded a formal dining experience, instead the switch has been in offering both formal and informal dining experiences. It should be understood that this change in dining room ambiance has not necessarily mandated the alteration or construction of new facilities. To the contrary, this conversion process has typically been an exchange of the table dressings and altered member dress codes.

Private club industry

The private club industry has a very rich history of exclusive clubs that are designed to satisfy members' social, recreational, sports, political preference, professional, or other purposes. The richness of this history has been traced to clubs that catered to those of aristocratic backgrounds as noted in the 1700s and forward in clubs located in England and Scotland. To affirm this need for affiliation and recreation the combination of a club setting and golf has been traced by various authors to the Royal and Ancient Golf Club of St. Andrews, Scotland. Clearly this makes the private club industry one of the more established segments of the hospitality industry. According to a study conducted by the Club Managers Association of America (CMAA), there are over 14,000 private clubs located throughout the USA generating $11.322 billion each year. In addition, 302,000 people are on private club payrolls for an annual payroll of $4.4 billion.

Private club management to leadership model

A model developed at the 2004 Club Managers Association of American (CMAA) that attempts to compartmentalize the club leadership process via identifying general manager leadership skills. The model is divided into three distinct components of (a) operations, (b) asset management, and (c) club culture. The operation dimension is subdivided into the skill areas of: property management, human and professional resources, management, marketing, food and beverage operations, golf/sports and recreation management, accounting and financial management, building and facilities management, and knowledge of government and external influences. The asset dimension consists of financial management skills, physical plant management of assets, and human resource asset management. The final and culminating dimension is culture as comprised of vision, history, club tradition, and governance issues.

Private club merchandising

A comprehensive process that encompasses internal advertising, internal marketing, and the production of promotional materials with the intent being the provision of services that meets or exceeds membership needs. Examples can be found in the clubhouse via menu construction that offers a wide array of food and beverage items that appeal to a vast array of member palates. Perhaps the most prominent area of the club in which merchandising is the most pronounced is that of the pro-shop. The products in the pro-shop should indicate distinction that is sought by the membership via brand name or signature clothing and equipment. Furthermore, the pro-shop further follows tried and true merchandising rules by use of adequate lighting, layout design of the merchandise, use of indirect lighting, spot lighting, and diffused lighting for visual enhancements of products on display.

Private club overtime tax exemption

In the USA, overtime tax exemption for private clubs represents an exemption offered by the Internal Revenue Service relative to commissioned based wage earners. As with lodging and restaurant operations, taxation issues are a constant concern to the operator and the employee. Such is the case with overtime taxes seeing that this can be very costly to the private club and viewed by the employee as a negative because the income tax ramifications often offset the desire to work overtime. According to the US Department of Labor Fact Sheet No. 20 the following three conditions, if satisfied, would qualify the private club (employer) for overtime exemption: (a) the employee is employed by the private club; (b) the employee's rate of pay exceeds one an one-half that applicable minimum wage for every hour worked in the assigned work week; and (c) more than half of the employee's total earnings consists of commissions.

Private equity club committee types

There are two basic types of committees found within a private club; first is the standing committee and second is the ad-hoc committee. A standing committee indicates a permanent committee structure that deals with routine operations. Examples of standing committees include the: athletic committee, bylaw committee, entertainment committee, executive committee, finance and budget committee, golf course committee, house committee, membership committee, nominating committee, and strategic planning committee. An ad-hoc committee is a temporary committee that is established for the sole purpose of dealing with a pressing issue on a one-time basis. A good example of a one-time issue would be the renovation of the clubhouse. In general, the guidelines surrounding committee structure are: (a) membership is limited to a specific number (commonly an odd number) to promote discussion and resolution of issues; (b) committees set policy relative to a specific function (e.g. membership, clubhouse policies, golf, etcetera); (c) committees directly advise the board of directors; and (d) committees communicate and seek advice from club management so that pertinent issues are addressed and acted upon by the committee.

Private Residence Club

A membership concept in which a distinctive bundle of services and amenities are offered and provided to members/owners of a high-end real estate development; typically second homes or condominium resorts in which the members/owners have a fractional/interval ownership interest. Shares of the fractional ownership interests are generally 1/4th–1/13th of full interest in a given parcel or unit. Ownership of each fractional interest is usually evidenced by a deed representing a fee simple fractional interest in a specific housing unit, plus an undivided interest in the common areas. Private Residence Clubs (PRCs) generally offer and deliver services and amenities consistent with high-end vacation resort hotels but generally not found in traditional timeshare resorts such as room service and daily housekeeping. PRCs are further defined by the 'Club' rules and regulations, unique to each PRC, that govern the reservation process, owners association, and associated fees of membership in the PRC.

Prix fixe

The French term 'prix fixe' meaning fixed price is used to identify a meal at a set price that covers several courses (e.g. appetizer, entrée, and dessert). Used today synonymously with 'table d'hôte', prix fixe offerings are usually associated with upscale restaurants and haute cuisine. Prix fixe menus offer operators a number of advantages. First, there is substantial opportunity for maximizing profit since many of the lesser courses have a lower food cost while the large number of courses equate to a high perceived value to many guests. Second, if forecasts are accurate, an operator can monitor costs very closely since there is no waste or need for overproduction. Finally, the production and delivery of multiple courses can be streamlined owing to the limited number of menu offerings (compared to an operation with a lengthy menu). The challenge of the prix fixe format is that dining duration is long thereby reducing the opportunity for operators to increase seat turnover.

221

Pro-shop

An area within the clubhouse of a private club that is operated as a high-class boutique and addresses player game scheduling, training, equipment, or retail needs. The operation of a private club pro-shop comes in two formats: the first is where the club owns the merchandise and all members play or equipment service requests are done by club employees and the second is where the pro-shop is leased by the golf pro who in turn acts as an independent contractor. Under this latter scenario, the merchandise that is sold in the pro-shop is under the control of the pro with commissions being paid to the club for use of the pro-shop facilities. The key under either operational format the key is in providing the highest level of product quality and member service as possible.

Product life cycle

A marketing theory in which products or brands go through the following four stages: introduction → growth → maturity → decline. Each stage of a product life cycle is distinct and marketers may adjust different marketing strategies for each stage to maximize product's value and profitability. In the introduction stage, a new product is introduced into the market. Sales growth is normally slow because the customers are not aware of the product. A firm's objective is to create product awareness. Competition is at a minimum because the product is at the 'pioneering' stage. In the growth stage, sales increase rapidly. Competition increases as competitors see the product's profit potential. A firm makes profits and may expand market share. At maturity stage, sales volume is stable and sale growth rate is rather slow. Heavy promotion and cost reduction are required as competitors may lower prices and introduce improved version of the product. In the decline stage, sales continue to decline. A firm may maximize profit by lowering product costs or withdraw the product from the market.

Production company

A company that offers a wide variety of technical, creative, and logistical services to meet the event objectives and budget of corporate and association planners. Projects of various size and complexity can range from product launches, training programs, entertainment concerts, theme parties and galas, event marketing programs, and business meetings with video conferencing to multi-media campaigns. An event producer essentially can provide pre-conference planning, on-site management, and production services through complete turnkey program development or ala carte offerings.

Logistically, production companies assist with site selection, contract management, food and beverage menu creation and management, tradeshow sale, travel coordination, ground transportation, and other event services. Projects involving the services of a production company demand expert creativity, project management, and integration of talents to exceed expectations.

Production schedule

A schedule that shows the sequence and quantity of kitchen production for a given day. The schedule must take into account the equipment needed, the time of preparation, the quantities needed, and the staffing required to complete the production based on inventory and the delivery of needed ingredients. The goal is to eliminate over-purchasing and over-production, the chief causes of high food costs. The production schedule will contain the following:

- Menu item.
- Quantity needed (expressed in total yield or number of portions).
- The time the production needs to start and finish.

Without a production schedule in place for each item, management cannot accurately identify where unnecessary food-cost expenditures are occurring. Furthermore, these schedules ensure consistency of production, which can lead to increased customer satisfaction.

Productivity

A term used to describe the relation between the inputs and outputs of a productive system. Stated differently it is an overall measure based on a quantity of output generated by a given quantity of input. The intangible nature of hospitality services complicates productivity management and measurement. It is difficult to objectively define and measure the service outputs being provided (e.g. number of guest nights versus number of satisfied guests). The measurement and management of inputs/outputs are also complicated because of the simultaneous production and consumption of hospitality services as well as their perishability and heterogeneity. Low productivity in hospitality is identified as a major source of concern, which is mainly attributed to a lack of understanding and application of quantitative and analytical techniques. Robust productivity measurement is very critical, though, because it can be used for several purposes. For example, it can be used strategically as a basis for making longer-term comparisons with competitors.

Professional Congress Organizer

An independent person or organization specializing in all aspects of convention and meeting management. The term Professional Congress (Conference) Organizer (PCO) is commonly used in Europe and Asia for individuals or companies that offer services to inbound MICE (Meetings, Incentives, Conferences and Events) professionals – it is synonymous with terms like independent meeting manager, meeting planner or coordinator, conference manager, or event manager that are customary in North America. Furthermore, destination management companies (DMCs), primarily found in North America are similar to PCOs in that they provide services to inbound MICE professionals. They differ in that the types of services offered by DMCs are of a more social nature than those of PCOs. The former will guide meeting planners to services that will enable convention attendees to experience the unique attributes of a particular city or region. The services of PCOs are contracted by both associations and corporations that do not employ an in-house congress organizer, to manage either the entire event or specific tasks only.

Profit

Simply defined as the excess when revenues exceed expenses, profit is the residual monetary return to the hospitality operator (owner or investor) and as such is the driving force behind hospitality operations. This residual return is usually predetermined. From an economic perspective, profit does not include any of the return on labor, land, or capital, but is rather the surplus (predetermined or not) remaining after the full opportunity costs of these have been met (where opportunity cost is the value of that which must be given up to acquire or achieve something). Economists distinguish two types of profit: normal profit and excess profit. Normal profit is the minimum amount of profit necessary to attract the potential foodservice operator to venture into business and to remain in it. Excess profit is any profit over and above the normal profit.

Profit and loss statement

The profit and loss statement or P&L provides an overview of the profit earned by the reporting entity over a specific period of time. The P&L is also referred to as the income statement in the USA. Net profit represents the excess of revenues over expenses for the time period in question. If expenses exceed revenues then a net loss results. At least two levels of profit are generally referred to in profit and loss statements: gross profit (which is calculated by deducting cost of sales from sales revenue) and net profit (which is calculated by deducting all expenses from all revenue).

An example of a profit and loss statement is presented in the figure below:

ABC Hotel:
Profit and loss statement for the year ended December 31, 2007

Sales revenue		$1,000,000
Less: Cost of sales		250,000
Gross profit		750,000
Less: Other expenses		
Administration	300,000	
Depreciation	150,000	450,000
Net Profit		300,000

Promotional mix

An integrated marketing communication program that develops a consistently clear message or set of impressions through the use of the communication tools. The promotional mix consists of paid advertising, sales promotion, publicity and public relations, direct marketing, personal selling, and interactive marketing. Each of the above components of the promotional mix is synchronous part of the Interactive Marketing Communications (IMC) program. An appropriate IMC program is an important part of the overall marketing plan for companies and organizations in the international hospitality and tourism arena.

Promotional pricing

The primary objective of this strategy is to 'pull' consumers toward a product or service by offering temporary economic incentives. This strategy is effective only if it is supported by strong operational efficiency, effective distributional channels, and high consistency in product/service quality. It is effective only as a short-term solution. If an organization is not well prepared to deliver the goods and services as promised, promotional strategies do more harm than good. So it is not recommended when an organization is not operationally competent. In that case, more consumers may try the promoted product to take advantage of the economic incentives and may be disappointed by poor execution. This strategy is often noted in the tourism/hospitality industry. It is very common to promote a product at a reduced price for a short duration to increase product trials. Promotional pricing is often practiced effectively in introducing a new product at an existing establishment or when entering a new market by an established brand.

Property management systems

Sometimes referred to as 'front-office systems', the property management systems (PMS) forms the core of all the computerized systems used in a hotel. While a PMS's primary functions are to track which rooms are currently occupied or vacant, and to maintain the guests' folios by recording details of all sales and payment transactions, they also act as the information hub of all the other ancillary system used to improve customer service, and interface with reservation systems such as the computer reservation systems and Internet Bookings Engines to support the management of the distribution process.

Proprietary

A term that means held in private ownership. In the context of information technology, the term is used in relation to technology such as software algorithms restricted by patent or trademark, for example, Unisys' LSW, used in GIF files. Proprietary technology is therefore neither 'free' nor 'semi-free'. Hence unless specifically authorized, it is not permitted to use, copy, modify, or redistribute proprietary software either for a fee or gratis because the source code is copyrighted. Proprietary software is used extensively in the hospitality industry for example, 'general purpose' software like Microsoft Word, used for menu production, or 'dedicated' software applications like property management systems (PMS) such as Micros' FIDELIO or ASI's general purpose FrontDesk, which help to manage interdepartmental interactions.

Psychological contract

Psychological contracts are different from written contracts; they are implicit in the relationship between employer and employee and concern a series of mutual expectations and needs arising from the relationship. The precise content of the obligations and expectations on both parties are difficult to define, because they change over time and may well vary between individuals. Indeed the individual employee and the employer may not be consciously aware of the terms, but they do have expectations of the other party. These expectations should be largely satisfied within the relationship; otherwise it will break down resulting in unplanned staff leaving or employee dismissal. This unfortunate outcome is common in hospitality because of the prior knowledge and skills employers assume (experienced) candidates possess.

Psychological pricing

This pricing strategy emphasizes consumer psychology and attitude about pricing rather than economics. Typically, consumers tend to ignore the right most digits in making purchase decisions. Thus, hospitality firms may use price endings as marketing tools. High-end restaurants prefer to use 0 endings to present high-*quality image* and low-end restaurants prefer to use 9 endings to project *high value image*. Some ethnic restaurants, mostly Asian, tend to avoid using digits 9 and 4 as price endings since they consider even numbers as lucky numbers and odd numbers as bad luck numbers. Budget hotels and motels usually follow psychological pricing. Some of the high-end hotel companies have also begun practicing psychological pricing, especially after the 9–11 tragedy in the USA.

Public offering statements

A statement which summarizes the salient features of a timeshare plan. Timeshare legislation in most countries and states generally requires that the developer or seller of the timeshare interests deliver this to the purchaser. The statements contain disclosures in conspicuous type and attaches exhibits of important documents related to the creation and use of the timeshare plan. The summary and disclosures focus on such details as a description of the facilities and amenities of the timeshare property or properties, a description of use rights and rules and regulations governing owner use, a description of the developer and managing entity, and financial and budgetary descriptions for the property. Exhibits attached to the public offering statement include the restrictive covenants establishing the plan, the annual budget for operating the timeshare plan, and governing documents of any managing entity.

Public relations

The process of building good relations with the hospitality or tourism company's various publics by obtaining favorable publicity, creating and sustaining a strong corporate image, and dealing with unfounded rumors, stories, and events. By its very meaning, public relations (PR) connotes dealing with the public; however, the public takes many different forms of groups who may have some relationship with hospitality or tourism organizations. Usually the customers, both current and potential, are the most obvious public group, but constituents will also comprise of government agencies, suppliers, citizen action groups including environmental or cause-related groups, the media, and the financial community including bankers and investment partners. Hospitality and tourism companies must also be involved with 'internal publics' which will consist of employees, board of directors or internal advisory groups, stockholders and subcontractors. Major PR activities include press relations and press releases, product and service publicity, corporate or business communications, lobbying and legislative review, and counseling.

Purchase order

A hard copy or electronic form specifying particular products or services to be purchased from a purveyor. In many cases, the purchase orders are sent out to competing companies for bid. While not all products are sent out for bid, those used on a regular basis or those that tend to have higher prices may be. Purveyors will submit bids to the purchaser, possibly along with a sample of the product for comparative purposes. In other cases, the purveyor uses the purchase order to bill the buyer for products delivered or services rendered, as the purchase order contains an official identifying number. In this case, the purchase order – in addition to product specifications – will also include the exact amount to be purchased and the price to be paid. Today many hospitality distributors offer electronic purchasing, which automate the purchase-order process thereby reducing paper handling and increasing productivity related to the purchasing process.

Purchasing

The process of buying goods necessary for the operation of a business. These purchases are made through purveyors after negotiations regarding issues such as price, quality, and delivery dates/times are completed. As many inventory items are perishable, it is critical that 'just the right amount' of a particular product is in stock. Carrying too much inventory can lead to increased spoilage and theft, higher carrying costs, and overstocked storage space. An effective purchasing program utilizes par stock levels of inventory items. These par stocks are based on counts of each product used between delivery dates, plus 10–25 per cent extra to have on hand as a safety net. Par stock specifies a reorder point – the least amount of an item that can be held in storage before ordering additional inventory.

Purveyors

Vendors or suppliers of goods and services to others. In most cases, purveyors compete for business based on price, quality, and service. Establishing solid relationships with reputable purveyors is critical to the success of hospitality operations. Today, many view purveyors more as partners than vendors, and consider such relationships critical to long-term profitability. To this end, most purveyors send out sales representatives on a regular basis to help ensure that the needs of the operator are being met. While these representatives may take orders during personal visits, technology has allowed purchasing agents to complete most of their ordering via the Internet or through the use of a fax machine.

Qualitative research

Based on a phenomenological paradigm, qualitative research refers to observation and analysis of data that are not predetermined by the researcher. It assumes that reality is socially constructed through individual or collective definitions of the situation or environment. The goal of qualitative research is to capture the understanding of the social phenomenon as participants experience it. Therefore, qualitative research is not mainly concerned with establishing cause-and-effect relationships among variables of interest. Rather, it helps to identify new variables and questions for further research. The researcher is part of the phenomenon of interest. Another school of thought argues that qualitative research can also develop causal explanations of the phenomenon. Common qualitative research designs include ethnographies, grounded theory, case studies, participant observation, interviewing, and focus groups.

Quality control

Quality control evaluates actual quality by comparing performance to quality goals and then acting on the detected differences. Based on the process control system established in the planning phase, quality control is part of the quality management process. Quality management involves three steps: quality planning, quality control, and quality improvement. Quality planning refers to steps taken to develop products and services that meet customers' needs. While planning is concerned with setting goals and establishing the means to achieve these goals, quality control is concerned with operating the business in order to meet the goals. It monitors operations in order to detect discrepancies between actual performance and quality goals, and it undertakes actions to remedy the discrepancies. To keep up with the emerging competition, quality improvement aims at raising quality performance to the next level. A notable example of a hospitality organization that has strived for quality is the Ritz–Carlton hotel company, which has been awarded the Malcolm Baldrige Award twice in the past.

Quality of work life

The concept of quality of work life (QWL) deals with the issue of how rewarding or satisfying the time spent in the workplace is. As such, QWL may reflect working conditions and contextual issues such as relationships with work colleagues and the intrinsic satisfaction of the job itself.

Social scientists identified the following six requirements for job satisfaction, also termed 'psychological job requirements':

1. Adequate elbow room.
2. Opportunity of learning on the job and going on learning.
3. An optimal level of variety.
4. Conditions where workers can and do get help and respect from their work mates.
5. A sense of one's own work meaningfully contributing to society.
6. A desirable future.

These factors were at the core of the QWL programs initiated in the 1970s and 1980s, that represented a comprehensive effort to improve the quality of the work environment by integrating employee needs with the firm's need for higher productivity.

Quantitative research

In social sciences, the goal of quantitative research is to explain the causes of changes in social facts, primarily through objective analysis of data that are treated in magnitude. Quantitative research is more concerned with developing and empirically testing hypotheses. The researcher focuses more on established procedures rather than the individual judgment. Quantitative research attempts to reduce the amount of error in the study by designing and implementing appropriate sampling procedure (preferably random sampling) and instrumentation. Common quantitative research designs include surveys and experiments.

Quick service restaurants

What the restaurant industry calls a quick service restaurant (QSR) the rest of the world refers to as *fast food*. The food itself is not fast; it is the service that adds the quickness, generally taking less than five minutes from the time an order is placed until it is presented to the diner. Early restaurants in this segment included the dining cars on USA transcontinental railroad trains during the end of the nineteenth century. When retired, these cars became urban diners, where short-order cooks were masters at fixing meals quickly. Then in 1922, the Ingram family created a collection of small hamburger stands called White Castle. The McDonald's brothers experimented during the late 1940s in streamlined mass production of hamburgers which created a new hybrid form for restaurants, one that also required the customer to provide a significant involvement in his or her own 'quick' service.

Ratio analysis

A ratio represents a numeric relationship that compares one measurement with another in the form of a multiple, fraction, percentage, or rate. For example:

Multiple	5:1
Fraction	5/1 (or 1/5)
Percentage	500%
Rate	5 per 1 (or 5 for 1, or 5 times – expressed as $5\times$)

Thus, for instance, in the case of a hospitality business such as a hotel, room occupancy is normally calculated as a percentage of total room capacity, whereas restaurant occupancy is often calculated as a seat turnover figure (i.e. the average number of times each seat is sold). Ratio analysis is a tool often used to interpret information presented in financial statements. It is, therefore, important that the relationship between the elements used in ratios is clear, direct, and understandable.

Receiving

The practice of inspecting, accepting, and routing products when they arrive on-site at a hospitality facility is termed 'receiving', as is the department typically responsible for these activities. Tight controls and rigorous management of the receiving function can help protect an operation from *shrinkage*, reduce opportunities for unsafe food handling, and save the operation money through reduced waste. The receiving process is as follows: first, when a delivery arrives at a facility, a member of the hospitality staff meets it and the relevant paperwork is obtained from the delivery driver. The delivery then is checked against purchase orders to ensure that what is being delivered has been ordered. The receiver then inspects the items for quality, quantity, and condition, which may involve weighing boxes, opening and inspecting cases or crates, and in some cases counting items piece by piece. Lastly, accepted goods are moved into storage quickly, particularly if the items require a refrigerated environment or have a significant value.

Recipe costing

Recipe costing is at the core of all pricing functions. In order to price a menu item properly, the first step is to calculate the cost per edible portion (EP), which is the cost per servable pound or kilogram, based on the standardized recipe. One lists the recipe ingredients, quantities, and respective costs for each recipe. One then calculates the total cost of the recipe yield. This cost is then divided by the number of standardized portions to determine the cost per portion. In order to properly cost a recipe, one must understand the difference between 'as purchased'(AP) price per pound or kilogram and EP. For most ingredients, the cost per servable pound or kilogram is always more than the AP price per pound or kilogram because of trim waste and cooking shrinkage. In order for recipe yields and portion costs to be accurate and consistent, a restaurant must have standardized purchase specifications, standardized recipes, and standardized portioning controls.

Recipe standardization

A set of instructions for producing a particular menu item in a consistent manner so that the quality, quantity, and cost will be approximately the same each time it is prepared. Such a recipe lists ingredients, amounts, preparation method, cooking instructions and times, portion size, and serving instructions for a given menu item. Some standardized recipes include how leftovers are to be stored or incorporated into other recipes. They might also list the types and sizes of utensils, pots, pans, and equipment needed to produce the recipe. It is 'customized' to the ingredients, equipment, and utensils used by a specific operation. Today, standardized recipes also incorporate plating instructions, usually including a photograph to ensure that a given item will be plated in a consistent fashion. A typical standardized recipe format is shown below.

Recruitment

The process of attracting a pool of qualified job candidates from which an appropriate selection decision can be made. Internal recruitment strategies (e.g. promotion from within, lateral transfers) are often supported by career planning, human resource information systems, or internal job-posting systems and are helpful for motivating, developing, and retaining employees. External recruitment approaches are useful when significant numbers of new employees are required or for introducing new ideas and skill sets to the organization. External recruitment methods have traditionally included employee referrals, walk-ins/write-ins, advertisements, head hunters/employment agencies, job fairs, and liaising with educational institutions. Online methods include using the company's own website to post jobs. Potential candidates may be invited to respond to advertisements by e-mail or listservs, to submit their résumés electronically, and/or to complete an online pre-screening instrument to help assess compatibility. E-recruitment can also involve posting jobs on private employment websites and reviewing résumés posted by those looking for work.

Redundancy

A term used in the UK, Australia, and other British heritage countries that refers to an employer's decision leads to the termination of the worker's employment. Grounds for redundancy are fulfilled if the employer decides that it no longer wishes the job a worker has been performing to be done by anyone; the employer's decision is not due to the ordinary and customary turnover of labor; and the termination is not due to any personal act or default of the employee. A job may become obsolete (or redundant) if tasks and duties are deconstructed to become internal elements of other positions so that the original occupier of that job has nothing left to perform. Additionally, redundancies may result from a substantial decrease of responsibilities, a geographical change in the location of the job, and the sale or transfer of a business. In the hospitality industry, some redundancies have occurred through increased levels of autonomy afforded to staff.

Reference checks

Reference checks are used to confirm past employment and assess any uncertainties about that employment – position, duties, strengths, weaknesses, competencies, reasons for leaving previous employment, and suitability for present position. Reference checks are considered one of three ways to do background checks. Other ways of performing background checks are to confirm candidate credentials and assess candidate training needs. Given the importance of the customer service interaction in hospitality, checks can also be used to confirm past behaviors used in service situations. Often reference checks are used to determine criminal background and credit worthiness. Given the mobility and youth of hospitality industry employees, reference checks can be a valuable and low-cost source of accessing a variety of information on a potential candidate. Generally, information conveyed from a reference check must be based on objective facts and not opinions, and the discussion should be related to job issues and not deal with personal information.

Reference group

An individual(s) or group(s) that influences the shaping of an individual's opinion, belief, attitude, and/or behavior. There are two major types of reference groups: normative reference group and comparative reference group. Normative reference group influences an individual's norms, attitudes, and values through direct interaction. Parents, teachers, associates, peers, and friends belong to this group. Comparative reference group refers to an aspirational group to which an individual does not belong, but is used as a standard for self-evaluation. Comparative reference group serves as a reference point that an individual compares himself/herself to other individuals or groups. Celebrities or heroes are examples of comparative reference groups that indirectly influence an individual's attitude or behavior. Marketers accept the reference group as an important concept that can exercise an influence on information processing and consumer purchasing decision. Advertising is one of the marketing fields that heavily use this reference group influence.

Reference price

The price for which consumers'believe the product should sell. The reference price is formed when consumers consider such things as the price last paid, the price of similar items, the price considering the brand name, the real or imagined cost to produce the item, and the perceived cost of product failure. The last item is of considerable importance for they reflect consumers' imaginations. For example, the reference price for a meal where one is celebrating a special occasion is higher than the reference price for a meal with some old college friends, even though the restaurant may be the same. The risk of failure is critical in the first case and less critical in the second.

Refreshment break

A break during a meeting or convention so that attendees may refresh and sharpen their attention. It also helps alleviate boredom that tends to develop when guests are engaged in tedious business activities during the day. Breaks provide learners with an opportunity to reflect on what they have just heard. It is common to have breaks between sessions where participants are going from one room to another. The break allows for participant movement, as well as for refreshments. A break can be set up in the pre-function space just outside the meeting room if the space is secure and the area is large enough to accommodate the group. If the room is large enough, the break can be set up at the back of the room, if the space is available. However, noise during setup can be distracting to both the speaker and the audience.

Registration

The process of checking a guest into his/her hotel room. Registration is an activity that usually takes place at the hotel's reception (front desk) and upon the guests arrival at the hotel. The registration process, irrespective of the type of the hotel, can be divided in a series of activities. These activities typically include greeting the guest, creating a registration record, distributing a key, and finally fulfilling any special requests (such as wake up calls) that the guest might have. In some countries, it is the legal obligation of the hotel to obtain and retain information, including identification or passport number, from the hotel guests during registration.

Registration card

Also called a 'reg'card, a registration card is presented to the hotel guest for signature and verification at check-in. A typical registration card requires the guest to furnish personal data including name, billing address, length of stay, and method of settlement. From the registration card, credit can be established or verified during check-in as well. Most governmental jurisdictions require the guest's signature on the registration card before the relationship between the hotel and the guest is considered legal. In some governmental jurisdictions there may be specific requirements printed on the card relating to the availability of safe storage for guest valuables. The registration card will also show the room rate, allowing the guest to confirm it and a place for the guest to initial an agreement and confirmation of the rate. Such information reduces questions about the price of the room at check-out.

Relationship marketing

A customer-centric strategy that selectively builds long-term, mutually profitable customer relationships through interactive and individualized interactions that maximize customer lifetime value. Relationship marketing also referred to as customer relationship management (CRM) and closely related to one-to-one marketing and aftermarketing has become one of the leading business strategies in the new millennium. The objective of relationship marketing is to selectively turn existing, new, or prospective customers into loyal ones through a good understanding of needs and individual preferences, a superior service designed accordingly and a long-term, mutually beneficial relationship. Relationship marketing is all about making customers happy and bringing them back. It represents a comeback to the roots of traditional hospitality: knowing every single customer intimately, providing one-to-one solutions to customers'requirements, and developing a continuous relation that does not expires at the end of the customer's stay. The result is to make customers feel part of the 'family' and convincing them that the hospitality company truly cares about them and their problems.

Renewable energy

Energy that is provided by the capture of solar energy, wind energy, falling water, biomass, and some other sources such as geothermal heat. These are called renewable because they are constantly being renewed by short-term natural processes. This is in contrast to fossil energy sources such as natural gas and oil where the process of renewal takes thousands to millions of years. Hotels fairly easily use solar energy for heating domestic water or for pool heating.

235

Some hotels also use solar energy with photovoltaic cells to produce electricity. Others access geothermal energy through the use of ground source heat pumps and a few, in active thermal areas, are able to use geothermal heat directly. A few hotels may be using wind power to produce electricity although it is probably more likely they will buy wind powered electricity.

Renovation

In the hospitality industry renovation is the process of improving the image of a property by modifying its tangible product or by making changes in the property's layout, such as a new extension or replacing furniture and equipment. Renovation may be essential for a number of reasons, such as improving operational efficiency, reducing costs, improving corporate image and standards, responding to new trends and technology in the market, complying with government requirements, and recovering from accidents and disasters. Through renovation, the original reputation of the property and market share can be retained. In some cases, renovating may be faster more economical than building a new property. Renovation may range from minor renovations, which may only involve replacing furnishings, to master renovations or restorations that involve the entire property and results in extensive changes to the physical layout, and may take a long time to complete.

Request for proposal

An invitation to submit a competitive bid soliciting hospitality services and/or products. The request for proposal (RFP) specifically details the major needs and requirements for services or provides description of products to be procured. The document typically lists specifications and application procedures to be followed and serves as a precursor to a legal agreement. Related terms include invitation to tender, request for quote (RFQ), bid solicitation, and invitation to bid.

Rescission

The cancellation of a contract by mutual agreement or by law. In timeshare contracts the rescission period is fixed by the company or by statute. Also known as a 'cooling-off period' this allows a consumer to cancel a purchase contract for a timeshare property without incurring a penalty, and with full refund of any money paid up front. The right to rescission is now a universal provision in countries with substantial numbers of timeshare resorts. Purchase contracts used by companies may exceed statutory requirements, but all must provide at least the minimum time for 'cooling off'. To a large extent the now universal legal requirement for a rescission (cooling-off) period is a response to concerns about high-pressure selling techniques that have been used by some unscrupulous operators in the past. The cooling-off period allows the customer time to reflect on the decision made during the site visit and sales presentation.

Research and development

The process of discovering new knowledge about hospitality products and services and then applying that knowledge to create new ones that satisfy customer needs. Successful hospitality operations must continually examine their production and service methods to ensure that it is knowledgable about customers'needs and desires while maximizing efficiency and effectiveness. Many hospitality organizations dedicate significant resources to research and development (R&D) in their efforts to optimize their operations' potential. Larger hospitality organizations may create an R&D department that modifies and/or creates new products and services that reflect the needs and tastes of their existing and potential customers.

Reservation file

A computer-based collection of reservation records that are compiled prior to the arrival of hotel guests. Based on this file guests may be sent a letter or electronic confirmation to verify that a reservation has been made and that its specifications are accurate. The confirmation permits errors in communication to be corrected before the guest arrives and verifies the guest's correct mailing or electronic address for future correspondence. Many hotels often provide confirmations via a word processor in the form of letters, making the process seem more personal. The reservations software may directly interface with a central reservations network and perform many pre-arrival activities and calculations from the reservation file. In addition to automatically generating letters, electronic folios can be established from the reservation file and pre-registration transactions can be processed for guests with confirmed reservations. From the reservation file an expected arrivals list, occupancy and revenue forecasts can also be generated.

Reservation price

The maximum price the customer will pay for a product. For instance, if the customer's reservation price for a can of soda is $1.00 and the price is $1.01, the customer will not buy the product. If the selling price is less than the reservation price, the customer will buy the product. Firms that price exactly to the reservation price are said to extract the entire consumer surplus. Firms that price less than the reservation price are said to be leaving money on the table. Obviously, firms do not want to leave money on the table.

The desire to set prices by individual customer further implies that each customer has a different reservation price and by selling to that price, the firm maximizes revenue because everyone will buy the product. By having a limited number of prices, there will always be some people whose reservation price is less than the selling price and hence, they will not buy and vice versa.

Reservation record

The reservation record identifies hotel guests and their occupancy needs before the guests arrival. This record enables a hotel to personalize guest service and more accurately schedule staff. In addition the reservation record can be utilized to generate multiple management reports. Typically a reservation record includes guest name; guest home or billing address; guest telephone number including area and country codes; guest corporate address and telephone numbers as appropriate; name of and pertinent information about the person making the reservation; number of people in the party; arrival date and time; number of nights required or expected departure date; whether the reservation is guaranteed or not guaranteed with some form of payment; special requirements such as non-smoking or services for an infant or disabled guest; and additional information about transportation requirements, late arrival, room preference, etc.

Reservation reports

Reports generated by an in-house computerized system proving information regarding future reservations of a hotel. Regardless of the degree of automation, the number and type of management reports available through a reservation system are functions of the hotel's needs and the system's capability and contents. Typically reservation reports include reservation transaction reports which summarize daily reservations activity in terms of reservation record creation, modification, and cancellation; commission agent report which tracks the amount a hotel owes to each agent who has a contractual agreement with the hotel to book business; turnaway report which tracks the numbers of reservation requests refused because rooms were not available for the requested dates; and revenue forecast report which projects future revenue by multiplying predicted occupancies by applicable room rates. In addition, expected arrival and departure lists are typically generated from reservation data; advance deposits for reservations can be identified; and reservation histories.

Reservations

An essential aspect of any hospitality business is reserving space – a hotel room, a restaurant seat, a conference room, and a banquet hall – for customers. This ensures that the customers'needs are satisfied when they require it, and the hospitality providers know the quantity of demand for their products on a daily basis, which assists in planning labor and consumable requirements for that day. Recording of reservations can range from writing them manually in a bound book, which can still be seen occasionally in small hotels, *pensions* and especially in restaurants to electronically recording them in an establishment's computer reservation system, which is generally part of its property management system (PMS). Much useful marketing data can be gathered from the reservation records, depending on the amount of information requested from the guest, which forms the basis for much of the marketing activity of an establishment – customer relations management; yield management; market segmentation.

Reserve for replacement

The replacement reserve refers to funds in various stages of liquidity set aside by a firm and targeted for future major refurbishments and replacements of the physical assets (e.g. building exterior and interior, mechanical, electrical and plumbing systems, and major equipment), where the assets'expected lives are less than the expected property life. The replacement reserve enables the firm to maintain property value both as an operating concern and a real estate asset, and to handle required improvements while hedging against unforeseen increases in costs of capital. There are two types of reserves: *contingency* and *capital reserves*. *Contingency reserves* are set aside to handle unforeseen significant expenditures. *Capital reserve* amounts are based on a reserve study of each major physical asset that can be expected to need repair or replacement at some point in the future.

Resident manager

A title that was historically given to the senior management representative who actually resided on property. In today's hotel environment there has been a movement away from live-in statues. The title however has remained, and is most often given to the individual recognized as the assistant general manager of the property. The term resident manager is used to describe that person who acts on behalf of the general manager in his/her absence and sometimes resides 24/7 on the hotel property. The general manager may promote any executive to relieve the general manager of some operational duties; however, a resident manager may take on these duties without being relieved of her/his regular departmental responsibilities. Additional responsibilities of the resident manager may include representing the general manager on various hotel interdepartmental committees, and taking responsibility for important special projects such as major hotel renovations, VIP guests, or operating reports that require in-depth analysis for the regional or perhaps corporate offices.

Resignation

This refers to when employees give notice unilaterally to employers of their intention to quit their job (or terminate their employment) with or without notice. Whether verbal or written, a key element of a resignation is the date from which it becomes effective. This must be explicit and understood clearly by both parties. Workers should also give an appropriate notice period; usually this is the same length as the pay period. This allows both employer and worker to make arrangements. Employers have an option of either allowing the employee to work out their notice period or paying them in lieu of notice. However, should workers refuse to work out their notice, they are not entitled to be paid for the period of notice. In some instances, failure to report for duty can be considered a repudiation of the contract of employment.

Resource-based view

A strategic management term that stresses the importance of resources in delivering the competitive advantage of the firm. The resource-based view (RBV) of the firm posits that firm performance is ultimately a return on unique assets owned and controlled by the firm. The focus of RBV categorizes resources into three main groups: physical capital resources (such as plant and equipment), human capital resources (such as training, intelligence, and experience), and organizational capital resources (such as reporting structure and coordinating systems). These resources are employed to support the firm's quest for a competitive advantage, or a sustained competitive advantage. Competitive advantage is defined as the ability to use firm resources for implementing a value-creating strategy that is not simultaneously being implemented by any competitor. Similarly, sustained competitive advantage is a competitive advantage that the competition cannot copy or simulate. More specifically, a competitive advantage becomes sustained only if it continues to exist after efforts to duplicate that advantage have failed and ceased.

Resource planning

Resource planning for the hospitality industry may be divided into two major streams:

1. *Material resource planning (MRP)*: The practice of calculating what materials are required to create a product by analyzing bill of materials data, inventory data, and/or a master production schedule.
2. *Enterprise resource planning (ERP)*: The practice of consolidating an enterprise's planning, manufacturing, sales, and marketing efforts into one management system. Implementation of ERP systems is not difficult. A company stores the fixed information needed

to run its business – materials inventory, order lead times and quantities, safe stock levels, etc.), and adds processes such as sales, works and purchase order processing, and inventory control.

Responsibility center

An organizational unit with a manager responsible for the relationship between input (resources/ costs) and outcome. The combination of the outcome of each unit results in the outcome of the organization as a whole. The assumption is that if each manager achieves his or her own target, the organization as a whole achieves its financial goals. Responsibility centers are traditionally classified into five groups: cost centers, revenue centers, expense centers, profit centers, and investment centers. Responsibility centers might be projected over organizational units, but always result in a hierarchy, which matches the structure of the organization. Responsibility is assigned accordingly with the decision-making power of each unit because managers are accountable only for what they can control. Therefore, responsibility is both a direct consequence of the actual control over resources and of the decision-making power assigned to a specific manager.

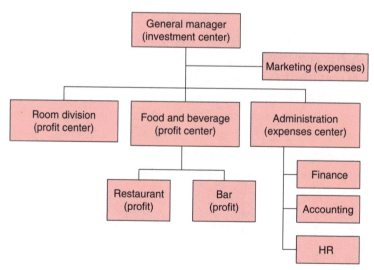

Responsibility centers identified in a hotel.

Restaurant systems

Restaurant systems describe the Information Communication Technology used for the effective running of the business, namely procurement, stock control, production and service, revenue control, and payroll systems. The procurement system includes the ordering and receipt of a food or beverage requisition, the selection of reputable suppliers, the creation of electronic invoices, and the acceptance of goods and the transfer of goods to stores. The stock control system facilitates storing and issuing of food or beverages, stocktaking and receiving food or beverages. Production systems support production methods, such as Cook hold serve, Call order, Cook to order, Batch, Cook chill, Cook freeze, Standard refrigeration, Sous vide to name a few. Revenue systems include electronic points of sales and support staff record keeping, such as commission payments, rotas, training achieved, or sick leave. The introduction of computer software has enabled even small restaurants to have efficient systems at low cost and has provided significant benefits for restaurant management.

Resume/curriculum vitae

Two terms that are often used interchangeably. However, curriculum vitas are usually much longer documents with greater detail. Resumes are generally two or three pages, and therefore, more widely used in the hospitality industry. Resumes are open ended in how they are structured and the information provided, enabling the applicant to reflect their personality and tailor information for specific situations. Resumes contain information on the candidate's work-related history, including job duties, job-related accomplishments, and educational background. Especially important to the hospitality industry are indications of one's service-oriented accomplishments. There are two basic types of resumes: chronological and experiential (or functional). Chronological resumes list applicant accomplishments in reverse chronological order. Experiential resumes list candidate accomplishments in some topical order without reference to employer. Employers are listed at the end of the experiential resume. There appears to be a greater preference in the hospitality industry for chronological resumes.

Return on investment

A widely used measure of overall performance. There are two key approaches to return on investment (ROI), firstly, return on total assets (ROTA) or return on capital employed (ROCE) focus on operating efficiency of the total enterprise, and secondly, return on equity (ROE) which concentrates on this efficiency as translated into return to owners of the business (shareholders). ROCE and ROTA provide overall measure of operational performance, linking profits generated to the value of assets in the business. ROCE is calculated by expressing Profit before Interest and Tax (PBIT) as a percentage of capital employed, which is calculated by taking fixed assets (FA) plus current assets (CA) and deducting current liabilities (CL).

Example	FA	$960,000
	CA	$640,000
	CL	$480,000
	PBIT	$224,000

$$\text{ROCE} = \text{PBIT} \div (\text{FA} + \text{CA} - \text{CL})$$
$$= 224{,}000 \div (960{,}000 + 640{,}000 - 480{,}000) \times 100 = 20\%.$$

ROTA is calculated by expressing PBIT as a percentage of total assets, which is FA plus CA. Using figures from the example above:

$$\text{ROTA} = \text{PBIT} \div (\text{FA} + \text{CA})$$
$$= 224{,}000 \div (960{,}000 + 640{,}000) \times 100 = 8.75\%.$$

ROTA compares the PBIT to the total value of total assets being used by the business. Total assets include FA and CA, as such it excludes the effect of CL which reduce the needs for operational demands on funding, the result is that ROTA will produce a lower figure for return that ROCE for the same company. In the example above it can be seen that ROTA is 8.75 per cent and ROCE is 20 per cent.

Revenue

The amount of money that a company actually receives from its activities, mostly from sales of products and/or services to customers. For most hotels, the largest portion of revenue comes from sales of services such as accommodation and restaurant meals. Revenue can be robustly defined as occurring when there is an inflow of assets. In most cases, the asset received following a sale is cash or an increase in accounts receivable (debtors) if the sale is made on credit. Other examples of revenue that increase assets include interest revenue (where the hotel has interest-bearing investments), dividend revenue (where the hotel has share investments), and rental revenue (where the hotel has rented out one or more properties). Under accrual accounting revenue is recognized at the time it is earned, which does not necessarily coincide with the cash receipt associated with the revenue.

Revenue center

In the context of a hotel, a revenue center is a department that generates revenues and costs that are directly related to the department. The biggest revenue center for most full-service hotels is the rooms division. In addition other major revenue centers include food and beverage serving facilities such as restaurants, bars, lounges, room service, and banqueting facilities; telephone; gift shops; newsstand; valet; laundry; barbershop or beauty salon; and recreation centers among others. Specialized hotels have other additional revenue centers such as health clubs, golf courses, casinos and gaming facilities, and conference facilities. It is very important for the hotel's profitability to promote all revenue centers to all arriving and in-house guests. Most hotels promote these facilities through the hotels front desk employees (upselling) and through printed material in strategic places within the hotel such as elevators and the guestrooms. Each revenue center is subject to internal controls ranging from manual systems to semi-automated systems to fully automated systems.

Revenue management

The business practice of selling the right inventory to the right customer at the right price at the right time so as to maximize total revenue, profit, and market share. With the emergence of Internet travel websites, the definition may be extended to include '…through the right channel'. Moreover, the above definition truly describes the objective of revenue management. In the context of hotels, revenue management is dependent on an accurate demand forecasting of future arrival dates at a granular level as well as a relative understanding of the demand and rate positioning of competitors. To achieve optimal revenue performance over time, hotels must forecast total arrivals demand by rate, market segment, length of stay, and distribution channel while positioning the rates within each channel and market segment giving consideration to several factors such as seasonal market demand, city-wide events, competitors' rate positioning, and demand levels. In the context of restaurants, revenue management can be defined as selling the right seat to the right customer at the right price and for the right duration, with right entailing achievement of the highest revenue while delivering the greatest value. Two main strategic levers can be used to manage revenue: price and meal duration. Price is a fairly obvious target for manipulation, and many operators already offer price-related promotions to augment or shift peak-period demand (e.g. early bird specials, special menu promotions, happy hours, and minimum cover charges or higher priced menu items during peak periods). As far as meal duration is concerned, one should not think only of reducing diners' average meal length. Quite often the factor interfering with revenue management is the variability in meal lengths, and not just their duration. These issues can be addressed by, for example, streamlining the service-delivery process, changing reservation policies, redesigning menus, pacing service processes, and making those processes more efficient.

Revenue per available room

Revenue per available room or REVPAR is determined by dividing room revenue received for a specific day by the number of rooms available in the hotel for that day. REVPAR can also be calculated multiplying average daily rate by occupancy percentage. REVPAR is used in hotels to determine the amount of dollars each hotel room produces for the overall financial success of the hotel. REVPAR is the best way a hotel has to compare its competition and is a reflection of the way occupancy and average daily rate are being managed. REVPAR can alert a manager to how well the reservations department is selling during slow periods and/or how successfully reservationists are upselling hotel guests to higher-rated rooms or packages during peak periods.

Revenue per available seat hour

A measure used in the restaurant industry that is calculated by dividing revenue for the desired time period (e.g. hour, day-part, day) by the number of seat hours available during that interval. Because it embraces capacity use and check averages, revenue per available seat hour (RevPASH) is a much better indicator of the revenue-generating performance of a restaurant than the commonly used measures of average check per person or food and labor margins. RevPASH indicates the rate at which revenue is generated and captures the tradeoff between average check and facility use. If seat occupancy percentages increase even as the average check decreases, for instance, a restaurant can still achieve the same RevPASH. Conversely, if a restaurant can increase the average check, it can maintain a similar RevPASH with slightly lower seat occupancy.

The following table presents a hypothetical illustration of this principle. The four restaurants in the exhibit all have the same RevPASH ($7.20), but each achieves it in a different manner.

Various calculations of RevPASH

Restaurant	Seat occupancy (%)	Average check per person	RevPASH
A	40	$18.00	$7.20
B	60	$12.00	$7.20
C	80	$9.00	$7.20
D	90	$8.00	$7.20

Right-to-use ownership

A type of interest in a timeshare plan in which the owner receives the right to use the accommodations and facilities of the timeshare plan during the term of the timeshare plan but does not receive an ownership interest in the underlying property included in the timeshare plan. If timeshare plan terminates the owner of a right-to-use interest will not have any on-going use rights or ownership interest.

The purchaser of a right-to-use ownership interest is conveyed the interest through the execution and delivery of a purchase contract which governs the purchaser's rights under the timeshare plan.

Since the owner does not receive an underlying property interest, right-to-use timeshare plans may be regulated to a greater degree than deeded ownership interests, including requiring that the developer record in the applicable public records a notice to creditors and non-disturbance agreement putting potential creditors of the developer on notice of the right-to-use purchasers'interests in the timeshare plan. This type of interest is also referred to as a timeshare license.

Risk-return tradeoff

The risk-return relationship is a key concept related to the valuation of stocks, bonds, and new projects. In investment, the required rate of return (RRR) has two components: reward for delaying consumption and compensation for bearing risk. The risk associated with different hospitality investments varies. Some investors may choose to invest in risky assets because those investments generate higher returns. The higher the perceived risk associated with an investment, the greater the RRR and vice versa. An increase in the perceived risk of an investment will raise the RRR and hence lower the value of the asset or project. On the other hand, if the perceived risk associated with an asset or project decreases, the investors' RRR will be lowered and the value of the asset or project will increase. Major national or international events such as the 9.11 terrorist attacks can change the perceived risk of investors, hence having a significant impact on RRR and assets valuation.

Role playing and simulations

An interactive training technique in which participants experience real or exaggerated workplace situations involving the reenactment of certain parts or roles. This training technique is particularly effective for practicing and developing interpersonal skills such as hospitality employees appropriately responding to guest requests or complaints. In that employees assume the roles of guests, as well as workers, this technique helps in building empathy toward guest needs and perceptions. Simulations also involve interactive training techniques in which there is a scaled-down enactment of reality. Typically this training approach utilizes technology such as CD-ROMs or the Internet. Simulations offer many benefits including providing a realistic learning experience that enhances the transfer of learning to the workplace. The duplication of the working environment also allows for training not to interrupt business operations. Many hotels now have simulated front office training programs involving computer applications in which employees are trained in the process of rooming or checking-out a guest.

Roles

Whilst role formally refers to an organized collection of behaviors and is used to define the tasks and activities undertaken as part of work, one of the key issues in the discussion of role is how individual work performance and job satisfaction is shaped by employees' expectations with regards to role. There are three aspects to role of which we must be aware because of their implications for role performance, job satisfaction, and staff turnover. They are *role ambiguity* which is a person's lack of understanding about the rights, privileges, and obligations of a job. *Role conflict* which refers to the conflict between what one prefers to do as an individual and what one believes he has to do in the execution of his job role. *Role set* is the set of expectations people have for the behavior of an individual in a particular role.

Room rate

A hotel or lodging enterprise will usually designate a standard rate for each room. This rate is typically called the rack rate because traditionally the standard rate was the one posted on or near the room rack. The rack rate is considered the retail rate for the room.

Other room rate schedules may reflect variations of the rack rate and relate to the number of guests assigned to the room, service level, and room location. Rates might include corporate rates for business people staying in the hotel or lodging enterprise; commercial rates for business people who represent a company and have infrequent patterns of travel but collectively this group can represent a major segment of the hotels guest; complimentary rates for business promotion; group rates for a predetermined number of affiliated guests.

Room setups

The organized design of tables, chairs, audio-visual equipment, food and beverage stations, other furniture and equipment in a room that allows for the favorable environment of an event. There are a number of room setup standards in the industry including theater or auditorium style, schoolroom or classroom, reception, banquet, boardroom, hollow square, U-shape, and variations of these styles. The different room setups are appropriate for different types of events. Additionally, events with different types of objectives or desired outcomes may require different room sets. They each require different amounts of square footage per person. A number of criteria go into a room setup and considerations should be made to comply with national disabilities acts (such as the American with Disabilities Act in the USA) and facility capacity requirements. In addition, fire codes dictate the number of people (load) that a room can accommodate. There are a number of software programs available to help with design and placement of furniture and equipment in the room.

Room system automation

Hotel rooms are becoming increasingly wired with a wide range of electronic and information technology-based systems being used to both enhance the guest experience and generate incremental revenue. They may be broken down into two categories: structural systems (such as electronic door locks, energy management systems, mechanical curtains and blinds, and even to a limited extent systems that regulate air quality and odor) and guest service systems (such as in-room bars, entertainment systems that deliver music, movies or video games on demand, guest information systems, and Internet access facilities). As technology becomes more persuasive and guests become more familiar with such facilities in their own homes, provision of such facilities will become essential if a property wants to remain competitive. Opportunities also exist to personalize the guest experience by interfacing in-room systems of this kind with customer relationship management databases to allow guestrooms to be configured precisely to match guest preferences.

Rooms, status of

The state of the guestrooms. Before a guest arrives at the hotel the front desk needs to know the status of the rooms so as to check guests into rooms which are vacant and clean rather than inconveniencing the guest by sending them to an occupied or dirty room. It is important for both the front desk and housekeeping staff to be familiar with these terms and information in relation to room status must be communicated to the front desk from housekeeping as soon as possible in order for the room sales to be maximized. Listed below are some of the terms used in relation to room status:

- *Did not check out*: The guest did not actually come to the front desk to check out but had made arrangements previously to settle their account. This guest is not a skipper (explained below).
- *Do not disturb*: The guest does not want to be disturbed. Usually indicated with a sign left hanging on the guestroom door knob or electronically by a red light indicator outside the guestroom door.
- *Due out*: The guest is expected to vacate the room after the following day's check-out time.
- *Late check-out*: Hotels have a normal check-out time (usually 11 a.m. or 12 noon) and in this situation the guest has made arrangements with the front desk to check out later than this normal check-out time.

- *Occupied*: A guest is registered to the room and is not due to check out yet.
- *On change*: The guestroom is in the process of being cleaned. The guest has vacated the room but it is not as yet ready for resale.
- *Skipper*: This refers to a guest that has not made arrangements with the front desk to settle their accounts and has left the hotel without paying. Also known as a walk-out.
- *Sleeper*: This situation occurs when the front desk has not updated their room status information. The guest has settled their account and left the hotel but this is not recorded in the front desk records.
- *Stayover*: This refers to a room that is occupied by a guest but they are not checking out on that day. A guestroom is known as a stayover from the date of arrival to the date of departure.

Rooms, types of

The following are some of the common terms used in relation to room types:

- *Adjacent room*: Rooms that are close to each other (e.g. across the hall). This type of room is possibly suitable for families.
- *Adjoining rooms*: Two rooms beside each other with a common wall but they do not have a connecting door between them. This type of room is possibly suitable for families.
- *Connecting rooms*: Two rooms beside each other with a common wall and they do have a connecting door in between them, which allows access to each room without the use of a public corridor. Also known as communicating rooms. This type of room is possibly suitable to a family with young children.
- *Double*: This type of room may have one or two people in it. It may have two singles in the room or one double bed in the room. In American terminology this can also be referred to as a twin.
- *Double-double*: A room that has two double beds in it. One or more people can be accommodated in this room type.
- *En suite*: A room that has bathroom facilities included within.
- *Family room*: A room that can accommodate a family. Can be a double-double, a triple, a quad, or a suite. It depends on the number of people being accommodated. Family rooms can get a child's cot or a Z-bed added.
- *Junior suite*: A room that has a sitting/living area and a bed. The sleeping area can be separate from the sitting/living area but this is not always the case.
- *King*: A room that has a king size bed. One or two people can be accommodated in this room type.

- *Mini suite*: Same as junior suite above.
- *Quad*: A room that can be assigned to four people. It may have two or more beds (e.g. double-double).
- *Queen*: A room that has a queen size bed, which can accommodate one or more people.
- *Single*: A room that is assigned to one person. It may have one or more beds in it.
- *Studio*: A single or double room with a studio bed. A studio bed usually converts to a couch during the day. In a studio room there may also be an additional bed.
- *Suite*: A room that has one or more bedrooms and a living room. All of these rooms are connected.
- *Triple*: A room that can accommodate three people. It may have two or more beds in it.
- *Twin*: A room that has two or more beds and may accommodate one or more people.

Routine maintenance

The process of repairing devices and facility components within a scheduled period of time. Upon receipt of a device or facility breakdown the request is prioritized as emergency, routine, or backlogged. Some examples may include replacing electric light bulbs, guestroom equipment, or furnishings repairs and adjusting thermostats in public areas. Most repairs are handled as routine and are corrected within a 24-hour time period. In addition, when the device is being repaired it should be inspected for premature wear–tear and if potential defects are found, these should be repaired and included as routine maintenance. Emergency repairs are necessary because of safety reasons or need and are corrected immediately. Backlogged maintenance is scheduled when resources become available. Automation has increased the efficiency of managing routine maintenance. Automation of the routine maintenance function prompts the managers of the maintenance function with the tasks required to complete a routine maintenance order.

Ss

Safety

Safety involves preventing employees and customers within the hospitality property from potential death and injury, such as from accidental slips, falls, cuts, burns, and so forth, as well as preventing related property damage. Failing to provide a safe environment can be costly monetarily, in terms of reputation, as well as in the time required to deal with the consequences. Hospitality organizations have many concerns about safety such as fires, food poisoning, infectious diseases, accidents, problems with electronic equipment, physical attacks on guests and employees. Certain safety issues need to be considered for bedrooms, baths, lifts, kitchens, restaurants, bars, discos, casinos, lobbies, swimming pools, sport areas, etc. In order to improve safety, hospitality organizations now install electronic locks, fire sprinklers, smoke detectors, and closed-circuit televisions. However, providing safety requires extensive and ongoing investment, training, and the improvement of physical conditions.

Sales promotion

An activity, material, or technique that stimulates interest, trial, or purchase by offering added value to or incentive for the product to resellers, salespeople, or consumers. There are at least four types of sales promotion activities in the hospitality industry. (1) *Sampling*: This is an attempt to pre-sell the activity or service to the patron in order to promote the item being sampled, that is desert in a restaurant. (2) *Coupons*: A coupon gives the patron the opportunity to participate in an activity at reduced or no cost. (3) *Contests*: Contests usually provide some form of prizes. An example of a contest to promote enthusiasm and interest in a particular activity is a chili cook-off, held at the snack bar, judged by the staff, and a featured menu for a period of time. (4) *Demonstrations*: A good example would be a cooking demonstration arranged at the exchange mall or at a booth during a festival, in hopes to create interest in menu specialties or new Chef.

Scripts and schemas

The term 'script' refers to a schema that is retained in memory. The 'schema' describes sequences of events or behaviors that are appropriate in a particular context. In the hospitality industry, customer scripts serve as antecedents of what customers expect to happen when they visit a hospitality operation. Scripts are developed and altered, according to the typicality of a situation. If a situation is unusual, intensive conscious processing is required to decide appropriate

251

behaviors and actions. Since there is no script that exists for the unusual situation, little or no script processing can occur and intense conscious processing must take place. In contrast, when a situation is very familiar, little or no conscious processing occurs because the situation already is highly scripted. Scripts are important to hospitality managers and researchers because the hospitality industry involves a wide array of situations that demand employees and customers fluidly move from intensive conscious processing to less active processing.

Seasonality in foodservice

In terms of foodservice, seasonality has two meanings. The first refers to the time of year a product is in its highest period of abundance, availability, quality, and usually lowest price. Seasonality often refers to produce, but it can also refer to protein types of entrée dishes. Examples include, but are not limited to finned fish, shellfish, wild game, and turkey. Fruit can be seasonal as well, for example, a restaurant located in Southern California, will pay as much as 60–70 per cent less in the spring for strawberries than at other times (when strawberries must be trucked in or shipped from remote areas). The second meaning pertains to seasonality of business. Business seasonality exists when guest counts (and correspondingly, revenue) fluctuate according to some seasonal pattern. The 'season' may be one of the four seasons of the year, or may be interpreted similarly but applied to days of the week or months of the year.

Secondary data

Data and information that is obtained from existing records of past data collection or from an outside source. This is in contrast with primary data, which are collected for the specific project at hand. Secondary data may be obtained internally from a company's existing records or through external sources. Internal sources in the hospitality industry may include resources such as guest registration records, point-of-sale systems, internal financial reports, forecasting and budgeting reports, and hotel management's daily reports. External sources of secondary data are numerous and diverse. Examples of external secondary data sources are the Internet, publications, government reports, public records, such as competitors' annual reports; demographic records collected from national, state, or local government agencies; information available through the media, such as newspapers, magazines, or television/radio broadcasts; and data purchased through information gathering services and consulting firms.

Security

The protection of the assets of an individual or a business. Hospitality firms, especially hotels, have a legal as well as a moral obligation to keep their employees and guests/customers safe.

Proper security measures not only keep the guest safe but they also assist in minimizing the hotel's legal liability. Hotel guests expect security measure to be taken to ensure their safety when staying at a hotel. Internal security devices that are used by hotel to provide security are recodable locks, alarms systems, surveillance systems, as well as emergency plans. Emergency plans are imperative to have in place in order to provide property security for hotel guests. Emergency plans should be written and practiced often to ensure proper execution at the time of an emergency. There should be separate emergency plans for the many different types of crises that can arise. Hotel assets can be threatened by internal (employees) or external (outsiders) sources.

Self-check-out

Self-check-out provides guests with an opportunity to check themselves out of the hotel from lobby terminals and/or guestrooms via the television. In either case, the terminal or in room system is interfaced with the property management system. Guest access the proper folio and reviews its contents. They may be required to enter a credit card number or insure the accuracy of a credit card number. Settlement can be automatically assigned to an acceptable credit card as long as the guest presented a valid card at registration. In-room folio review and check-out utilize the room's television with a remote control or guestroom telephone access via an in-room television. The guest can confirm a previously approved method of settlement for the account since the in-room television is connected via the property management system to the front office.

Self-development

Individuals improving their knowledge, skills and abilities through their own self-directed efforts. According to some experts, there are three critical questions that must be answered in the self-development process: (1) Where am I now? (2) Where do I want to be? and (3) How will I monitor progress? In the process of answering these three questions, the ability to engage in self-analysis including objectivity of one's own strengths and weaknesses is of great importance. In addition to self-analysis, the learner must have the ability to formulate learning objectives, target dates for completion, and determine methods and resources to be utilized. For example, one goal, for an individual desiring to become a hotel general manager, in addition to the completion of a hospitality degree, may be to achieve certification through a professional industry association. Self-development is a lifelong process which can include attendance at professional conferences, executive education programs, and embracing leadership positions in professional associations.

Self-service technologies

Services produced entirely by the customer without any direct involvement or interaction with a service firm's employees. As such, these services represent the ultimate form of customer participation. Advances in technology, particularly the Internet, have allowed the introduction of a wide range of self-service technologies (SSTs), including automated teller machines, hotel check-in and check-out, automated car rental, and Internet shopping. Services can be viewed along a convenience continuum, from those that are produced entirely by the firm, to those that are produced entirely by the customer. SSTs occupy the latter portion of this spectrum.

Semantic Web

A range of standards, languages, development frameworks, and tool development initiatives aimed at annotating Web pages with metadata, so that intelligent agents can reason effectively about services. Agent development and website annotation are based on ontologies (consensual, shared, and formal descriptions of key concepts in given domains). The ultimate aim is to be able to handle user requests such as: '*Arrange a vacation for me, somewhere in Victoria (Australia), during March*'. An intelligent agent needs to determine an appropriate time slot, make airline and book rental cars, find a hotel and book tours, etc. The user's personal website needs to be accessed to obtain details of preferences: ranging from the general (such as her preferred airline, favorite restaurants, and car rental preferences) through to detail trip-specific detail (such as she would like to do some surfing and visit a favorite restaurant).

Semi-variable costs

A semi-variable cost tends to vary partially, rather than in proportion, with the volume of activity. Payroll for a hotel is an example of a semi-variable cost, where the minimum (skeleton) staff is required in order for the property to function and accept guests (fixed cost element) and additional staff are employed on an 'as needed' basis as activity increases beyond the capacity of the minimum staff level to absorb. Payroll will, thus, increase 'stepwise' with volume. It will be a fixed cost within a limited range of activity, but will have to step up to a higher level once activity increases above that range. The classification of cost types into fixed cost or semi-variable cost is not easy, the main methods available to analyze semi-variable costs into their fixed and variable elements are by technical estimate (using managers' intimate knowledge of their businesses), graphical analysis (charting using a scatter graph), and statistical cost analysis (using regression and correlation analysis).

Service failures

Service failures can be assigned to one of three categories: service delivery system failures, customer needs failures, and unsolicited employee actions. *System failures* refer to failures in the core service offering of the firm (i.e. an airline mishandling a passenger's luggage). *Customer needs failures* are based on employee responses to customer needs or special requests (i.e. a hotel guest may want to have a pet in the room).

Unsolicited employee actions refer to the actions, both good and bad, of employees that are not expected by customers (i.e. a hotel front desk clerk gives a free upgrade to a guest who waited in line too long). When customers complain, firms are presented with the opportunity to recover from service failures. Service recovery occurs when a firm's reaction to a service failure results in customer satisfaction and goodwill.

Service profit chain

The chain illustrates relationships between service firms' profits and customer satisfaction and loyalty, as well as employee satisfaction and loyalty. The 'service profit chain' concept was developed through an analysis of successful service organizations. There are three components in the service profit chain. First, work environment and hiring practices are designed to foster employee satisfaction, loyalty, and productivity. Satisfied and loyal employees drive service quality, which in turn drives customer satisfaction and then customer loyalty. A stable base of loyal customers ultimately results in continuing profits and growth. The 'service profit chain' is a particularly important concept for the hospitality industry because of the positive relationship between good human resource practices and profits. Hospitality industry employees are a major component of the service product and successful management of human resources is a clear source of competitive advantage in a highly competitive business climate.

Service system

Services in hospitality and tourism firms manifest primarily through the contribution of people serving people. People-focused services have become the recognized value enhancement variable for successful service firms. It is therefore imperative to seek ways to assist firms to nurture employees' mental contribution over and above their manual input. This necessitates cohesion between the systems that support the activities and the processes that manifest as service. In this age of information, technology not only supports service personnel with knowledge, but it helps the entire organization to disseminate valuable information (knowledge) across international borders and create organization-wide strength through interdependency. However, collective efficiency will manifest only when there is interdependency between the people, processes and systems that make up the service organization. The service system is specifically designed to create this collective focus of the three independent but interrelated strategies, namely, service empowerment, service guarantees, and service recovery.

Shrinkage

The loss of assets in a foodservice operation, usually food or liquor, which is usually the result of inadequate internal controls. Restaurants suffer greater losses associated with shrinkage than other businesses because the majority of assets are consumable and easily usable. For example, food and liquor has demonstrated value to employees as well as plates, silverware, glassware, cleaning supplies, tablecloths, napkins, and candles. It is for this reason that shrinkage is the leading cause of business failure for restaurateurs.

Shrinkage also results in increased costs for the respective categories on a firm's income statement. Take, for example, the effect of stolen steaks. Since the food cost for a given period is calculated by assessing what was taken from inventory during the period, it is difficult to distinguish what was sold to guests and what was stolen.

Single and double loop learning

The process of learning to simply solve problems whereas double loop learning is not merely solving the problem but increasing learning by asking and understanding why the problem occurred in the first place. An example of single loop learning would be the case of a kitchen porter who attends chemical safety training to simply ensure the correct measures are used in the dishwasher. Double loop learning would occur if the learner was asked to consider what would happen if the correct measures were not used or if the chemicals were not stored properly.

Site inspection

Personal, careful investigation of a property, facility, or area by meeting planners. A site inspection allows the planner to assess everything from the general condition of the hospitality facilities to the attitudes of the service personnel who manage them. Site inspections for meeting are normally done at least a year or two in advance for large meetings, although many associations book as far as 10 years in advance of their annual conventions. During the site inspection meeting planners set a time to meet with the hotel sales representative or if several hotels will be visited, the convention and visitors bureau representative for the destination. Meeting planners determine in advance the parts of the facilities they wish to tour and set a firm schedule. They review the meeting requirements and history with department managers. A checklist is prepared by the planner during the site inspection to ensure that the hotel meets the needs of the meeting or convention.

Site selection

Before a meeting venue is selected a geographical destination is chosen. The destination for a meeting must be carefully considered, looking at factors including geographic regions, accessibility, affordability, urban or suburban, resort destination, gaming destination. It is important to prepare the meeting specifications prior to opening discussions with prospective destinations. Meeting specifications include requirements for space, dates, rates, and services. Space would include sleeping rooms, suites, number of complimentary rooms per paid occupied room, number and size of meeting rooms, exhibit space, registration area, audio-visual requirements, computer and technology requirements, suitable storage space, office space, meeting dates, and types of events requiring banquet space. Historical data from previous meetings is important to show the type of attendance expected. Location specifications take into consideration the accessibility of the location by plane, train, bus, and/or automobile, as well as the number of seats on all planes flying into a destination per day, month, or year.

Smart card

A card that is embedded with either a microprocessor and a memory chip or only a memory chip with non-programmable logic. The microprocessor card can add, delete, and otherwise manipulate information on the card, while a memory chip card can only undertake a predefined operation. Smart cards, unlike magnetic stripe cards, can carry all necessary functions and information on the card. Therefore, they do not require access to remote databases at the time of the transaction. The size and shape of a credit card, smart cards have many of the attributes of a miniature computer. A single card can contain multiple applications and functions that are protected by advanced security features to prevent unauthorized use. Today, there are three categories of smart cards, all of which are evolving rapidly into markets and applications: (1) Integrated Circuit (IC) Microprocessor Cards; (2) IC Memory Cards; and (3) Optical Memory Cards.

Smoke detectors

A device used to detect smoke and sound an alarm to warn of impending fire. Smoke detectors react to the solid and liquid aerosols created by a fire. Each of the four types reacts to a specific aspect of smoke. The four major types of smoke detectors are: (1) *spot-type ionization*, (2) *spot-type light scattering*, (3) *line projected beam*, and (4) *air sampling*.

Ionization smoke detectors have two electrically charged plates arranged in a parallel manner with an air gap between. Smoke particles slow down the ionized air (creating an electrical current) and the detector measures this change. *Spot-type photoelectric* smoke detectors contain a small light source that shines into the detection chamber. Smoke particles entering the detector chamber cause additional light to be scattered so more reaches the photosensitive receiver. *Projected beam* detectors contain a light source that projects a beam through a space to a receiver. When the percentage of light obscured (from smoke crossing the beam) reaches a preset threshold, an alarm sounds. *Air-sampling* detectors use separate detection chambers to sample air from a room. The detection chamber may use a cloud chamber to detect minute particles in the air. A second type of air-sampling detector uses a sensitive photoelectric light-scattering detector.

Smorgasbord service

A type of food service which is similar to buffet service except that the guests are allowed to serve themselves from the smorgasbord. Also, a true smorgasbord comprises dishes from Scandinavian countries and features hot and cold seafood delicacies, which are often smoked or pickled.

Social influence

A change in behavior due to the real or imagined influence of other people. There are three types of social influence: *informational, normative, and interpersonal. Informational social influence* occurs because of people's desire to be correct and to know how to best behave in a given situation. Persuasion is the most common type of informational social influence. *Normative social influence* occurs because of people's desire to conform to social norms in order to be liked and accepted. Normative social influence occurs when people adopt the behaviors, attitudes, and values of members of a reference group. *Interpersonal social influence* occurs as the result of direct pressure from another person. Two types of interpersonal social influence are obedience and compliance. Of the three types of social influence, information social influence results in long lasting attitude and behavior change and is the type most sought after by marketers.

Socialization

The process whereby new employees are inducted in to the culture of an organization. Within the hospitality context, the socialization process involves the transmission of values, beliefs, and attitudes embraced by individuals already within an organization, particularly those holding positions of power, influence, and salience. Such individuals would include hotel general managers, human resource managers, and also divisional managers. The concept of person-environment fit holds considerable explanatory power in the understanding of how employees take on their new hospitality work culture and the norms embedded within it. Socialization is regarded as the process that seeks to make this fit as precise as possible, comfortable for all, and generally enduring for the newly employed. It may also be understood as a continuous process that will periodically occur throughout a person's career in hospitality.

Soft branding

A branding strategy of independent operators who wish to maintain their uniqueness, yet also wish to gain immediate positioning and credibility through a branded affiliation. They are able to deepen relationships with their existing customers, acquire new markets through the 'soft' brand's global distribution systems, as well as benefit from other marketing services that are normally only enjoyed by hotels that are part of larger more standardized hotel groups. The term soft branding was first used in 1991 by Slattery to refer to middle of the road branding strategies of large hotel chain companies that found it difficult to achieve a strong consistent brand offer across all of their properties. This initial usage of this term 'soft branding', was in contrast to 'hard branding' that referred to those hotel chains that had very consistent and highly standardized products and services.

Software

The general term used to describe the methods of using and controlling computers. The four main task-related categories based on the type of operating instructions provided are: '*language software*', '*system software*', '*applications software*', and '*network software*'. *Language software* provides computer programmers with a set of commands to write programs. *System software* includes operating systems and programs that support applications software. It controls the allocation and use of hardware resources such as memory, central processing unit (CPU) time, and disk space. *Applications software* is the programs that perform tasks computer users want to do, such as hotel reservations or client billing. *Network software* enables computers to communicate with each other to perform tasks such as program and data sharing or interpersonal message transmissions; this allows personnel from different departments to work together more effectively.

Solvency ratios

Solvency is the ability of a business to pay its debt. While liquidity ratios measure a business's ability to deal with short-term obligations, solvency ratios, therefore, measure a business's ability to pay its long-term debt. Long-term solvency is normally measured by four ratios: *debt ratio, debt-equity ratio, capital gearing ratio*, and *interest coverage ratio*.

The *debt ratio* is expressed in a percentage form of a business's total debt over its total assets:

$$\text{Debt ratio} = \frac{\text{Total debt}}{\text{Total assets}}$$

It is generally preferable to have this number in the region the 40–50 per cent.

The debt-equity ratio, is expressed as a multiple:

$$\text{Debt-equity ratio} = \frac{\text{Total debt}}{\text{Total equity}}$$

If there is less debt than equity, the ratio will be less than one. If there is more debt than equity, the ratio will be larger than 1.0. Therefore, it is better to have a debt-equity ratio of less than 1.0.

The *capital gearing ratio*, is also known as the 'capital structure' or 'leverage' ratio. The capital structure ratio is:

$$\text{Capital gearing ratio} = \frac{\text{Long-term debt}}{\text{Owner's equity + long term debt}}$$
$$= \frac{\text{Long-term debt}}{\text{Total capitalization}}$$

This ratio measures the degree a business depends on borrowed capital as compared to investor's capital. Generally, when the long-term debt exceeds 40 per cent of total capital, the structure may become unsatisfactory.

The *interest cover ratio*, also known interest coverage or times interest earned, indicates how adequate the earnings of a business are to cover the obligations of bond/debt/loan interest. The higher this ratio, the better the business is able to meet its interest payment.

$$\text{Interest cover ratio} = \frac{\text{Income from operations}}{\text{Interest}}$$
$$\text{or} \quad \frac{\text{Earnings before interest + Tax}}{\text{Interest}}$$
$$\text{or} \quad \frac{\text{EBIT}}{\text{I}}$$

Speaker

In the field of event management, an individual of interest or stature who can speak to the theme of an event who presents a session on a specific topic or topics, including a convention keynote address; a general session or seminar leader who is a topic specialist; a trainer or workshop leader who facilitates for group participation and interaction; a change of pace speaker such as a humorist, entertainer or sports figure, industry insider educational, interactive. Types of speakers best suited for meetings' audience include humorists, athlete, futurists, economists, local executives, politicians, media personalities, authors, etc. Speakers are usually invited based on expertise on subject, contribution to the program, and appropriateness for the audience and because they are accomplished orators. When selecting a speaker the most important factors to consider are the purpose and/or objective of the meeting, the message that is to be communicated, the audience mix (gender, age, socio-economic background) and the audience interest.

Special markets

Special or niche markets consist of two primary categories: *Government* and *SMERF* meetings. When combined with the two most prominent market segments – corporate and association – they make up the total mix of the meetings industry.

'*SMERF*' identifies the category of meeting marketing segments consisting of Social, Military, Education, Religious, and Fraternal. This market encompasses much of the not-for-profit sector. In general these groups hold meetings and events that are very similar to those of trade and professional associations – conventions, board and committee meetings, training, and educational seminars. In a category unto itself, and separate from the SMERF market, is the government market segment. *Government meetings* bring together attendees who are civil servants, elected officials or service providers to governmental entities. These meetings are held by the agencies or departments of city, county, state or province, national or international governments. It is in this category that quasi-government meetings, such as political party conventions or lobbying groups, can also be found.

Staging guide

A guide composed of all documents relating to an event such as function sheet, instructions, room setup, diagrams, directory of key personnel, etc. *A Meeting and Exhibition Specification Guide* is a key component of the staging guide and is comprised of three sections: (1) the narrative, a general overview of the meeting; (2) schedule of events, a timetable outlining all functions that compose the overall meeting; and, (3) meeting event orders (function sheets) detailing the requirements for each specific event within the meeting. These specifications are sent to the facility 30 days prior to the meeting so the facility's convention service manager can communicate the meeting's needs to their staff. The meeting planner uses the staging guide to maintain the smooth flow of the logistical and programmatic aspects of the meeting. Some planners refer to this collection of documents as their Bible or the Production Manual.

Standard cost accounting in foodservice operations

Cost accounting relates the expenditure of a foodservice organization to its food and beverage sales. Cost accounts, while they can be directly related to financial accounts, are concerned with the detailed make-up of cost in identifiable output for purposes of pricing, budgeting, control of food and beverage production and service, purchasing and control of food and beverage materials, and control of labor expenditure, rather than the overall financial results of the foodservice operation. In a standard cost system, the following accounts are always recorded at budgeted cost: food and beverage held in inventory, finished food and beverage inventory, and cost of food and beverage sold. Hence, if actual costs exceed budgeted costs the variance is unfavorable, while if actual costs are less than budgeted costs, the variance is said to be favorable.

Storage

Facilities used to hold products under optimal conditions to prevent spoilage. Protecting a foodservice organization's investment in inventory depends on its having effective and efficient storage facilities. Storage is a vital function that is given too little attention: well-planned and well-managed storage areas encourage employee productivity, reduce product loss, and improve food safety. Storage needs vary depending on the scope and size of an operation, its menu offerings and level of service, anticipated meal volumes, the frequency of deliveries, and the configuration of the building. In general, storage for foodservice operations can be classified into three distinct groups: temperature-controlled storage such as refrigerators, freezers, and wine rooms; ambient temperature (or 'dry') food storage for bulk goods and packaged items that do not require refrigeration; and non-food storage, typically for service ware, utensils and cookware, paper goods, linens, and cleaning supplies.

Strategic choice

Strategic choices relate to decisions about the future of an organization and how it should respond to environmental pressures and influences. Strategic choice involves three stages: (1) formulating options for future development; (2) evaluating available options, and (3) selecting which options should be chosen. As a result of the complexity of the environment, scope and scale of many hospitality and travel and tourism organizations, it is common to distinguish between various levels of strategic choices: corporate level, business level, and operational (or functional) levels. Accordingly, there are numerous strategic options to consider. Most normative approaches to strategic choice emphasize the requirement that the chosen strategy take advantage of environmental opportunities, while attempting to avoid threats. At the same time, the choice should be based on organizational strengths and unique resources that will result in a sustainable competitive position.

Strategic direction

Those policies required to provide a clear mandate for action, whether at the individual firm or at the community and government level. A strategic direction determines where an organization is going over the next year or more, how it is going to get there, and how it will know if it got there or not. A strategy will be embodied in an existing business approach (to customers or to suppliers) or may be developed in response to issues identified in relation to the development of a new approach to the management of the hospitality industry. What then is a desirable strategic direction? In simplest terms the direction set by an organization must meet the needs of all stakeholders and do so in a way they value. Each stakeholder group will define its needs in different ways depending on the relationship it has with the organization.

Strategic evaluation

The strategic evaluation process assesses whether the organization is achieving the desired performance and following the correct path to remain competitive into the future. Evaluation takes place at all levels of the firm. Managers obtain clear, thorough and accurate information from the frontline and throughout the organizational hierarchy. By synthesizing this information, managers compare actual outcomes with expectations established during the strategy formulation stage. The evaluation process creates a feedback loop to assess the success of implemented strategies and action plans. Poor performance usually indicates that something has gone wrong at the formulation stage, implementation stage, or both. This feedback may become a learning process to improve planning systems or the implementation process to ensure greater success in the future.

Hospitality organizations' strategies are traditionally assessed using quantitative measures such as profits or cash flow but should also be evaluated on more qualitative measures such as customer satisfaction or employee turnover rates.

Strategic formulation

The process of determining a value-based strategy that considers external opportunities and threats as well as internal capabilities and constraints. This process has generally been perceived as an analytical approach, driven by formal structure and planning systems. The deliberate perspective of strategic formulation, also known as the comprehensive process, is based on an early view of strategic management that assumes a predictable environment and perfect foresight by managers. The ideas underpinning the emergent approach to strategy formulation reflect the idea that strategy formulation is both learning and maneuvering process, which allows managers to respond to the vagaries of a dynamic environment. As such, a change between what was intended (deliberate formulation) and what strategies are realized represents emerging changes. Realized strategy can be conceptualized as the combination of deliberate components (intentions defined in advance) and emergent components (the level of replacement and additive strategies).

Strategic groups

A group of companies in the same industry who follow the same or similar business model or strategies. Strategic dimensions are essentially those decision variables which underpin the business strategies and competitive positioning of the firms within an industry. These include product market scope, distribution channels, level of product quality, degree of vertical integration, choice of technology, and so on. Research into strategic groups has primarily focused upon analyzing the differences in profitability between firms.

Strategic management

The term strategy is derived from the military, as part of war relations between nations and communities. Management theory adapted the term to competitive business situations between firms in terms of economic, technological, or managerial dimensions. The meaning of strategy in the organizational context involves an amalgam of decisions, characterized by unique features, aimed at reaching the goals of the organization. Strategic management is an organization-wide process that involves the development of a strategy that determines how an organization is to accomplish its objectives in such a way as to capitalize on the opportunities that present themselves. Strategic management entails specifying objectives, developing policies and plans to achieve these objectives, and allocating resources to implement the plan. It provides overall direction to the entire organization.

Strategy implementation

The process of putting the formulated strategy into action in hospitality organizations. Strategy implementation may also be defined as carrying out essential activities to make strategy work. Strategy implementation in the hospitality management field is often treated as a tactical activity and it is usually taken into consideration after strategy has been formulated. However, lately it has started receiving more attention since it has been realized that in hospitality organizations the main difficulty is the implementation of strategies rather than the development of them. There are a number of implementation variables/factors such as organizational structure, culture, programs, resources, people, communication, rewards, and control and constructed strategy implementation frameworks for hospitality organizations. It has been emphasized that there should be a 'strategic fit' among the above implementation variables. However, strategy implementation is a complex and dynamic process in which achieving a fit among the implementation variables is almost impossible.

Strategy marketing planning

A management tool used to help determine where an organization is going and how it is going to get there. The strategic planning process attempts to address three core questions: (1) Where are we? (2) Where do we want to be? and (3) How are we going to get there?

Situational analysis

The first stage of strategy planning involves answering the question, 'Where are we?' This stage requires a company to identify the company's strengths and weaknesses by looking internally at the organization and then to identify the current or potential opportunities and threats by scanning the external environment. This activity is referred to as a SWOT (strengths, weaknesses, opportunities, and threats) analysis or situational analysis.

Goals and objectives

The second stage of the strategic planning process is to decide where the organization wants to be and to establish the overall mission and objectives that will guide the strategy. Drawn from the SWOT analysis and market opportunities, the organization's strategic goals and strategies to achieve the goals must be identified. This process involves identifying or updating the organization's mission, vision, and/or values statements.

Marketing plan

The third stage of the strategic planning process involves creating a marketing plan. The marketing plan, or 'marketing strategy', consists of identifying the target markets and developing the marketing mix. Once the target markets have been identified, the organization must define its positioning statement. The positioning statement defines the customer's perception of the total product in light of the other competitive product and service offerings. The final step of the marketing plan is to develop the marketing mix. A separate marketing mix should be created for each identified target market. The marketing mix consists of the '4Ps' – product, promotion, place, and price.

Submetering

The function of using additional utility meters, other than the main meters at the boundary of the building. The purpose of submetering is to identify where utilities are used. Without submetering, there can be no valid basis for operational control and cost allocation. Likewise, there can be no way to verify efficiencies and quantify savings. In a hotel, submetering of electricity, steam, chilled water, hot water, and cold water are all practiced. The reduced cost of chilled water metering in the past 10 years has made it viable to identify where air conditioning is being used down to the level of individual rooms. Installing submeters is significantly cheaper when done during construction or major renovation, so decisions about submetering are best made prior to these activities. Consistency of meter readings is generally more important than absolute accuracy.

Sustainability

The protection and conservation of resources for future generations, as opposed to current users' undue depletion. Behavioral standards have been developed in an effort to assist tourism and hospitality operators in developing practical environmental impact monitoring measures, or to regulate their activities. Within the hospitality industry such standards are usually self-regulated unless they are mandated by law, as for example in the fire protection and health areas of operation.

Switch companies

Switch companies (sometimes called 'Universal Switches') act as a bidirectional translator, converting electronic messages between the unique languages used by each of the four major global distribution systems (GDS) and the large number of proprietary central reservations systems

(CRS) used by the hotel companies (and vice versa). GDS are used extensively by travel agents to make reservations for airline seats and, to a lesser degree, hotel rooms. Two major Switch companies currently operate in the hotel sector – THISCo (The Hotel Industry Switching Company) and Wizcom. In the absence of a switch, each hotel company would have to develop costly individual interfaces between its CRS and each of the GDS in order to make their product available to travel agents electronically. Using a switch means that only a single interface (between the CRS and the switch itself) needs to be developed to give access to all of the major GDS systems.

Switching costs

These are one time costs facing a hotel or restaurant as it contemplates switching from one supplier's product to another's. Such costs may include direct expenses as a different purchase price, modifications in equipment used plus any related testing and retraining expenses. Good customer or volume discounts, generated over time by combining different purchases, could be lost. Indirect costs such as building or ending relationships and time factors may also be involved. If switching costs are high, the hospitality firm must perceive a major benefit to changing suppliers – but such a benefit would have to clearly outweigh the high costs involved in such a switch. Otherwise, the firm would likely remain with the current supplier. If switching costs are low, the hospitality firm may more readily change suppliers. The goal of suppliers is to build relationships with customers so that they perceive large costs in changing suppliers and are thus encouraged to continue existing relationships.

Systematic risk

A financial term that describes the stock volatility caused by the capital market volatility, or the covariance of stock return with market return. This type of volatility or risk cannot be eliminated via portfolio diversification because the volatility is due to factors that affect all securities such as changes in the nation's economy, tax reforms, or a change in the world energy situation. Even if an investor holds a portfolio consisting of all the stocks in the capital market, he or she will still be exposed to systematic risk. The non-diversifiability of systematic risk determines that it should be priced on the capital market. High systematic risk should be compensated by high return, and vise versa. For an individual investing in a hospitality firm, the systematic risk of the firm is the relevant factor in determining his or her required rate of return within the capital asset pricing model (CAPM) framework.

Tt

Table d'hôte

The literal interpretation of the French term 'table d'hôte' is 'table or offering of the host'. It stems from a bygone period when nobility and people of means entertained their guests in their homes (see also Prix fixe). A contemporary table d'hôte or 'set' menu offers a fixed price for a limited number of courses and dishes. It can also be offered for a set dining period (e.g. lunch). Table d'hôte menus may change daily, weekly, or even monthly, and they may be used in rotation, as they are for cycle menus in on-site foodservice. Table d'hôte menus offer a complete meal of three or more courses with or without a choice of dishes in each course. Guests usually pay full price for all courses whether or not they consume all of them. Some foodservice operators who offer special gourmet table d'hôte menus for events such as Christmas dinner or wedding banquets require a deposit when making reservations.

Tableau de Bord

A management control system that has been used in French enterprises for more than 45 years. Tableau de Bord literally means 'dashboard' or 'instrument panel' and was developed to monitor the progress of the business and, where necessary, take corrective action. The approach entails three-dimensional communication between managers, peers, and subordinates and is described as being 'nested' because of the high interaction between different levels of responsibility. The main objective is to give managers certain key parameters to support their decision-making. It does not give a major importance to accounting-based information and is equally important to use operational indicators with the financial indicators. Additionally, the reporting frequency is not limited to a specific accounting cycle; information is provided as per decision-makers' requirements.

Tables per server

The number of tables that are assigned to each server or server station in a foodservice operation. For example, if a restaurant has 50 tables, it may assign four or five tables to each server. Typically, fine dining restaurants assign fewer tables per server than casual dining restaurants and as a result offer a higher level of service. Some foodservice managers prefer assigning a certain number of seats to each server rather than assigning a certain number of tables. In this case, all servers might have a mix of 2-tops, 4-tops, and 6-tops, but would be serving approximately the same number of guests. One of the major factors involved in determining the appropriate number of tables per server (or servers per table in rare situations) is the use of bussers. Bussers may be employed to simply clear and reset tables; such use increases somewhat the amount of time available for the server to spend with guests.

Target pricing method

A pricing method that is based on the rule that each product must contribute a certain amount of profit. Target pricing practice is based on the principle of break-even analysis. Some hotels try to reach breakeven points by lowering or increasing prices as the supply and demand changes with a consideration to variable costs. In the foodservice industry, this method is appropriate for institutional foodservice and catering where each customer is charged a set amount. Usually, companies that follow this method calculate the total food cost and overhead and add a desired amount of profit. The total amount is divided by the total number of customers to arrive at a menu price for each meal. This method may or may not be appropriate for commercial restaurants as they follow a la carte pricing practices.

TCP/IP

TCP (Transmission Control Protocol) and IP (Internet Protocol) are protocols governing the handling and the formatting of data in an electronic communications system; they are the main protocols used on the Internet. The messages (files) exchanged over the network are divided into small units (called packets) by TCP, while IP takes care of managing the actual delivery of the data. All is needed in order to access another system is an 'Internet address' (called IP address), a 32-bit number, normally written as 4 decimal numbers. A specific service, called DNS (Domain Name Service), provides a database containing the correspondence between numeric addresses and alphabetic domain names. TCP/IP uses the client/server model of communication in which a computer user (a client) requests and is provided a service by another computer (a server). In the hospitality industry, beside these applications, many internal networks are using TCP/IP protocols to connect not only computers, but also other electronic equipment.

Telephone systems

Telephone systems are used to link people together within an organization, and to the outside world. Most hotels provide telephones in guest rooms, which allow guests to ring reception or other numbers within or outside the hotel. The system usually has a private automated branch exchange (PABX) where calls are received, perhaps by a receptionist, and then transferred to the appropriate person within the organization. Many systems allow Direct Dial In (DDI) so that calls can be made direct to the correct extension without being processed by the receptionist. Hotel telephone systems allow guests to make calls, recording details automatically, and passing charges to the guest's bill. With the increased use of mobile phones, and the premium rates often charged by hotels, there may be reduced demand for voice telephony. Telephone systems also allow a range of other facilities, including automatic wake-up calls and voice-mail for guests.

Tennis professional classifications

These are classifications designated by the United States Professional Tennis Association (USPTA) for tennis professionals in a private club setting. USPTA's Career Development Program offers tennis teachers three certification levels, culminating with the master professional designation. To earn the *Professional 1* designation the applicant must be 22 years or older, have successfully passed the certification examination at the Pro 1 level or higher, hold a score of 4.5 on the National Tennis Rating Program (skills test), and have three or five seasons of full-time instructional experience. An individual holding the *Professional 2* designation must be at least 18 years old, have successfully completed an apprenticeship program or an equivalent combination of experience, successfully passed the written examination at a Pro 2 or higher, and passed the National Tennis Rating Program at 4.0 or higher. If a tennis pro holds a *Professional 3* designation, he or she is at least 18 years old, must pass the written certification examination at the Pro 3 level or higher, must hold a National Tennis Rating Program of 4.0 or higher (skill test) and is not required to have tennis-teaching experience. The *master professional* must hold a *Professional 1* designation for a specified period of time, has maintained continuing education hours, and has completed a variety of service activities as recognized by the USPTA. To receive this designation, the tennis pro must submit an application to the master professional review board of the USPTA for ratification and certification.

Tennis tournaments

A tennis event organized as a competition between players. In a private club setting, for the tennis enthusiast tennis tournaments are essential to maintaining the member's needs for competition, social bonding, physical invigoration, and fitness concerns. The common tournaments offered at private clubs are: (a) men's and women's singles, (b) men's and women's doubles, and (c) mixed doubles. To make any of these tournaments a success, the tennis pro engages the tennis committee in securing the use of the courts for tournament play, confirming that the tournament will be sanctioned by the appropriate tennis association, deciding the hours of play, deciding which courts will be used for the tournament and which courts will remain accessible to the members, arranging publicity (if this is to be public event), and ensuring that all registrant information is completed in advance and so that rosters of play can be established.

Third-party meeting and event planners

An independent meeting or event professional who provides conference, event or meeting services for a third party, meaning a corporation, a non-profit, an educational institution or an association, as an outsourced vendor. These individuals may be self-employed and/or operate a division within a company specifically designed to administer various facets of design, planning, strategic consultation, support services and/or logistics for meetings, conferences and/or exhibitions. The services that third parties perform range from managing small parts of an event (task or service specific), to the full-service deliverable: 'soup to nuts'. Full-service meeting or event planners are hired by their client organization to take the complete meeting from the very beginning, determine goals and objectives, to the end, the thank you letters and budget reconciliation. In the case of task or service specifics, the third-party planner may be contracted to perform a piece of the meeting or event. For example registration, housing, site selection, etc.

Timeshare financing

The three predominant types of financing that are available to a timeshare developer is *hypothecation, sales of receivables*, and *securitization. Hypothecation* in the timeshare industry refers to the process of pledging an asset as collateral (security) for a loan. This occurs when a borrower assigns rights to a piece of real estate (such as a hotel and the land on which it stands) or other asset (such as accounts receivable, inventory, etc.) to a lender. If a timeshare developer chooses to *sell its receivables* to create cash flow, he/she will need to make a decision; to whom to sell the receivables. A financier who specializes in the purchase of receivables is traditionally called a factor, and the sale is referred to as 'factoring the receivables'. *Securitization* in the timeshare industry is a process in which a number of financial assets (typically loans of some specific type) are sold to a legal entity called a special purpose vehicle, which then sells new securities to investors based on the assets it holds in trust.

Timeshare industry

Also called a vacation ownership, this lodging type involves the sale of rooms for a specific period of time or a percentage of interest in a vacation home or resort. The timeshare business in the USA pours in $5.4 billion dollars annually into the collective communities where they are located. The average US travel party spends $1, 205 in the local economy during their visit on average. Currently only 12–15 percent of the timeshares are brands, but this will change as major brands are looking for alternative sources of income. Growth has extended to international arena although to date Marriott Vacation Club International is the only international brand represented.

Most timeshare buyers in the USA are female, white, married, are 37 years old or older, and have household incomes of $50,000. Most timeshare resorts in the USA are located in Florida, California, South Carolina, Colorado, Hawaii, and North Carolina.

Timeshare resales

A legal timeshare interest that is sold by a purchaser to a third party. If the timeshare interest is fee-simple property, an owner can dispose of it by sale, lease, or in a will within the limits set forth by applicable laws or in the purchase documents. If the product is not sold as a fee-simple interest, the owner may not have a right to resell their timeshare interest and must refer to their original purchase documents for a 'resales' clause exists. Resales are problematic for developers because as a resort reaches sellout, the developer's prices rise as a reflection of product demand. As a result, the owner who purchases at a lower price early in the resort development process has bargaining power in setting the resale price. Hence, the owner sells his or her timeshare interest at a lower price, therefore entering into direct competition with the developer.

Tipping

Tips are voluntary payments made to service providers after they have delivered a service product. In American restaurants, it is customary to tip a waiter or waitress 15–20 percent of the check amount. These restaurant tips amount to approximately $20 billion a year and represent nearly all of US waiters' and waitresses' take-home pay. Even in countries with less generous tipping norms, tips often make up a substantial portion of servers' incomes. Thus, tipping is an important issue to restaurant servers around the globe. Tipping is also a concern of restaurant managers as well, since it affects servers' attitudes and behaviors as well as customers' dining experiences. Thus, it should be managed properly to maximize employee motivation and customer satisfaction. Tipping also affects restaurants' legal responsibilities with respect to income and social security taxes, therefore it needs to be carefully monitored and recorded by managers.

Total quality management

Total quality management (TQM) was developed by W. Edwards Deming, a management theorist, in the early 1950s. Deming sought to offer a new way for American manufacturers to improve the quality of their products by reducing defects through worker participation in the planning process. TQM in a hotel or lodging enterprise is a management technique that encourages managers to look with a critical eye at processes used to deliver products and services. Managers must ask front line employees and supervisors to question each step in the methods they use in providing hospitality for guests. Some examples might be asking guests why they are unhappy about waiting in line at check-out or why a guest might feel the table service in a hotel restaurant was rushed or why guests are dissatisfied when their room is not ready on check-in.

Trade show

An exhibit of products and services that are targeted to a specific clientele and are not open to the public. A marketing activity that provides the exhibiting company the opportunity to do market research, talk to customers, and promote products, and/or services. Trade shows are usually held in convention centers but may be held in convention hotels, armories, arenas, or other venues. Some trade shows also offer educational sessions. Attendees visit the shows to learn about products, compare products, find out about new trends in their industry, and make buying decisions. Exhibitors at the shows may give away product samples, demonstrate products and/or talk to attendees about how their products can be used. The models for trade shows are differ around the world. In the USA they tend to be short-term events, lasting from three to five days. In other parts of the world, these events may last weeks or months.

Trade show organizer

The individual, who plans a trade show, reserves the space, markets to exhibitors, and promotes attendance by buyers. Several different people may actually accomplish these activities but one person would have overall responsibility for the success of the event. The organizer must create a business plan for the event that includes goals and objectives, operational plans, and evaluation methods. Frequently, they also negotiate contracts with a variety of suppliers and with hotels for blocks of sleeping rooms for attendees. They may also negotiate contracts for shuttle buses to run between the convention venue and hotels. The show organizer hires a general services contractor to handle the freight for the event, create the graphics and look of the show, design the registration area, create an exhibitor services kit, and act as the liaison between show management and the venue.

Trade union

An organization of employees formed to engage in collective action and membership, usually based on a particular industry or occupational group. The goals of trade unions are usually to enable their members to purse their industrial interests, but some unions may also seek political and social goals. Unions as 'ex parte' agents on behalf of their members generally have recognition under most industrial legislative, particularly in collective bargaining, for pursuing wage claims and grievance handling with employers. Unlike employer associations, trade unions tend to be more cohesive as they share common goals. In some countries unions are also called employee associations or guilds. Employers may also form trade unions to represent their broader interests, in the form of employer associations. Union representational rights tend to do better under pluralism. In most industrialized countries, union representation in the hospitality industry is lower than that of other industries.

Training

A process of developing knowledge and skills, through instruction, observation, or practice which leads to skilled behavior. Within the hospitality industry training focus is often on the development of specific skills related to behavior and performance that will ultimately have an impact on guest satisfaction. In developing training to address these areas organizations will use a process often referred to as the training cycle. This is a continuous process involving the following activities: (1) identification and analysis of training needs; (2) planning and design of training interventions; (3) delivery of training interventions; and (4) monitoring and evaluation of outcomes. The delivery of the training interventions can be through a variety of means. On the job training can be a mix of one or all of the following: instruction, coaching, counseling, delegation from a manager, or guided processes.

Turnover (of employees)

Employee turnover occurs when an employee leaves his or her organization either voluntarily or involuntarily. Operationally, turnover is often expressed as a percentage either within a hospitality organizations department or the organization as a whole, or sometimes both. Turnover in percentage and department/organizational terms may differ between hospitality organizations depending on natural business seasons, organizations location, external forces, for example international or domestic and staff themselves. Turnover rate is typically expressed as an annualized percentage. While turnover rates in the hospitality industry vary considerably by country, they tend to be significantly higher than in most other industries. High rates of voluntary turnover have been linked to many factors including job dissatisfaction and lack of connection between subordinate and supervisor. Turnover costs include: (1) replacement costs such as those associated with recruitment, selection, and training; (2) reduced customer service and product quality; and (3) poor morale resulting from insecurity and increased workload for remaining employees.

Turnover culture

As stated previously, employee turnover is generally acknowledged as particularly high within the hospitality industry. Indeed, some fast food chains have annual turnover rates in excess of 200 per cent. Turnover culture tends to be correlated with poor communication within organizations and more autocratic styles of management. Turnover culture is a product of a number of factors, including the seasonality of employment, the limited career structure in smaller establishments, the semi- or unskilled nature of some jobs and finally, the percentage of employees from secondary labor markets. Many employees who leave a job voluntarily move from establishment to establishment with little organizational loyalty. This perpetuates a high turnover culture. Because the industry has tended to turn to labor from foreign countries, the turnover problem in the hospitality industry has perpetuated since these employees are often more motivated by extrinsic rewards such as pay and conditions and are therefore more likely to be lured to another employer.

Uu

Understay

This refers to a guest who leaves the hotel prior to the departure date that they had originally indicated. It is also known as early departure or curtailment. Pleasure travelers may find their tourist attraction less interesting than anticipated. Urgent business may require the corporate client to return to the office sooner than expected. Like overstays, this situation has to be monitored especially in periods when the hotel is busy. Understays create a situation where the hotel is left trying to sell a room that had previously been reserved and represents a loss of revenue. Understays are lost revenue in that the hotel had not anticipated the departure and thus may be unable to sell the room to another guest to recoup the revenue. To minimize understays upon check in a guest is often asked to initial the departure date and thus may be charged for an early departure.

Undistributed Operating Expenses

The expenses of various service or cost centers – for example, administrative and general, information systems, human resources, marketing, security, property operation and maintenance, etc. – are normally grouped under the heading 'Undistributed Operating Expenses'. The costs comprising the two principal subcategories of each cost center's expenses, namely payroll and related expenses and other expenses, are direct costs of their respective cost centers, but indirect costs (overhead expenses) of the property's revenue centers. Thus, in the usual departmental accounting presentation under the Uniform System of Accounts for the Lodging Industry, undistributed operating expenses are treated as overhead expenses, and there is no attempt to allocate them to revenue centers. Thus, in the case of a hotel property, the undistributed operating expenses essentially reflect the resources put in place to support the business as a whole (including cost and revenue centers), rather than to focus on any one particular department or aspect of the property's business activities.

Uniform Resource Locator

Uniform Resource Locator (URL) – also known as Uniform Resource Identifiers (URIs), Uniform Resource Name (URN), and previously called URL is the global address of documents and other resources accessible on the World Wide Web. These resources include Hypertext Markup Language (HTML) pages, image files, virtual tours, or any other file supported by Hypertext Transfer Protocol (HTTP). URLs are typed into the browser window to access Web pages and are embedded within the pages themselves to provide hypertext links to other pages. The URL contains the protocol prefix, port number, domain name, subdirectory names, and file name. URLs may also be numbers but words are easier to use and remember. To access a home page on a website, only the protocol and domain name are required. In the URL http://www.expedia.com, for example, the first part of the address indicates what protocol to use 'HTTP' while the second part 'www.expedia.com' specifies the IP address or domain name.

Uniform System of Accounts

Standardized charts of accounts developed to reflect the specific operating and financial characteristics of individual hospitality industry segments. The Uniform System of Accounts for the Lodging Industry (USALI) is by far the most widespread in its use, but the Uniform System of Accounts for Restaurants (USAR) and the Uniform System of Accounts for Clubs (USAC) are also widely used. Uniform systems of accounts are designed to meet four distinct yet overlapping objectives:

1. *Comparability*: Because uniform systems provide carefully developed formats reflecting evolving operating and financing trends in their segments, the comparisons of financial results among adopters' operations are more reliable.
2. *Responsibility accounting*: Uniform systems distinguish between direct and indirect costs, thus permitting the assignment of costs to the activities – and their managers.
3. *Adherence to accounting standards*: Helps ensure that property-level accounting personnel are reporting transactions according to generally accepted accounting principles (GAAP).
4. *Flexibility*: Typically contains far more classifications and accounts than are used by most adopters, but this feature permits individual operations to customize the system to their needs while preserving comparability and accuracy.

Uniform System of Accounts Income Statement

Income statements for hotels and restaurants are organized above all to provide responsibility accounting information to users, although restaurant operating statements provide a lesser degree of detail. The *hotel income statement* communicates the dual retail real estate nature of lodging. In its most useful format, entitled 'Summary Statement of Income' the income statement is readily divided into three panels or levels.

The first level, summarized at the line 'Total Operated Departments', reports the combined results of the property's revenue centers. The second level describes the costs of the various service centers supporting the operating departments of the hotel, and is captioned 'Undistributed Operating

Expenses'. The third level, summarized at the net income line, is the province of ownership and reports the expenses related to the hotel's real estate component and capital structure. A common industry term for these expenses is 'fixed charges'.

Unit week

The traditional use period that is conveyed to and used by the purchaser of a timeshare interest. It consists of seven days in a particular accommodation in a timeshare property. A unit week generally begins and ends on the same day of the week, but that day may vary from accommodation to accommodation in the timeshare property, especially in larger resort properties where there is a need to stagger check-in times to avoid overloading the front desk. If the unit week is the unit of measurement used, there are fifty-two seven-day unit weeks created with a fifty-third unit week created for years with excess days. The fifty-third unit week can be conveyed separately, given to the purchaser of the fifty-second unit week, or retained by the developer for his/her own use or the use of the management company.

Unsystematic risk

The stock volatility caused by firm-specific events such as lawsuits and labor disputes. This type of volatility or risk can be diversified away because it is independent of economic, political, and other factors that affect all securities in a systematic manner. For hospitality investors, firm-specific volatility or unsystematic risk can be eliminated by holding a well-diversified portfolio that includes both hospitality and non-hospitality stocks. Since unsystematic risk is avoidable via diversification, those hospitality investors need not to be compensated for bearing it. In reality, however, hospitality investors are unlikely to ignore unsystematic risk completely because of imperfections of capital markets. In the real world, market imperfections, such as transaction costs, costly information, and unequal borrowing and lending rates, limit the effectiveness with which investors are able to diversify away unsystematic risk.

Upscale restaurants

The most traditional segment of the restaurant and foodservice industry is fine dining. Historically, the idea of an upscale restaurant (fine dining) included certain key organizing principles: efficiency in the production of freshly prepared food and professionalism in service. Prices are typically the highest of any segment, because the food is almost exclusively 'hand-made', not unlike a Rolls Royce automobile or a man's tailored suit. Fine dining is defined by having a well-trained and professional staff of waiters, usually including a dining room managed by someone in the role of Maitre d' Hotel.

This type of restaurant will almost always have an extensive wine list, as well as a full range of other alcoholic beverages. Meals are most often created by a culinary artist called an executive chef with dishes best described as consisting of elaborately and freshly prepared food. The décor and ambiance of the restaurant is usually distinguishable with a setting to enhance the dining experience.

Upselling

The efforts of reservation agents and front desk agents to convince guests to rent rooms in categories above standard rate accommodations. Hotels typically have several rate categories based on such factors as décor, size, location, view, and furnishings. Often the difference in rate between two similar guestrooms can be substantial. Although the majority of upselling is conducted during the reservations process, front desk agents are likely to have similar sales opportunities with walk-in guest. To upsell, front office and reservations staff must be trained to be professional sales people. Front office staff have to learn effective techniques for suggesting room options to guests. This involves knowing how and when to ask for a sale in a non-pressuring way and how to direct the sale from the guest's perspective. To create guest acceptance, the front desk agent has to know how to describe the hotel's facilities and services in a positive manner.

Urban timeshare

A high rise, condominium with a penthouse exposure that is located in thriving business districts within major cities. Timeshare resort developers have been successful in certain demographic markets by pricing the urban timeshare product against other vacation long-term stay alternatives. Current examples of urban timeshare locations include The Manhattan Club in New York, Marriott's Custom House resort in Boston; and The Edinburgh Residence in Scotland. The urban timeshare product is not for everyone. According to industry research there are four distinct markets. These markets encompass: upscale urbanites that exchange for the purpose of meeting friends and/or relatives; people that live within a 150 miles radius that want to take advantage of the cities arts, entertainment, and retail outlets; an international tourist market that is drawn to the arts and educational offerings of the city; and businesses that have long-term need stays for national and international travelers.

US Environmental Protection Agency

The US Environmental Protection Agency (EPA), which is located in Washington, DC, is an independent executive agency of the US federal government responsible for the formulation and enforcement of regulations governing the release of pollutants and other activities that may adversely affect the public health or environment. The EPA also approves and monitors programs established by state and local agencies for environmental protection and is also concerned with noise pollution and sponsors research into the effects of pollution on ecosystems. The EPA also works with other nations to identify and solve trans boundary pollution problems and to ensure that environmental concerns are integrated into US foreign policy, including trade, economic development, and other policies, as well as provide technical assistance, and scientific expertise to other nations.

Use period

The generic name given to the defined period of time in a timeshare plan during which an accommodation in a timeshare property is subject to reservation and use by the timeshare owner. Use periods can be as short as a single day or as long as a larger fractional interest which commonly refers to more than one week of timeshare interest. The use period traditionally used in timeshare plans is the week, consisting of seven days starting and stopping on the same day, and with or without the option to split the week into a three-day and a four-day stay or into other usage increments. Depending on the jurisdiction and the documents underlying the timeshare plan, the use period may be tied to the underlying timeshare interest, such as a fixed week, or may not be tied to the underlying timeshare interest, such as a floating week.

Vacation exchange

Vacation exchange allows timeshare owners the opportunity to trade their vacation week(s) for different vacation experiences at other comparable resorts around the world. The history and evolution of vacation exchange is directly tied to the history and evolution of the timeshare industry, which dates back to the 1960s in the French Alps. Demand for the vacation pleasures of a 'second home' were extremely limited, prices were high and consumers did not want the financial burdens of year-round second property ownership. In order to expand the potential customer base, companies began marketing a concept which involved buying only specific weeks of time in a resort condominium unit. The idea spread to the USA in the early 1970s. From the beginning it was clear the product still had one basic flaw: vacation owners were unwilling to buy an inflexible product that limited their vacation options by locking them into taking their vacation at the same time and at the same place year after year. Timeshare owner and entrepreneur Jon DeHaan recognized that timeshare owners wanted more flexibility to take a vacation when and where they wanted. The idea of an exchange network took hold. Jon and his wife Crystal were convinced the exchange component was needed to facilitate timeshare sales, and in 1974 they founded Resort Condominiums International (RCI), the world's first exchange network. In 1976, Interval International was formed to compete in the timeshare exchange marketplace.

Vacation ownership

See Timeshare industry.

VALS

VALS® an acronym standing for values and lifestyles is a psychographic segmentation approach developed at Stanford Research Institute International. The VALS® system consists of eight different segments to which a consumer may belong, based on the consumer's primary motivation and his or her access to resources to fulfill their needs and motivations. These segments include innovators, thinkers, achievers, experiencers, believers, strivers, makers, and survivors. The VALS® system may be used in new product development by comparing the company's proposed targeted customer base with the profiles most closely associated with the target. VALS® can offer insight into the likes and dislikes of the proposed target group, as well as offer suggestions on how best to structure and present an advertising message. VALS® may also be used for existing products and services, where the current customer base is surveyed using the VALS® survey to gain greater insight into the current customer.

Value-added statement

The difference between what a hotel pays for the goods and services that it sells and the price that it sells them for represents the hotel's value added. Preparation of a value-added statement can allow management to consider what proportion of value added is consumed by expenses such as staff costs, rent paid, etc. As can be seen from the example below, this can be facilitated in a value-added statement by stating all elements of the statement as a percentage of the total value added. A value-added statement should not be confused with 'Economic Value Added' which can be calculated by taking an organization's operating profit minus its annual cost of capital.

ABC hotel
Value-added statement for the year ended 31 December, 200X

	$	%
Sales revenue	85,000	
Bought-in goods and services	35,000	
Value added	50,000	100
Applied the following way		
To pay employees		
Wages, pensions, etc.	24,000	48
To pay providers of financial capital		
Interest on debt capital	4500	9
Dividends	6500	13
To pay providers of physical capital		
Lease payments	5000	10
To pay for fixed asset maintenance and expansion		
Depreciation	9000	18
Retained profit	1000	2
Value added	50,000	100

Value drivers

Indicators of a company's core values. Expressed in terms of measurable operating variables or activities that approximate the potential and often intangible assets of companies, changes in value drivers significantly impact the market value of a company. For example, a hotel company's value drivers may include growth, market share, technology, level of service, and amenities. The main utility of a value driver lies in its function to measure an overall corporate performance and estimate the company's market value by adding non-financial aspects to the evaluation process. To this end, value drivers are of interest to anyone concerned with measuring corporate performance such as investors, operators, and shareholders. The significance of value drivers may be inferred from the estimation that non-financial performance accounts for as much as 35 per cent of institutional investors' valuation for public companies.

Value pricing

A marketing tool that bases product prices primarily on the consumer's perception of value for a given product. The application of value pricing is an effort to satisfy consumer demand for value without decreasing the quality of the product. There are several value pricing strategies that a hospitality firm can apply, such as everyday value pricing, bundling, and special offers at given times. However, value pricing can be a risky technique if hospitality firms apply it merely as a discounting strategy in order to increase their market share, hoping to achieve a profit with increased sales volumes. In order to make value pricing a financial success, hospitality operators have to learn what represents value in their customers' minds and set prices accordingly. Value pricing strategies ideally are based on knowledge of how relationships between price and quality affect perceptions of value.

Variable costs

A type of cost that varies in direct proportion to the level of business activity. Thus, where the level of business increases by 10 percent, variable costs can be expected to rise by approximately 10 percent. Examples of variable costs include cost of casual labor, guest supplies, travel agents commission, laundry in a hotel, beverage cost of sales, and the cost raw material such as food in a restaurant. If variable costs are linear, then the cost per unit is independent of the volume (remains constant) and there are no economies or diseconomies of scale effects. When variable cost per unit is decreasing (e.g. if there are discounts for the purchases of larger quantities of raw material) there are scale advantages, but when variable cost per unit is increasing (e.g. need for more overtime work if the volume increases) there are scale disadvantages.

Vending

The process of providing products through an unattended machine that accepts a form of payment then dispenses the products. Vending machines can be found in many locations ranging from schools to businesses to medical facilities to hospitality properties.

While vending operations are very impersonal, they are also very convenient for customers whose purchasing needs fall outside of traditional business hours or where desired services and products are not otherwise available. A major advantage from an operator's perspective is the ability to provide food/drink/snack service while incurring low or no labor costs. The four most common items distributed through vending machines are candy, cigarettes, soda, and coffee. Through technology and innovation the industry has evolved to include such products as hot and cold entrees, frozen foods, and dairy products, which may be purchased using coins, bills, or credit cards.

Ventilation system

A system that replaces stale air with fresh air from the outside. Ventilation contributes to human comfort. Air inside an occupied building can become stale and stagnant. In hotel, activities such as smoking and cooking tend to magnify this problem. Consequently, the air in the building needs either to be filtered or to be replaced with fresh outside air. The replacement of inside air with air from the outside will raise heating and cooling costs because this outside air must be brought to the inside air temperature; thus a good air filtration system may be a cost-effective investment. In addition, building surroundings that allow free movement of winds may have positively impact on ventilation. The ventilation system also interacts with the heating and cooling systems. Heated or cooled air is sometimes distributed around a building by ventilation-assisted air movement; when this occurs, the ventilation system becomes a part of the heating and/or cooling system.

Vertical transportation

There are many ways of moving people and equipment vertically through a multi-story building. The most common method is using the stairs. Most modern commercial buildings have one or more pieces of equipment that allow them to move people and objects mechanically. This equipment falls into the general category of vertical transportation. Vertical transportation systems that are most commonly found in the hospitality buildings include elevators, escalators, and dumbwaiters.

Elevators

Hydraulic elevators are the most prevalent type of elevator. They are designed to be used in buildings with a relatively low vertical rise, usually serving between 2 and 6 stops.

Buildings that require greater speed and travel height typically turn to geared and gearless elevators to accomplish the task. In a geared and gearless elevators, the elevator cab is attached to a 'rope', or wire cable, that travels over a grooved sheave at the top of the hoistway. The other end of the rope is attached to a counterweight that travels in the opposite direction of the elevator.

Escalators

Escalators are moving staircases that carry passengers from one floor to another. They are complex mechanical systems that are very effective at moving large volumes of people over relatively short distances.

Dumbwaiters

Dumbwaiters are small elevators that are designed to carry materials only. Dumbwaiters are usually hoisted using a drum-style machine, where a cable is wrapped around a drum.

Virtual reality

A computer simulation that offers the user the opportunity to experience different kinds of pre-produced programs, as if in real time. It enables users to enjoy computer-generated environments that offer three-dimensional perspectives through the use of sound, sight, and touch technology. Using virtual reality, it is possible to simulate the physical environment of almost any tourism destinations or hospitality facility at low cost. It can also provide tourism experiences to those who are unable to travel because of physical disabilities or illnesses, lack of skills, or lack of sufficient time. Regarding the impact of virtual reality on the future of the hospitality industry, some commentators argue that people will have no need to visit a hospitality facility because 'virtual' conditions can provide the perfect experience. Others suggest that the chance to test or practice an experience will generate higher demand to visit the real place.

Vortals

A gateway to Web content on a particular subject area. A vortal may also be more simply defined as the industry-specific equivalent of the general-purpose portal (e.g. Yahoo.com) on the Web. Vortals are also known as vertical portals, VEP or Vertical Enterprise Portals, vertical market websites, Vertical industry portals, or voice portals. Vortals can be corporate portals, business intelligence portals, Web hub, or Interest Community website. Vortals provide information and resources including research, and statistics, discussions, newsletters, online tools, and many other services that educate users about a specific industry such as travel, insurance, automobiles, food manufacturing, and healthcare. Vortals also give users a single place to communicate with and about a single industry. Some vortals may be accessible by telephone hence the term voice portal. Examples of hospitality vortals are www.hospitalityindia.info and www.hotelshop.co.za that provide information for suppliers to the hospitality industry and their purchasers.

Walk-in

A person who arrives at a lodging facility without a reservation. Walk-in is an excellent opportunity to increase sales and occupancy. Walk-in guests take more time to check-in because all the information that is usually taken during the reservation process needs to be obtain at check-in. The walk-in guest is also an excellent opportunity to practice upselling and maximizing potential revenue for the property. A person who says they have a reservation but cannot be found would also be treated as a walk-in.

Walking the guest

When a guest arrives at a lodging facility with a guaranteed reservation and there are no rooms available, this is a direct result of the hotel overbooking it rooms. Overbooking is a common hotel practice to cover for no-show guests. When the guest is walked, they should be sent to a similar lodging facility at the expense of the facility that did not honor the reservation. The guest should be given free transportation to the facility and one free long-distance phone call to notify someone of the change in where they will be staying. If the guest had a reservation for more than one night, every effort should be made to move the person back to the property the next day. The key to minimizing the negative impact of walking a guest is preparation. The front desk should make arrangements at a similar properties prior to the guest's arrival and messages should be forwarded to the displaced guest.

Wall reader

An important part of the smart card system. By holding a small fob or card near the reader, from 4" to 24" depending on the model, an electric strike or magnetic lock opens. The reader can be mounted inside or behind the wall in areas where vandalism is a problem. Each reader has a unique identification number. Some of the readers have a keypad built in to use for programming. The wall reader is programmed at the reader itself or through a laptop or PC. The system can provide audit trails to provide who entered the location and when. In hotel operations, it can lower operation cost through fewer handling errors, decreasing production time, and minimizing excess programmed proximity cards in inventory. It is simple to use and the software allows the administrator to set usage permission for the users.

Warnings

Cautions, either written or verbal, given to correct improper employee behavior in an attempt to improve employee performance.

A *verbal* warning given to a hospitality employee usually represents the first step of the disciplinary action process relating to management action aimed at controlling, punishing, modifying, or inhibiting undesirable employee behavior (e.g. absenteeism, poor performance, inefficiency, negligence, safety violation, etc.). In most instances where there is a strong Human Resources Management (HRM) focus, there is a formal disciplinary code or procedure to be followed. A *formal* warning or reprimand of a hospitality employee usually represents the second stage of the disciplinary process. Whilst there are no specific legislative guidelines in most countries, as a rule, there is a verbal warning, followed by either one or two written warnings alerting the employee that their behavior is unsatisfactory and may lead to the termination of their employment should they not improve.

Waste factor/yield

When calculating recipe and portion costs, allowances need to be made for unavoidable waste when calculating the recipe yield. Failure to do so will result in understating portion costs. Subsequently, instead of figuring on 100 per cent yield from a recipe, one should assume that only 98 per cent will be actually used, allowing 2 per cent for evaporation, over-portioning, and quality control waste. This percentage of waste will differ depending on the menu item. There is a higher allowance for waste on items prepared from scratch than on items that are purchased preportioned. For example, if a steak is purchased pre-cut then there will be no waste; if the kitchen has to cut the steaks then the yield will depend upon the skill of the butcher. Furthermore, yield calculations are most critical for more expensive items, such as meats, since these have a more dramatic impact on cost and profit outcomes.

Water and waste water systems

Water is used by hotels in guestroom areas for bathing and sanitary purposes, in foodand beverage operations, laundry operations, grounds and landscaping, swimming pools, and cooling towers. Water systems require water at a proper pressure and in adequate quantity. Pumps may operate on the water system within the building to provide pressure and quantity as needed. The hot water system also needs water supplied at an appropriate temperature. Each usage of water within the building has requirements regarding the quality of the water. Waste water is the used water and solids from the facility flowing into a septic system or treatment plant. Storm water, surface water, and ground water are included in the definition of waste water and depending on location, may also enter a waste water treatment plant. In facilities there are essentially two waste water systems: the sanitary sewer system and the storm sewer system.

Weighted Average Cost of Capital

The Weighted Average Cost of Capital (WACC) calculates the overall cost of capital for a company. The funds of capital of a company are divided into equity capital (E) and debt capital (De). The costs of each of the funds are different because they bear different levels of risk for the lenders. Namely, dividend (D) is the cost of the use of equity capital provided by the shareholders and interest (I) is the cost of the use of debt capital provided by capital lenders. The average between the rate of dividend (total dividend paid divided by equity capital) and the rate of interest (total interest paid divided by debt capital) is the average cost of capital. Such a measure can be calculated as follows:

$$\text{WACC} = I \times [De/(De + E)] + D \times [E/(De + E)]$$

The WACC is also used to calculate the economic value added (WACC) of a project, which is the after-tax residual operating income after a figurative cost of capital has been deducted, where the figurative cost of capital used is the WACC multiplied by the capital employed (CE) (which is the working capital plus the fixed assets).

$$\text{Figurative cost of capital} = \text{WACC} \times \text{CE}$$

Wireless

Telecommunications in which electromagnetic waves – as opposed to wire – carry a signal. Early wireless transmitters used radiotelegraphy to transmit Morse code and later voice. Information Communication Technology (ICT) developments have proliferated the use of wireless applications and devices, including cellular phones and pagers; Global Positioning System; cordless computer peripherals and telephones; home-remote control and monitor systems. Many hotels make Wi-Fi (Wireless Fidelity) networks available, through the installation of wireless hotspots for hotel guests and employees. These hotspots allow individual users to access the network via wireless cards in their laptops or wireless-enabled Internet Protocol (IP) telephone handsets or other mobile devices such as a Personal Digital Assistant (PDA). From the hotel operations point of view, wireless technologies play an increasingly vital role for hotels, linking together everything, from point-of-sale terminals to housekeeping and security management systems allowing employees to be more productive.

Wireless Application Protocol

An international application environment and a set of communication protocol for applications that use wireless communication. Its principle application is to allow access to the Internet from a mobile phone or a personal digital assistant (PDA). A Wireless Application Protocol (WAP) provides all the basic services of a land based computer Web browser but simplified to operate within the mobile phone and PDA environment.

The WAP Forum was founded in 1997 on the initiative of Ericsson, Nokia, Motorola, and Phone.com. The goal was to by-pass transmission bottlenecks through a simplified transmission language. The content is represented in WML (Wireless Markup Language) for which a WAP capable microbrowser is needed. Cut down Internet sites thus can be displayed on WAP browsers on mobile phones, organizers, palmtops, or pagers with a standard speed of 9.6 kbit/s. The most relevant WAP Applications for tourism and hospitality are: providing information on flight delays, the traffic situation, weather and road conditions, flight schedules, and restaurant information.

Work order

A key document used by the engineering department in hospitality organizations. It is a report stating that an engineering system or piece of equipment needs to be inspected, repaired, or replaced (i.e. a request for work to be done). This document is sequentially numbered and contains the following information: a description of the problem, the location of the problem, the name of the individual who reported the problem, the date and time the problem was reported, the name of the engineer assigned to the task, the time and date the task was completed, and any comments the engineer may have concerning the task. If a work order cannot be fulfilled in a timely manner the engineering department needs to communicate with the department or person who reported the initial problem and alert them of when the request will be fulfilled. In addition, once the work order has been completed the engineering department notifies the department or individual that the work requested has been completed.

Work orientation

The concept of work orientation refers to individuals' attitudes toward work. It emphasizes how people construe their roles and work environments. Work orientation draws on what work means to each individual employee incorporating his/her goals, career aspirations, wants and outlooks, desired rewards, and personal goals. Three main types of orientation to work are as follows. *Instrumental* – viewed as 'a means to an end' rather than the central focus of their life. *Bureaucratic* – considered critical component of employee life. There is positive involvement with work issues because work is considered as a profession. *Solidaristic* – enjoyed for its associated social and group activities. There is a strong involvement with work groups such that work and non-work activities are closely linked.

Worker's compensation

See Compensation.

Working capital

The monetary value of current assets less the current liabilities. When the value of the current assets exceed the current liabilities this is known as positive working capital (vice versa for negative working capital) where current assets are funded partly from the current liabilities such as accounts payable (creditors) and bank overdrafts and also from long-term sources of funds such as bank loans or equity. In the case of negative working capital, current liabilities are funding both current assets and a proportion of long-term assets. The current ratio is calculated as follows:

$$\text{Current ratio} = \frac{\text{Total current assets}}{\text{Total current liabilities}}$$

Working capital (working capital cycle) is required to fund the time lag between expenditure being made for the purchase of raw materials and the subsequent collection of cash for the sale of the finished product.

Xeriscape

Derived from the Greek word 'xeros', meaning 'dry' and 'landscape'. Xeriscape means gardening with less than average water. Xeriscape is landscape consisting primarily of native, drought-resistant species, less than average turf, and other practices that require little or no maintenance, watering, or fertilization. Xeriscape landscaping incorporates seven basic principles which lead to saving water: planning and design, soil analysis, practical turf areas, appropriate plant selection, efficient irrigation, use of mulches, and appropriate maintenance. A Xeriscape-type landscape can reduce outdoor water consumption by as much as 50 percent without sacrificing the quality and beauty of the environment. Xeriscape is particularly beneficial to hotels that can use anywhere from 100,000 gallons (378,000 liters) to 1 million gallons (3.78 million liters) of water for irrigation each month.

XML

XML or EXtensible Markup Language is an open standard for describing data from the World Wide Web Consortium (www.w3.org). XML is written in Standard Generalized Markup Language (SGML), the international standard meta language for defining the structure of different types of electronic documents. It is used for defining data elements on a Web page using a similar tag structure as HyperText Markup Language (HTML). However, whereas HTML defines how elements are displayed by using predefined tags, XML allows the tags to be defined by the website developer, allowing Web pages to function like database records.

The design and use of XML by Web developers improves functionality providing more flexible and adaptable information identification, as well as a more robust and verifiable file format for the storage and transmission of data on and off the Web. XML removes two major constraints of Web development that of the dependence on a single, inflexible document type (HTML) and the complexity of full (SGML).

Yield management

A technique of allocating the right type of capacity or inventory unit to the right type of customer at the right price so as to maximize revenue or 'yield'. Yield management (YM) is a management tool or technique which is currently being utilized by an increasing number of groups and independently owned hotels in order to maximize the effective use of their available capacity and ensure financial success. YM is not an entirely new innovation and most hoteliers practice some form of YM such as the adjusting of room rates to temper fluctuations between peak and off-peak seasons, mid-week, and weekend rates. The airline industry has been credited with the development and refinement of YM following deregulation of the US airline industry in the late 1970s. The resulting heavy competition led to a price cutting war with some airlines going out of business. In response large carriers began to offer a small number of seats at even lower fares whilst maintaining the higher-priced fares on the remainder of the seats. This strategy allowed them to attract the price sensitive customers and still retain their high-paying passengers. Consequently, YM was introduced as a method of utilizing capacity and maximizing revenue or 'yield' where airline companies sought to fill their planes with the optimum mix of passengers. In similar highly competitive circumstances, YM began to be adopted in the hotel industry around the middle of the 1980s. At this time the industry was being confronted with excess capacity, severe short-term liquidity problems, and increasing business failure rates. Major hotel chains such as Hyatt, Marriott, Quality Inn, and Radisson endeavored to redress these difficulties by adopting YM. Today many medium- and small-size hotels are utilizing YM as well.

Yield statistic

The ratio of *actual revenue* to *potential revenue*. *Actual revenue* is the revenue generated by the number of rooms sold. *Potential revenue* is the amount of money that would be received if all rooms were sold at their rack rates. *Potential revenue* can be determined in more than one way. Some hotels calculate their *potential revenue* as the amount that would be earned if all rooms were sold at the double occupancy rate or by taking into account the percentage mix of rooms normally sold at both single and double occupancy. The second method results in a lower *total potential revenue* figure, since double rooms are sold at a higher rate. While it is unlikely that a hotel will attain a 100 percent double occupancy, a hotel using the second method may actually be able to exceed its potential if demand for double rooms exceeds sales mix projections.

Zz

Zoning codes

Codes regarding the construction of buildings developed by the local government. The objective of zoning codes is to promote the safety and welfare of the public. Topics covered in zoning codes include land use, setback, building codes, easements, parking restrictions, density, and building heights. Some include regulations for the esthetics of buildings. The earliest zoning ordinance on record in the USA was enacted in 1913 in New York City to regulate the height, size, and layout of buildings. In 1916, a more comprehensive ordinance was adopted to control the density and uses of land. In the USA zoning codes are developed by a town's council and enforced by the zoning officer, sheriff, or police officer. When necessary, they are interpreted by the judicial system, beginning with a Zoning Board of Appeals and then to the county, state, and federal court system.

Index

Main entries are in bold type. Regular type is used for all other entries.

301

S

Contributing Authors to the International Encyclopedia of Hospitality Management

Jim Ackles
USA

Debra Adams
UK

Julie Adams
Australia

Sekeno Aldred
USA

Judy Allen
Canada

Robert Allender
Hong Kong SAR China

Tommy D. Andersson
Sweden

Helen Atkinson
UK

Rodolfo Baggio
Italy

Billy Bai
USA

Patricia Baldwin
USA

Seymus Baloglu
USA

Deborah Barrash
USA

Paul Beals
USA

Suwathana Bhuripanyo
Thailand

David Biel
USA

Kemal Birdir
Turkey

Ruth Blackwell
UK

David Bojanic
USA

Frank Borsenik
USA

Debbi Boyne
USA

Jackie Brander Brown
UK

Deborah Breiter
USA

Anthony Brien
New Zealand

Dimitrios Buhalis
UK

Cathy Burgess
UK

Sally-Ann Buriss
Australia

Liping A. Cai
USA

Grant Cairncross
Australia

Debra F. Cannon
USA

Bonnie Canziani
USA

Amanda Kay Cecil
USA

Benny Chan
Hong Kong SAR China

Eric Chan
Hong Kong SAR, China

Steve Chan
Hong Kong SAR, China

William N. Chernish
USA

Julia Christensen Hughes
Canada

Olgun Cicek
United Arab Emirates

Candice Clemenz
USA

Paolo Collini
Italy

Catherine Collins
UK

Jennifer T. Condon
USA

Malcolm Cooper
Japan

Jerry Daigle
USA

Agnes Lee DeFranco
USA

Frances & Adrian Devine
UK

Ron Dowell
Australia

Suzette Eaddy
USA

Roman Egger
Austria

Raymond Clinton Ellis
USA

Dominique Faesch
Switzerland

Trish Fairbourn
Australia

George Fenich
USA

Raymond Ferreira
USA

Reed Fisher
USA

William Fisher
USA

Jose Manoel Gandara
Brazil

Morgan Geddie
USA

Don Getz
Canada

Jim Gilkeson
USA

Pat Golden-Romero
USA

Ian Graham
UK

Susan Gregory
USA

Kurt Gruber
USA

Zheng Gu
USA

Chris Guilding
Australia

311

Sigal Haber
Israel

Mine Haktanir
Turkish Republic of Northern Cyprus

Bob Harrington
USA

Peter Harris
UK

Shelley T. I. Harris
USA

Michael Haushalter
USA

Flavia Hendler
USA

G. Keith Henning
Canada

M.T. Hickman
USA

Tyra W. Hilliard
USA

Nicole Marie Holland
USA

Connie Holt
USA

Sonja Holverson
Switzerland

William R. Host
USA

Judy Hou
Switzerland

Krista Hrin
Canada

Dieter Huckestein
USA

Michael Hughes
USA

David Inaneishvili
Finland

Aviad Israeli
Israel

Robert Jenefsky
Switzerland

Colin Johnson
USA

Eleri Jones
UK

Juli Jones
USA

Tom Jones
USA

Jay Kandampully
USA

Bomi Kang
USA

Kurtulus Karamustafa
Turkey

Tammie Kaufman
USA

Gillian Kellock Hay
UK

Ashish Khullar
USA

Hyunjoon Kim
USA

Sherri Kimes
USA

David Kirk
UK

Jaksa Kivela
Hong Kong SAR, China

Frederick J. Kleisner
USA

Bozidar Klicek
Croatia

Sheryl F. Kline
USA

Metin Kozak
Turkey

Vira Krakhmal
UK

Robert Kwortnik
USA

Jerry LaChappelle
USA

Carolyn Lambert
USA

Conrad Lashley
UK

Rob Law
Hong Kong, SAR, China

Stephen LeBruto
USA

Suna Lee
USA

Darren Lee-Ross
Australia

Eric O. Long
USA

Erwin Losekoot
UK

Paul Lynch
UK

Ann Lynn
USA

Wm. Michael Lynn
USA

Angela Maher
UK

Hilary C. Main-Murphy
UK

Alan Marvell
UK

Gillian Maxwell
UK

Karl Mayer
USA

Vivienne McCabe
Australia

Ian McDonnell
Australia

G. Michael McGrath
Australia

Brumby McLeod
USA

Una McMahon Beattie
UK

Edward A. Merritt
USA

Brian Miller
USA

Juline E. Mills
USA

Asad Mohsin
New Zealand

Marco Mongiello
UK

Christopher Muller
USA

James Murphy
Australia

Eunha Myung
USA

Kathy Nelson
USA

Richard Nelson
USA

John Nightingale
UK

Peter O'Connor
France

Fevzi Okumus
USA

Barry O'Mahony
Australia

William O'Toole
Australia

Robert Owen
UK

Ioannis S. Pantelidis
UK

Alexandros Paraskevas
UK

H.G. Parsa
USA

David V. Pavesic
USA

Gabriele Piccoli
USA

Annemarie Piso
UK

Jeff Pope
Australia

Josephine Pryce
Australia

Samantha Quail
UK

Carola Raab
USA

Arie Reichel
Israel

Dennis Reynolds
USA

Paul Reynolds
Australia

Noel Richards
Australia

Chris Roberts
USA

Marco Antonio Robledo
Spain

Stephani K. A. Robson
USA

Pimrawee Rochungsrat
Australia

Glenn Ross
Australia

Chantal Rotondo
USA

Denney G. Rutherford
USA

Naz Saleem
Turkey

Steve Sasso
USA

Udo Schlentrich
USA

Raymond Schmidgall
USA

Peter Schofield
UK

Junwon Seo
USA

Kimberly Severt
USA

Margaret Shaw
Canada

Linda J. Shea
USA

Atul Sheel
USA

Patti Shock
USA

Stowe Shoemaker
USA

Mariana Sigala
Greece

Aram Son
Australia

Beverly Sparks
Australia

David Stipanuk
USA

Sandy Strick
USA

Alan T. Stutts
USA

Alex Susskind
USA

Nancy Swanger
USA

Irene Sweeney
Switzerland

Joy Talbot-Powers
USA

Cheng-Te Tan
USA

Karen Tang
UK

Masako Taylor
Japan

J. Stephen Taylor
UK

Mustafa Tepeci
Turkey

Lyle Thompson
Canada

Nils Timo
Australia

Horatiu Tudori
Switzerland

Randall Upchurch
USA

Gary Vallen
USA

Jean-Pierre van der Rest
The Netherlands

Cynthia Vannucci
USA

Constantinos S. Verginis
United Arab Emirates

Gerard Viardin
USA

Richard Vickery
USA

Peter Walton
France

Rod Warnick
USA

Karin Weber
Hong Kong SAR, China

Paul Weeks
Australia

Paul A Whitelaw
Australia

Charles Whittaker
UK

Karl Wöeber
Austria

James Wortman
USA

Chiemi Yagi

Ian Yeoman
UK

Darla Zanini
USA

Dina Marie V. Zemke
USA